> The author should be something of a prophet, tracing a thing before it is fully apparent, grasping a subject before it becomes a trend, stretching out one's antennae into the universe to sense its most subtle vibrations.
>
> **Doris Lessing**

ZEBRA

Published by Zebra Press, an imprint of Southern Books
(a division of the New Holland Struik Publishing Group (Pty) Ltd)
PO Box 3103, Halfway House, 1685
Tel: (011) 315 3633
Fax: (011) 315 3810
E-mail: zebrastaff@icelogic.co.za

First published in October 1998

© Zebra Press 1998
Text © Jenny Hobbs

All rights reserved. No part of this publication may be reproduced, stored in a retrieval system or transmitted, in any form or by any means, electronic, mechanical, photocopying, recording or otherwise, without the prior written permission of the copyright owners.

Editor Marika Truter
Cover design and photograph Micha McKerr
DTP and design Micha McKerr

Reproduction by Remata, Halfway House
Printed and bound by National Book Printers, Drukkery Street, Goodwood

ISBN 1-86872-227-9

Paper Prophets

A treasury of quotations about writers and writing

Compiled by
Jenny Hobbs

*In loving memory of Taffy & Cecilie Walters
who opened the magic door to books*

Contents

Preface xi
Introduction xiii

Section One: Writers & Writing

Chapter One: Writers 1

What is a writer? 2
Being a writer can be wonderful 6
Being a writer can be a trial 9
Great, good & bad writers 11
Writers of different nationalities 15
Women writers 17
Writers & age 20
Relationships with other writers 23
Writers' alternatives 25

Chapter Two: What Makes a Writer? 29

What is creativity? 30
Writing talent & skills 32
More necessary qualities for a writer 35
Influences 43
Inspiration 45
Why do writers write? 48

Chapter Three: Writers' Concerns 63

Writers' intentions 63
A writer's tasks & duties 68
Being individual 71
Being original 71
Being professional 73
Being serious 74
Output 74
The paradox of writers talking 75
Writers' failings 81
Writers' problems 84

Specific problems 86
    Booze & other stimulants 86
    Depression 88
    Drying up 90
    Exhaustion 91
    Exposure 92
    Failure 93
    Fear 94
    Hardship 95
    Health 96
    Insecurity 97
    Loneliness 98
    Madness 100
    Noise 101
    Partners 102
    Photographs 103
    Plagiarism 104
    Repetition 107
    Sacrifices 107
    Sickness & suffering 108
    Time 109
Last words on writers' problems 109
Writers' issues 110
    Freedom 110
    Life & death 111
    Work 112
Gnomic utterances 113
A few last words on writers 114

Chapter Four: Writing 117

Good & bad writing 132
The craft of writing 137
Can writing be taught? 141
Summing up 147

Chapter Five: The Nuts & Bolts of Language 149

Words 149
Sentences 160
Paragraphs 163
Language 164
Grammar 170
Split infinitives (ok or not ok?) 172
Adjectives 173

Adverbs 174
Spelling 174
Punctuation 175
Imagery 176
Metaphor 177
Symbols 179
Pace 180
Tone 181
Technique 182

Chapter Six: Style 185

Summing up 195

Section Two: Advice & Practicalities

Chapter Seven: How Writers Write 197

Writers' rites & rituals 198
Writers' routines 199
    Daily does it 199
    Time of writing 200
    Place 205
    Writers' tools 208
    Giving thought 216
    Getting started 218
    The writing process 222
    Order 226
    Working pace 227
    Amount 228
    Number of books or projects 231
    Stopping 232
Summing up 233

Chapter Eight: General Advice about Writing 235

First essentials 235
Read widely 236
Advice to new writers 238
Practice makes perfect 243
Be disciplined 245
Strive to write well 247
Write from the heart 247
Be yourself 248
Heed your subconscious 251
Use your imagination 252

Live life before trying to write about it 253
Give it all you've got 254
Be truthful 255
Be succinct 257
Write clearly & simply 258
Concentrate on communicating 260
Be objective 261
Be original 262
Avoid platitudes & clichés 263
Think before you write 263
Pay attention to the sense 264
More nuggets of practical advice 265
Ignore the opinions of others 265
Warnings 266
Rules of writing 267
Some final words of advice 272

Chapter Nine: Choosing a Genre 275

Autobiography 276
Biography 279
Travel writing 285
Summing up 286

Chapter Ten: Publishers, Publishing & Publicity 287

Publishers 287
Publishing 292
Publication 296
Publicity & promotion 299

Chapter Eleven: Critics & Criticism 305

Critics 305
Criticism 318

Chapter Twelve: Epilogue 325

Some closing quotes 325
Postscript 328

Bibliography 329
Author Index 331

Preface

If there is another book quite like *Paper Prophets* I do not know of it. There are plenty of dictionaries of quotations – they make fine birthday presents and thank-you gifts if you are ever stuck for an idea. Some of them are dedicated to a specialist focus but few specifically to writers and writing. If there are any that I have missed they will have to be very good to emulate this one.

Every reader will find something worthwhile here. The collection is useful for writers, for would-be writers, for those who just like to read; it even provides ammunition for those who dislike writing, or writers, or, in particular, those universal pariahs – the critics. Some of the quotations confirm our prejudices, others offend. Some will surprise. But about the art and craft of writing the book presents us pretty well with all we know and all we need to know.

It is full of characters, too. Some are bit-players, others grow familiar from frequent reappearance. Some speak sense, others nonsense. No theory is able to categorise writers: they can, on the evidence here, be astute, crass, arrogant, humble, accessible, obscure, acerbic, bitter, ardent, badgering, hypnotic, bloodless, candid, obtuse, evasive, impulsive, considered, perverse, seraphic, diabolical, natural, artificial, raffish, prudish, highfalutin, lowfalutin, honey-mouthed, poison-lipped, mean, petty, generous. Readers can take great delight in loving them or hating them. They can dip into the book for a light snack, or they can eat their way through the whole menu, getting a taste for the great variety of human endeavour and the intensity with which writers pursue their obsession.

In her introduction Jenny Hobbs, a practising writer, is characteristically modest but unacceptably deceptive when she describes this book as 'a magpie hoard'. This collection is not the random debris of a motor car's cubbyhole; it is more like the cherished lifetime accumulation of favourite threads and ribbons in a sewing basket. There is a personal touch here, but not an intrusive one. Firstly, it takes discipline and dedication – something we all envy but few achieve – to collect and keep these miniatures over a long time; secondly, it takes insight to lift them carefully out of the obscurity of chaotic context; thirdly, and this is the seminal achievement of *Paper Prophets*, it takes an organising mind and a quietly hidden hand to sort them out into such useful categories.

There is no such thing as a complete dictionary of quotations. This book silently begs the reader to fill in favourite quotations in the margins. The collection should become a classic. I hope it does. It does not need a preface from me. I told Jenny Hobbs this when she asked me to write one. But I did not refuse, only because I wanted to be first in line to get a copy.

Tim Couzens
Institute for Advanced Social Research
University of the Witwatersrand
October 1998

Introduction

This is a book of quotes for the person who wants to write, but doesn't quite know how.

Most of us believe that we have a book in us and that one day when we have the time – if we can ever find the time – we will sit down and write it. If you are one of these potential authors, this book is for you.

It is also for curious readers who want to know more about the writers they admire and the strange and infinitely variable processes of writing. And no less for those who love to browse among selections of other people's words, taking time to chew the mental cud of wit and wisdom.

It contains all the advice and encouragement a would-be writer needs to get started:
- Information about writers both literary and best-selling, and their often trenchant comments
- Observations on the craft of writing, its pleasures and problems, peaks and pitfalls
- Recommendations on the nuts and bolts of language, from words to grammar to style
- Practical hints from a broad selection of writers
- Both helpful and amusing comments about publishers and publishing, critics and criticism.

These quotes originated in a private collection assembled over many years: a magpie hoard of writing wisdom. Sources ranged across a whole spectrum of reading, from authors' memoirs to biographies to interviews to newspaper articles to anthologies.

As the collecting became a more serious quest, so the idea grew that the quotes would interest others. The criteria for inclusion have been consistent: that the quote be informative, interesting, relevant to a modern writer's concerns, and entertaining.

Though efforts were made to cover as many aspects of writing as possible, and to include writers from all parts of the English-speaking world, there are gaps. Indian, Canadian and New Zealand writers are poorly represented, as are writers living in post-colonial Africa. The compiler warmly welcomes further quotations from these countries – indeed, good short quotes about writing from any source – with a view to improving and expanding the second edition. Send us your favourites, please.

A companion volume will cover storytelling, literature and fiction writing, bringing would-be novelists a wealth of practical advice on how to set about writing a novel, revision, sending out the manuscript, agents and editors. Look out for *Playing God on Paper: A treasury of quotations about novels & novelists*.

Since fifty percent of the royalties on both books will go towards the Centre for the Book in Cape Town, both your purchase and any quotations you may contribute will support the best possible cause: the encouragement of a vibrant reading culture in our story-rich land.

May *Paper Prophets* find an honoured place on many desks and by many bedsides, preferably battered from being read often and with pleasure.

And now – on with the motley.

Jenny Hobbs
Johannesburg
October 1998

CHAPTER ONE
Writers

'Important soldiers in the fight for the survival of the human race'

Writers – like most lesser mortals – are as full of contradictions as they are fond of giving advice:

Harlan Ellison
First, is the big secret. The one no one ever tells you. And it is this: *anyone* can *become* a writer ... The trick is not in *becoming* a writer, it is in *staying* a writer. Day after week after month after year. Staying in there for the long haul.

Laurie Lee
There are roofless books in all of us, books without walls and books full of lumber.

Rod McKuen
The world needs writers ... We will always be necessary. There are few professionals that can claim that distinction.

Kurt Vonnegut
The real writer will write. He has something inside of him that must come out. If a person has a book in him, he will sit down and write it.

On the other hand:

Michael Legat
Everyone, they say, has a book in him. True, but in most cases it should stay there, principally because so few people have the ability to get it out of themselves in a form that anyone else will want to read.

Somerset Maugham
Women will write novels to while away their pregnancies; bored noblemen, axed

officers, retired civil servants fly to the pen as one might fly to the bottle. There is an impression abroad that everyone has it in him to write a book; but if by this is implied a good book the impression is false.

Paul Theroux
You can't want to be a writer, you have to *be* one.

Judith Rossner
Every asshole in the world wants to write.

· *What is a writer?* ·

'Writers, as a breed, [are] a bit odd'

The expressed views of those in the profession vary from sarcastic to savage, belying the fact that most writers love to be writers though they hate to admit it. Good definitions are those of:

A writer is ...

... his cause. **Ken Saro-Wiwa**

... a reader who is moved to emulation. **William Maxwell**

... a simple-minded person to begin with ... He's not a great mind, he's not a great thinker, he's not a great philosopher, he's a story-teller. **Erskine Caldwell**

... someone who can make a riddle out of an answer. **Karl Kraus**

... the Faust of modern society, the only surviving individualist in a mass age. To his orthodox contemporaries he seems a semi-madman. **Boris Pasternak**

... someone who always sells. An author is one who writes a book that makes a big splash. **Mickey Spillane**

Writers/authors are ...

... born, like painters and architects. **Doris Lessing**

... easy to get on with – if you are fond of children. **Michael Joseph**

... sometimes like tomcats: they distrust all the other toms, but they are kind to kittens. **Malcolm Cowley**

... very different from ordinary human beings. **John Mortimer**

... like cattle going to a fair: those of the same field can never move on without butting one another. **Walter Savage Landor**

... nothing if not opportunists. **John le Carré**

... egoists. All artists are. They can't be altruists and get their work done. **Ursula le Guin**

... always selling somebody out. **Joan Didion**

... interesting people, but often mean and petty ... Writers can be the stinkers of all time, can't they? **Lillian Hellman**

Malcolm Cowley
The writer ... is a person who talks to himself, or better, who talks in himself.

Leon Uris
To me a writer is one of the most important soldiers in the fight for the survival of the human race. He must stay at his post in the thick of fire to serve the cause of mankind.

Emile Zola
We simply paint humanity as we find it, as it is. We say let all be made known in order that all may be healed.

Nadine Gordimer
The function of a writer is to make sense of life. It's such a mystery, it changes all the

time, like light ... and you are trying to make something coherent out of it. Is not all art doing that? Assembling amorphous things and putting them into an order.

John Masters
A writer is one who, in writing, offers effectively phrased insights into the human condition. He is not a propagandist, nor a mechanic, or a communicator, and his work need not, indeed probably should not, have a meaning, a purpose beyond itself.

Less starry-eyed comments about writers include:

Frank Muir
From the early days of literature it was noted that writers, as a breed, were a bit odd.

Roald Dahl
Most writers are old farts who quickly become pompous and adult in their views.

Rod Serling
Every writer is a frustrated actor who recites his lines in the hidden auditorium of his skull.

Eric Linklater
Authors and uncaptured criminals are the only people free from routine.

Kenneth Patchen
Dogs with broken legs are shot; men with broken souls write through the night.

Wilfred Sheed
One reason the human race has such a low opinion of itself is that it gets so much of its wisdom from writers.

Irvin S Cobb
If writers were good businessmen, they'd have too much sense to be writers.

Saul Bellow
Our society, like decadent Rome, has turned into an amusement society, with writers chief among the court jesters – not so much above the clatter as part of it.

Henry Miller
For me the book is the man and my book is the man I am, the confused man, the negligent man, the lusty, obscene, boisterous, thoughtful, scrupulous, lying, diabolically truthful man that I am.

Nina Bawden
All writers are liars. They twist events to suit themselves. They make use of their own tragedies to make a better story. They batten on their relations. They are terrible people ... Writers are not to be trusted. Except in one thing. Most of us try to do our best for the sake of the story.

Paul Valéry
The writer consumes everything he is and everything around him. His pleasures and griefs, his business, God, his childhood, his wife, his friends and enemies, his knowledge and ignorance, all are tossed on to the fateful paper.

Carlos Fuentes
I've always said the writer in a way is the brother of Lucifer – he is rebellious and arrogant and condemned, but he is having a good time. Until the fires start burning.

George Sand
The trade of authorship is a violent and indestructible obsession.

John Irving
A writer is a vehicle. I feel the story I am writing existed before I existed; I'm just the slob who finds it, and rather clumsily tries to do it, and the characters, justice.

John Wain
Being a writer isn't a profession, it's a condition.

Writers are a species with such varying abilities, qualities, quirks and quiddities that they are difficult to categorise. Lots of people have tried, though:

Karl Kraus
There are two kinds of writers, those who are and those who aren't. With the first, content and form belong together like soul and body; with the second, they match each other like body and clothes.

Sidney Sheldon
There are two kinds of writers: those who want to write and those who have to write. *Wanting* to write is not enough, for it is a painfully difficult profession filled with rejections, disappointments, frustrations. *Having* to be a writer is something else again.

Jean Auel
There are two kinds of writers ... the organised ones and the organic ones. When you're organised, you do an outline, you do character studies ... *before* you write. The other approach is the organic one. You know where you're going and you kind of just let it take you there.

Walter Bagehot
Writers, like teeth, are divided into incisors and grinders.

V S Naipaul
I am the kind of writer that people think other people are reading.

· Being a writer can be wonderful ·

'A good day at the keyboard is the greatest high I've ever known'

The joys and glories of being a writer are manifold:

Jean Cocteau
When it goes well – the euphoria of such moments has been much the most intense and joyous of my life experience.

Robert Louis Stevenson
If any man love the labour of any trade ... the gods have called him.

Harlan Ellison
You're a writer. And that's something better than being a millionaire. Because it's something holy.

Gustave Flaubert
I love my work with a frenzied perverted passion, as an ascetic loves the hair-shirt that scrapes his body ... Last Wednesday I had to get up to find my handkerchief: tears were running down my face. I had moved myself to tears in writing, revelling deliciously in the emotions of my own conception, in the sentence which rendered it, and in the pleasure of having found it.

Graham Swift
There may be days and days of labour when ... the writer is all too aware of the self and its lonely effort, but there are those rare days too, of revelation, of ecstasy, when the writer can do no more than acknowledge with gratitude and wonder: this thing is bigger than me.

Peter Matthiessen
I think you're doing your best work when you're not even conscious of yourself. That's what's so thrilling about it – you're out of yourself.

Judith Krantz
I don't think anybody would write a novel if they weren't in some way psychologically driven, predisposed to write. There is terrible agony sometimes. But then, when a scene goes right first time, I feel such exhilaration. A good day at the keyboard is the greatest high I've ever known.

Joanna Trollope
When it's going well, there's nothing so exhilarating – apart from the immediate aftermath of childbirth.

Annie Dillard
Putting a book together is interesting and exhilarating. It is sufficiently difficult and complex that it engages all your intelligence. It is life at its most free.

Helen Garner
You start a paragraph sometimes and suddenly, boom-boom-boom-boom-boom! Out it comes, all these ideas are streaming through you and you can hardly keep up.

Hélène Cixous
Time and again, I, too, have felt so full of luminous torrents that I could burst – burst with forms much more beautiful than those which are put up in frames and sold for a stinking fortune.

Herman Melville (of Moby Dick):
I have written a very wicked story and I feel pure as a lamb.

James Dickey
That's what keeps it exciting for me. Not only to do something that nobody else has done before, but to do something that I haven't done before.

Agatha Christie
The most blessed thing about being an author is that you do it in private and in your own time.

D M Thomas
If the work is flowing then I'm basically happy. And I've become better at making sure that it does flow.

Dorothy Parker
It is nice to be a writer. 'And what does he do?' 'Why, he writes.' It is impossible to say it without shading the voice with awe. There is an air to it, a distinction.

Ptahotep
Be a scribe! Your body will be sleek, your hand will be soft ... You are one who sits grandly in your house; your servants answer speedily; beer is poured copiously; all who see you rejoice in good cheer. Happy is the heart of him who writes; he is young each day.

Jessica Mann
There can be few pleasures in the world to equal that of seeing a new book with one's own name on the cover.

Athol Fugard
You are looking at a radiantly secure person, because once I've started writing I know who I am, where I am, I know what my life's about. Because when I start writing, it's like going on a journey, on a great adventure; I set sail again on the great mythic voyage of discovery.

W B Yeats
All the excitement in my life is in my head.

Robert Frost
All the fun's in how you say a thing.

Shena Mackay
When there is time and space for ... mental pottering, for browsing in dictionaries, works of reference of all kinds, film and poetry books, being a writer is such fun.

Judith Krantz
My books are meant to be fun. Fun for me. If I'm not having fun I know I've gone off the track.

Katherine Mansfield
Oh, to be a writer, a real writer given up to it and to it alone!

Edna Ferber
Life can't ever really defeat a writer who is in love with writing, for life itself is a writer's lover until death – fascinating, cruel, lavish, warm, cold, treacherous, constant.

Ernest Hemingway
Once writing has become your major vice and greatest pleasure only death can stop it.

· Being a writer can be a trial ·

'What I can't stand is the paperwork'

The euphoria of creation notwithstanding, writing as a career has its downside:

Carl Gustav Jung
[The writer or artist's life] cannot be otherwise than full of conflicts, for two forces are at war within him; on the one hand, the justified longing for happiness, security and comfort, and on the other a ruthless passion for creation which may go so far as to override every personal desire.

Isaac Asimov
Writing is the most wonderful and satisfying task in the world, but it does have one or two insignificant flaws. Among those flaws is the fact that a writer can almost never make a living at it.

Clive James
A scholar takes a job. A writer takes a chance.

Fran Lebowitz
Contrary to what many of you might imagine, a career in letters is not without its drawbacks – chief among them the unpleasant fact that one is frequently called upon to sit down and write.

Michael Kanin
I don't like to write, but I love to have written.

Peter de Vries
I love being a writer. What I can't stand is the paperwork.

Truman Capote
It's a very excruciating life facing that blank piece of paper every day and having to reach up somewhere into the clouds and bring something down out of them.

Paul Sayer
If you're smart, if you want to survive, you'll mention nothing of the sweat, the dread, not even the fleeting joy, that lies behind this writing game.

Raymond Chandler
Writers ... live over-strained lives in which far too much humanity is sacrificed to far too little art.

Hilaire Belloc
The life of writing men has always been ... a bitter business. It is notoriously accompanied, for those who write well, by poverty and contempt; or by fatuity and wealth for those who write ill.

Basil Boothroyd
Writing a book isn't like any other sort of writing. It governs your whole life. Even to think about it is as terrifying as eternity.

Hilary Mantel
Once the process of becoming a writer is under way you can't stop it. Once you have begun, everything in the world is filtered through your writer's perception. You don't have a life any more; you just have writing opportunities.

J M Coetzee
It is not so much a life as a price or a currency. It is something I pay with in order to write ... I pay and I sell: that is my life. Sell my life, sell the lives of those around me ... A life without honour; treachery without limit; confession without end.

Franz Kafka
But what is it to be a writer? Writing is a sweet, wonderful reward, but its price? ... It is the reward for service to the devil ... And what is devilish in it seems to me quite clear. It is the vanity and the craving for enjoyment.

Norman Mailer
Most writers get smashed egos. They become like race car drivers in that sense. What happens is sooner or later the punishment they take stops them.

Mark Twain
There ain't nothing more to write about and I'm rotten glad of it, because if I'd knowd what a trouble it was to make a book, I wouldn't a tackled it.

Anthony Burgess
I don't much like writing, although it's the only thing I can do.

On the other hand:

Stanley Ellin
No one put a gun to your head and ordered you to become a writer. One writes out of his own choice and must be prepared to take the rough spots along the road with a certain equanimity, though allowed some grinding of the teeth.

· Great, good and bad writers ·

'A man may be a very good author with some faults, but not with many faults'

Blaise Cendrars
In truth, writers live alongside, on the margin of life and of humanity. That's why they're very great or very small.

Opinions as to greatness in writers vary from adulation to the mildly sarcastic:

Bobi Jones
The great writer runs before the moral standards of his age and creates the moral standards of a new age.

F R Leavis
Great writers are significant in terms of the human awareness they promote.

John Gardner
Great writers tell the truth exactly – and get it right.

Joseph Addison
Books are the legacies that a great genius leaves to mankind, which are delivered down from generation to generation, as presents to the posterity of those who are yet unborn.

Honoré de Balzac
It costs a lot to become a great man. The works of genius are watered with its tears... Whoever wishes to rise above the common level must be prepared for a great struggle, and recoil before no obstacle. A great writer is just simply a martyr whom the stake cannot kill.

Walter Savage Landor
Every great writer is a writer of history, let him treat on almost what subject he may. He carries with him for thousands of years a portion of his times.

J Middleton Murry
The great writer does not really come to conclusions about life; he discerns a quality in it.

André Gide
Great authors are admirable in this respect: in every generation they make for disagreement. Through them we become aware of our differences.

Cyril Connolly
A great writer creates a world of his own and his readers are proud to live in it. A lesser writer may entice them in for a moment, but soon he will watch them filing out.

Alexander Solzhenitzyn
For a country to have a great writer is like having a second government. That is why no regime has ever loved great writers, only minor ones.

Boris Pasternak
The greatness of a writer has nothing to do with subject matter itself, only with how much the subject matter touches the author. It is the density of style which counts.

Eugène Delacroix
A great man's book is a compromise between the reader and himself.

George Bernard Shaw
Great writers are always evil influences; second-rate writers are not wicked enough to become great.

Gore Vidal
In America the race goes to the loud, the solemn, the hustler. If you think you're a great writer, you must say that you are.

Attitudes towards good writers are (like any subject on which writers like to pontificate) a ragbag of opinions:

Isaac Bashevis Singer
A good writer touches the kinship between souls that transcends language and geography.

Logan Pearsall Smith
What I like in a good author is not what he says, but what he whispers.

Virginia Woolf
A first-rate writer respects writing too much to be tricky.

Mickey Spillane
If the public likes you, you're good. Shakespeare was a common, down-to-earth writer in his day.

Doris Lessing
Literary talents are common, as we live in a literate society. Reading turns you into a good writer. Many writers are nearly good, but they don't sit on it or keep at it.

V S Pritchett
I always look for the real voice of a writer because most good writers have a distinctive voice.

Voltaire
A man may be a very good author with some faults, but not with many faults.

Vladimir Nabokov
Among European writers you may distinguish the bad one from the good one by the simple fact that the bad one has generally one nightingale at a time, as happens in conventional poetry, while the good one has several of them sing together, as they really do in nature.

Alberto Moravia
Good writers are monotonous, like good composers. Their truth is self-repeating ... They keep trying to perfect their understanding of the one problem they were born to understand.

There are fewer quotes about bad writers, probably because they attract less envy than good writers:

Edward Albee
Good writers define reality, bad ones merely restate it. A good writer turns facts into truth; a bad writer will, more often than not, accomplish the opposite.

Jonathan Raban
The play of words on the page, the illusion of forming a fresh patter, crisply phrased, the heady sense of having nailed a fragment of the world with a telling metaphor, come more easily, if anything, to the bad writer than the good one.

Albert Camus
Bad authors are those who write with reference to an inner context which the reader cannot know.

Elizabeth Barrett Browning
> Many a fervid man
> Writes books as cold and flat as graveyard stones.

Malcolm Cowley
No complete son of a bitch ever wrote a good sentence.

Grace Metalious
I'm a lousy writer; a helluva lot of people have got lousy taste.

Molière
The only people who can be excused for letting a bad book loose on the world are the poor devils who have to write for a living.

Evelyn Waugh
Experiment? God forbid! Look at the results of experiment in the case of a writer like Joyce. He started off writing very well, then you can watch him going mad with vanity. He ends up a lunatic.

Writers of different nationalities

'In other countries, art and literature are left to a lot of shabby bums living in attics'

Generalising about writers in terms of their nationality is a favourite sport:

Geoffrey Cotterell
In America only the successful writer is important, in France all writers are important, in England no writer is important, in Australia you have to explain what a writer is.

William Golding *(on winning the Nobel Prize for Literature):*
It really means nothing in this country [England] whatsoever – but then being a writer here means nothing either.

Sinclair Lewis
In other countries, art and literature are left to a lot of shabby bums living in attics and feeding on booze and spaghetti, but in America the successful writer or picture-painter is indistinguishable from any other decent businessman.

Gore Vidal
American writers want to be not good but great; and so are neither.

George Malcolm Thomson
The Scots are incapable of considering their literary geniuses purely as writers or artists. They must be either an excuse for a glass or a text for the next sermon.

Brendan Behan
The English and Americans dislike only some Irish – the same Irish that the Irish themselves detest, Irish writers – the ones that *think*.

Maeve Binchy
Dublin is a small city and everyone loves talking. So you sit in a pub and tell me about the book you're going to write and I tell you about the book I'm going to write and we'd have lots of wine and neither of us would write our book at all.

Though some are more complimentary about Irish writers:

Carlos Fuentes
The English language has an unbroken tradition of excellence and when it goes to sleep there is always an Irishman who appears and wakes it up.

Kurt Vonnegut
Lucky indeed is the writer who has grown up in Ireland, for the English spoken there is so amusing and musical. I grew up in Indianapolis, where common speech sounds like a handsaw cutting galvanised tin, and employs a vocabulary as un-ornamental as a monkey wrench.

Dorothy Parker
English authors write better than Americans – and Irish authors write better than anybody.

Carlos Fuentes *(of Latin American writers)*:
We have to do more things in our culture than American writers do in theirs. They can have more time for themselves and for their writing, whereas we have social demands ... We have to assimilate the enormous weight of our past so we will not forget what gives us life.

Gomolemo Mokae
Medicine is my wife and writing is my mistress. I am African, so I can afford to be polygamous.

T T Moyana
An additional difficulty for the creative artist in South Africa, especially for the black writer, is that life itself is too fantastic to be outstripped by the creative imagination.

Clement Greenberg
The Jewish writer suffers from the unavailability of a sufficient variety of observed experience. He is forced to write, if he is serious, the way the pelican feeds its young, striking his own breast to draw the blood of his theme.

Women writers

'In writing, sex doesn't matter ... there is no sex in the brain'

Most women writers object to being categorised as such, preferring to be thought of as writers, period:

Charlotte Brontë
I wish critics would judge me as an author, not as a woman.

Simone de Beauvoir
A woman writer is first a writer who consecrates her life to writing and has no other occupation.

Natalia Ginzburg
A writer is a writer. You care about writing. It isn't men or women. I find these feminists very annoying, putting together these anthologies of women writers. As if there were a difference. You sit down, you write, you are not a woman, or an Italian. You are a writer.

Deborah Moggach
Novelists are hermaphrodites and should be able to slide into other people's skins regardless of gender.

May Sarton
In America, I think I'm pushed aside as that awful thing called a sensitive feminine writer. The very ingredient that makes me universal has kept me from being interesting to the critics.

Phyllis Rose
Women writers earlier in the century thought of themselves as alone and unique. Being a woman did not present itself to them as the communal, bonding experience which has been emphasised by feminist thinking since the 1970s but as a radically individual and rather lonely state, however much they hoped, as most writers do, that they spoke for more than themselves.

Nadine Gordimer
In writing, sex doesn't matter; it's the writing that matters ... There is no sex in the brain: being female is not a criterion of writing.

Eudora Welty
I don't really feel limitations in writing as a woman. I feel I can see the point of view of a man. Once you've leaped into looking at the point of view of another person, I don't think it matters whether it's a man or a woman.

Though, interestingly, gender doesn't seem to be a major issue with black women writers:

Terry McMillan
It doesn't bother me to be categorised as a 'black woman writer' because that's exactly what I am. I mean, hell, I'm black, female and I write. I write every day. It's a compulsion.

Ntozake Shange
I'm a playwright. But I'm a woman first. I am not a generic playwright. I am a woman playwright ... I don't have anything that I can add to the masculine perception of the world. What I can add has to be from what I've experienced. And my perceptions and my syntax, my colloquialisms, my pre-occupations, are founded in race and gender.

Male opinions of women writers vary in direct proportion to their level of misogyny ...

Michael Legat
Like many another dedicated reader, I do not choose my books according to the sex of the author, and I applaud the fact that no one any longer sneers, as they may have done in past generations, at women writers, or expects them to be any less capable as authors than men.

John Updike
The women writers interviewed [in *Writers At Work*] seem to have a warmer and more inspiring relationship with literature than the men. Most of the male writers interviewed are grim about the demands of their craft.

Roy Campbell
> Far from the vulgar haunts of men
> Each sits in her 'successful room',
> Housekeeping with her fountain pen
> And writing novels with her broom.

... while women writers' comments about themselves are a wry acknowledgment of the continuing battle for equal standing in the workplace:

Anne Finch
    Alas! a woman that attempts the pen,
    Such an intruder on the rights of men,
    Such a presumptuous creature, is esteemed,
    The fault can by no virtue be redeemed.

Rachel Billington
When people, women included, hear that you are writing, they assume that it is simply a hobby to fill in time between doing the washing-up and the ironing. It couldn't really be a profession.

Doris Lessing
No woman writer I know has a timetable. Only men have timetables because they have mothers, wives and sisters to manage their lives. We have to fit in.

Ursula le Guin
Most women's writing – like most work by women in any field – is called unimportant ... So if you want your writing to be taken seriously, don't marry and have kids, and above all, don't die. But if you have to die, commit suicide. They approve of that.

Alicia Ostriker
That women should have babies rather than books is the considered opinion of Western civilisation. That women should have books rather than babies is a variation on that theme.

Minette Walters
Women ... are particularly good at analysis because we are the ones who have the babies and we sit and say, 'Why are they doing that?' We tend to analyse more than men.

Mary Stewart
I hope all my books have a hard core of intellect in them: a real bite of intellect ... I'd like to think of myself as a romantic intellectual, with a tough kind of intelligence but romantic as well.

Virginia Woolf
A woman writing thinks back through her mother.

Hilary Mantel
Many people – women especially – feel guilty about writing. They feel it is self-indulgent. But it is not. It is a way of coming to grips with the world, and it is also a way of making money.

Lorrie Moore
[When I was younger] books by women came as great friends, a relief ... A book by a woman, a book that began up close, on the heart's porch, was a treat, an exhilaration ... I think that women who became writers did so to create more books in the world by women; to give themselves something more to read.

Anne Tyler
My family can always tell when I'm well into a novel because the meals get very crummy.

· Writers & age ·

'Writers age more quickly than athletes'

Young writers are seen as a mixed blessing:

William Faulkner
There are no young writers worth a damn.

Somerset Maugham
The trouble with our younger authors is that they are all in their sixties.

Cyril Connolly
The best that can happen for a writer is to be taken up very late or very early, when either old enough to take its measure, or so young that when dropped by society he has all life before him.

Tennessee Williams
Young writers. If they're meant to be writers, they will write. There's nothing that can stop them. It may kill them. They may not be able to stand the terrible indignities, humiliation, privations, shocks that attend the life of an American writer. They may not. Yet they may have some sense of humour about it, and manage to survive.

G K Chesterton
> And I dream of the days when work was scrappy,
>   And rare in our pockets the mark of the mint,
> And we were angry and poor and happy,
>   And proud of seeing our names in print.

Kingsley Amis
I was never an Angry Young Man. I am angry only when I hit my thumb with a hammer.

Some decide to write when they're very young ...

Charles Dickens
I dreamed my first dreams of authorship when I was six years old or so.

Jay McInerney
Writing is something I've wanted to do since I could remember, aside from a brief notion of being a trapper in the Hudson Bay, or a mercenary ... I fell in love with the image of being a writer – this Dylan Thomas, this roustabout, this bad boy, this perennial adolescent.

... and opinions are divided as to whether age improves writers:

Tennessee Williams
Writers age more quickly than athletes.

Georges Simenon
A writer has nothing to say after the age of forty; if he is clever he knows how to hide it.

Somerset Maugham
If, as most writers do, for it is a healthy occupation, he lives too long, his later work will show the decline due to advancing years, but there will be a period during which he will bring forth in the perfection of which he is capable.

Joseph Wambaugh
I don't think I was ready to write earlier; it took a little aging, at least for me, to acquire experience and a reasonable amount of maturity and discipline, although I don't know how much I have even yet.

E B White
How should one adjust to age? In principle one shouldn't adjust. In fact, one does. (Or I do.) When my head starts knocking because of my attempt to write, I quit writing instead of carrying on as I used to do when I was young.

James Thurber
The characteristic fear of the American writer is ... the process of aging. The writer looks in the mirror and examines his hair and teeth to see if they're still with him ... Coupled with this fear of aging is the curious idea that the writer's inventiveness and ability will end in his fifties.

Noël Coward
I don't write plays with the idea of giving some great thought to the world, and that isn't just coy modesty. As one gets older one doesn't feel so strongly any more, one discovers that everything is always going to be exactly the same with different hats on.

Oliver Wendell Holmes
An old author is constantly rediscovering himself in the more or less fossilised productions of his earlier years.

Mickey Spillane
If you're a singer, you lose your voice. A baseball player loses his arm. A writer gets more knowledge, and if he's good, the older he gets, the better he writes.

Harold Rosenberg
A writer who lives long enough becomes an academic subject and almost qualified to teach it himself.

Relationships with other authors

'Trifling with literary fools in taverns'

Since writing is a solitary occupation, most writers are by nature lone wolves and scorn social contact:

Cyril Connolly
The only way for writers to meet is to share a quick pee over a common lamp-post.

Nelson Algren
I've always felt strongly that a writer shouldn't be engaged with other writers, or with people who make books, or even with people who read them. I think the farther you get away from the literary traffic, the closer you are to sources. I mean, a writer doesn't really *live*, he observes.

Thomas Babington Macaulay
I hate the notion of gregarious authors. The less we have to do with each other the better.

May Sarton
I don't like writers. I don't like seeing writers. I'm not good at it. It upsets me. It's been too hard a struggle. I'm very competitive, and that side comes out. I'm uncomfortable with writers. I love painters and sculptors.

Joseph Heller
I don't think writers are comfortable in each others' presence. We can talk, of course, for five minutes or so, but I don't think we want to socialise ... I've noticed that the opening gambit in conversation between two writers – and I'm always very uncomfortable hearing it – is, 'I like your work.'

Ernest Hemingway
Writing, at its best, is a lonely life. Organisations for writers palliate the writer's loneliness, but I doubt if they improve his writing. He grows in public stature as he sheds his loneliness and often his work deteriorates. For he does his work alone and if he is a good enough writer he must face eternity, or the lack of it, each day.

Though there is at least one exception:

Isaac Bashevis Singer
When I lived in Poland, I used to hang out at the writers' club. I'd be there every day. But there is nothing quite like that in America. I know practically no other writers ... I am sorry about this. I would like to be friendly with more writers.

Writers are also notoriously waspish about their colleagues:

Saul Bellow
Writers seldom wish other writers well.

Walter Savage Landor
Authors are like cattle going to a fair: those of the same field can never move on without butting one another.

George Bernard Shaw
I have not wasted my life trifling with literary fools in taverns as [Ben] Jonson did when he should have been shaking England with the thunder of his spirit.

Oscar Wilde
Bernard Shaw has no enemies but is intensely disliked by his friends.

Quentin Crisp *(of Oscar Wilde):*
He festooned the dung heap on which he had placed himself with sonnets as people grow honeysuckle around outdoor privies.

Tennessee Williams
I think you judge Truman [Capote] a bit too charitably when you call him a child; he is more like a sweetly vicious old lady.

Gerald Brenan
[Henry] Miller is not really a writer but a non-stop talker to whom someone has given a typewriter.

Vladimir Nabokov *(of Ernest Hemingway):*
I read him for the first time in the early forties, something about bells, balls and bulls, and loathed it.

John Osborne
Vladimir Nabokov is surely the most preposterous Transylvanian monster ever to be created by American Academe. He is not a writer at all but a looming beast that stalks the Old Dark House of Campus Literature.

James Dickey
I'm put off by the great stuffed goats of English literature.

Though there are exceptions here too:

James Michener
I think about Tolstoy, Flaubert and Dickens, and I'm jealous of what those authors accomplished. Because I am jealous, I am a writer now. I remain jealous and this gives me a guide to what I might accomplish.

Truman Capote
I don't feel in competition with other writers. Because I don't write about the same things as any other writer that I know of does.

J P Donleavy
Your battle is not with other authors, your battle is with what you put on the paper.

· *Writers' alternatives* ·

'Install me in any profession save this damn'd profession of writing'

Like anybody in a chancy occupation, writers are much given to considering their alternatives:

Erskine Caldwell
I learned early in life that you can be a reader or a writer. I decided to be a writer.

Brooks Atkinson
Nothing a man writes can please him as profoundly as something he does with his back, shoulders and hands.

Frederic Raphael
Real men do things. They don't just write about them.

Carlos Fuentes
You have so much mental time on your hands when you are a bureaucrat: you have time to think and to learn how to write in your head.

Kurt Vonnegut
There is only one genuinely ghastly thing hack jobs do to writers, and that is to waste their precious time.

Joseph Wambaugh
I was never a wet-eyed, passionate writer; I was always a policeman. I'm still not sure what I am mostly, a writer or a policeman.

John le Carré
I was never a very good spook; I was definitely a writer who took up spying rather than a spy who took up writing.

Nathaniel Hawthorne
I don't want to be a doctor, and live by men's diseases; nor a minister to live by their sins; nor a lawyer to live by their quarrels. So I don't see there's anything left for me but to be an author.

Joan Didion
I wrote stories from the time I was a little girl, but I didn't want to be a writer. I wanted to be an actress. I didn't realise then that it's the same impulse. It's make-believe. It's performance. The only difference being that a writer can do it all alone.

John Cheever
Good writers are often excellent at a hundred other things, but writing promises a greater latitude for the ego.

Ezra Pound
> O God, O Venus, O Mercury, patron of thieves,
> Lend me a little tobacco-shop,
>   or install me in any profession
> Save this damn'd profession of writing,
>   Where one needs one's brains all the time.

Ernest Hemingway
I like to do and can do many things better than I can write, but when I don't write, I feel like shit. I've got the talent and I feel that I'm wasting it.

Georges Simenon
Everyone who does not need to be a writer, who thinks he can do something else, ought to do something else.

William Saroyan
If it were not for my good luck in having the profession of writing and the compulsion to write, the human experience would be for me a very different order of thing. I could never be a worker, a slave. So if I hadn't been a writer, I'd have been a bum.

More Quotes

CHAPTER TWO
What Makes a Writer?

Creativity

'The artist always wants to be the creator of the world'

The ability to think creatively is the essential quality all original artists require, whether they be painters, sculptors, composers, choreographers or writers:

David Malouf
The artist always wants to be the creator of the world. He wants to be God in that way, in the way in which he can breathe out of his mouth and all the world is there, all shiny new, with the breath just condensing on it.

Alison Lurie
One of the gifts an artist may have is the ability to create what J R R Tolkien called a 'secondary world' – a fully imagined universe, as consistent as our own or possibly more so.

William Plomer
It is the function of creative men to perceive the relations between thoughts, or things, or forms of expression that may seem utterly different, and to be able to combine them into some new forms – the power to connect the seemingly unconnected.

Jean Cocteau
The work of every creator is autobiography, even if he does not know it or wish it, even if his work is 'abstract'.

James Harvey Robinson
Creative intelligence in its various forms and activities is what makes man.

· What is creativity? ·

Rollo May
Creativity is a yearning for immortality.

Seon Manley & Susan Belcher
There is no simple answer as to what is creativity – certainly it seems to be a gift distributed almost indiscriminately.

Edward de Bono
Creativity is not a matter of inspiration, craziness or gimmicks but a form of logic – the logic of asymmetric patterning systems or lateral thinking.

Alex F Osborn
Creativity is so delicate a flower that praise tends to make it bloom, while discouragement often nips it in the bud. Any of us will put out more and better ideas if our efforts are appreciated.

William Safire
To write creatively is to come up with something new or at least to come at something differently. Whether in arranging fact or hatching fiction, originality is inner-directed, not audience-driven.

Alexander A Bogomoletz
One must not lose desires. They are mighty stimulants to creativeness, to love, and to long life.

Ray Bradbury
Surprise is where creativity comes. Allow your subconscious to come out into the light and say what it has to say.

Shirley Hazzard
All who have created well have had humility, however little it appeared in their daily personalities.

John Poppy
Discipline and focused awareness ... contribute to the act of creation.

Kingman Brewster
There is a correlation between the creative and the screwball. So we must suffer the screwball gladly.

Charles Frankel
Anxiety is the essential condition of intellectual and artistic creation ... and everything that is finest in human history.

Paul Johnson
The thrill of creation is never without its sinister döppelganger of anxiety, the unspeakable dread of artistic death.

Niki Daly
Fear is the enemy of creativity – one can start closing up through fear, seized by fear for daring to be creative.

Margaret Drabble
I've often worried about this – if one got really very happy in life, one might not want to write at all. I think grief is creative. And, in some awful way, boredom is creative ... One's got to rise out of it in some way. And the way I'm most familiar with is by writing.

Isaac Bashevis Singer
The pessimism of the creative person is not decadence but a mighty passion for the redemption of man. While the poet entertains he continues to search for eternal truths ... to find an answer to suffering, to reveal love in the very abyss of cruelty and injustice.

Bernice Fitz-Gibbon
Creativeness often consists of merely turning up what is already there. Did you know that right and left shoes were thought up only a little more than a century ago?

William Goyen
Since the writer is truly a seminal person (he spits out his own web, as Yeats said, and then ... gets caught in it), the truly creative writer is full of the fear and the pride that a maker of new things feels.

Peter Høeg
Our culture is the first one in history to think that it is the individual who achieves, the first to say, 'I work, I have accomplished this or that.' Our culture is the first one to say 'I'. All other cultures believe creativity comes from outside.

Henry James
To live *in* the world of creation – to get into it and stay in it – to frequent it and haunt it – to *think* intensely and fruitfully – to woo combinations and inspirations into being by a depth and continuity of attention and meditation – that is the only thing.

Anna Freud
Creative minds always have been known to survive any kind of bad training.

And creativity needn't fade with age unless you let it:

John Cassavetes
No matter how old you get, if you can keep the desire to be creative, you're keeping the man-child alive.

· Writing talent and skills ·

'Talent is like a grain of pearl sand shifting about in the creative mind'

Given the ability to think creatively, a would-be writer must also have specific inborn talent:

John Mortimer
I knew early on that I was going to be a writer. I think it's something rather like a curse that you're born with.

William Shakespeare
This is a gift that I have ... a foolish extravagant spirit, full of forms, figures, shapes, objects, ideas, apprehensions, motions, revolutions ... But the gift is good in those in whom it is acute, and I am thankful for it.

Being born with creative skills and a level of talent is no guarantee of success, however. The gifts need to be taken seriously and augmented by hard work and application:

Ernest Hemingway
Real seriousness in regard to writing is one of the two absolute necessities. The other, unfortunately, is talent.

Ned Rorem
A writer doesn't need to go out and live, but stay home and invent.

Jean Anouilh
Talent is like a tap; while it is open, one must write.

Jules Renard
Talent is a matter of quantity: talent doesn't write one page, it writes three hundred.

Nadine Gordimer
I think that if you distort whatever little talent you've been given, that's wrong, because talent is the one thing you have and it should be used faithfully in dealing with the world around you.

Marjorie Holmes
Talent is a gift. You had nothing to do with receiving yours, nor I with receiving mine. But each of us has everything to do with what becomes of that talent. I am firmly convinced that each of us is given his talent for a reason.

Rod McKuen
Talent is never enough in any field; it must be coupled with perseverance and the need for recognition.

William Kennedy
I always knew that (a) I wanted to be a writer and (b) if you persist in doing something, sooner or later you will achieve it. It's just a matter of persistence – and a certain amount of talent. You can't do anything without talent, but you can't do anything without persistence, either.

James Baldwin
Talent is insignificant. I know a lot of talented ruins. Beyond talent lie all the usual words: discipline, love, luck, but, most of all, endurance.

Though there are those who disagree:

Aldous Huxley
There is no substitute for talent. Industry and all the virtues are of no avail.

Dorothy Parker
I think that Aldous Huxley utters the loud truth when he says ... that industry can never substitute for talent. There exists, especially in the American mind, a sort of proud confusion between the two ... It is our national joy to mistake for the first-rate, the fecund rate.

And even the combination of talent, seriousness and hard work are not enough. Writers need other qualities too:

Joseph Wambaugh
Under talent, I don't know what to lump – maybe an ability with language, maybe an ability to handle it ... Maybe a logical mind ... an ability to perceive truth in things ... Maybe if you lump all those things under a heading called talent maybe that's half of it. The other half is discipline.

F Scott Fitzgerald
As a first premise you have to develop a conscience and if on top of that you have talent so much the better. But if you have talent without the conscience, you are just one of many thousand journalists.

Erica Jong
Everyone has talent. What is rare is the courage to follow the talent to the dark place where it leads.

Bill Adler
Most authors' talents are not equal to their egos.

*B*eyond talent is the lodestar, genius:

Malcolm Cowley
Talent is what you possess; genius is what possesses you.

Truman Capote
Talent, and genius as well, is like a grain of pearl sand shifting about in the creative mind. A valued tormentor ... When God hands you a gift, he also hands you a whip; and the whip is intended solely for self-flagellation.

F Scott Fitzgerald
Genius is the ability to put into effect what is in your mind.

Oscar Wilde
I've put my genius into my life; I've only put my talent into my words.

Lawrence Block
It's not enough just to have the ability, you have to want the life.

· More necessary qualities for a writer ·

'When I was a little boy they called me a liar but now that I am grown up they call me a writer'

*I*f one were to make a list of the essential qualities writers believe they need it would be a long one, starting with humanity:

Ralph Waldo Emerson
Talent alone cannot make a writer. There must be a man behind the book.

William Faulkner
No man can write who is not first a humanitarian.

John Steinbeck
A writer who does not passionately believe in the perfectibility of man has no dedication nor any membership in literature.

Heinrich Heine
If one has no heart, one cannot write for the masses.

Kurt Vonnegut
Writers ought to have a passion for and an engagement with something beyond the page.

E L Doctorow
The writer writes from an almost biblical anger, which is not much different from despair. It is a dire, driven state of mind which professes and, at the same time, refuses to accept the truth that, as individuals, humans are pitiful, and as groups, inhuman.

Athol Fugard
I don't think [anger] is the most meaningful dynamic a writer can have. I mean, it has been a subsidiary energy, but at the risk of sounding pretentious, I would like to say my dominant energy has been love.

Ethel Wilson
A writer's mind seems to be situated partly in the solar plexus and partly in the head.

Robertson Davies
The terrible truth will out ... Every writer is, in one way or another, a moralist. Not ... that he seeks to impose ideas of truth and conduct on his readers ... but because he observes life from the standpoint of his own spirit and personality, and he records what he sees.

Ray Bradbury
A writer must have the firm, hard ability to turn his eye inward upon himself.

Brian Moore
I think there has always been this dichotomy in a real writer. He wants to be terribly human, and he responds emotionally, but at the same time there's this cold observer who cannot cry.

Julian Barnes
The writer must be universal in sympathy and an outcast by nature: only then can he see clearly.

George Darien
A writer's eyes, to be clear, must be dry.

Though two writers at least disagree on the subject of tears:

Robert Frost
No tears in the writer, no tears in the reader.

Ring Lardner
How can you write if you can't cry?

Character traits considered important for a writer range from compassion to optimism:

Arnold Bennett
Essential characteristic of the really great novelist: a Christ-like, all-embracing compassion.

Tobias Wolff
To be a writer you need to see things as they are, and to see things as they are you need a certain basic innocence.

Robert Penn Warren
Context is all. And a relatively pure heart. Relatively pure – for if you had a pure heart you wouldn't be in the book-writing business in the first place.

Though **François Mauriac** *once wrote:*
Sin is the writer's element.

Ralph Waldo Emerson
Nothing great was ever achieved without enthusiasm.

Hilary Mantel
In my view the most helpful personal quality a writer can cultivate is self-confidence – arrogance, if you can manage it. You write to impose yourself on the world, and you have to believe in your own ability when the world at large shows no sign of agreeing with you.

John Barth
It's a combination of an almost obscene self-confidence and an ongoing terror.

Thomas Costain
I am convinced that all writers are optimists whether they concede the point or not ... How otherwise could any human being sit down to a pile of blank sheets and decide to write, say two hundred thousand words on a given theme?

good imagination is an obvious necessity ...

Albert Einstein
Imagination is more important than reason.

Jessica Anderson
I believe imagination is the primary necessity. It's not a process of reasoning, but letting one set of words fire off another, and another ... like improving a dance.

Henry Miller
A writer needs very little to stimulate him. The fact of being a writer means more than other men he is given to cultivating the imagination.

Ernest Hemingway
Nobody knows a damn thing about [imagination] except that it is what we get for nothing. It may be racial experience. I think that is quite possible. It is the one thing besides honesty that a writer must have. The more he learns from experience the more truly he can imagine.

Graham Swift
A true writer's imagination is always bigger than he is, it out-reaches his personality. Sometimes this can be felt palpably and thrillingly in the very act of writing, and perhaps it is for this infrequent but soaring sensation that writers, truly, write.

Doris Lessing
I'm tormented by the inadequacy of the imagination. I've a sense of the conflict between my life as a writer and the terrors of our time.

Gabriel Garcia Marquez
It always amuses me that the biggest praise for my work comes for the imagination, while the truth is that there's not a single line in all my work that does not have a basis in reality. The problem is that Caribbean reality resembles the wildest imagination.

... though (surprisingly) one writer doesn't think she has any ...

Hilary Mantel
I don't think I have much imagination. What talent I have is for seeing the connections between things, and in finding a dramatic form for abstract ideas.

... and another (tongue-in-cheek) finds imagination a positive hindrance:

Franklin P Adams
Having imagination, it takes you an hour to write a paragraph that, if you were unimaginative, would take you only a minute. Or you might not write the paragraph at all.

Writers also need a well-developed faculty for observation ...

Morley Callaghan
There is only one trait that marks the writer. He is always watching. It's a kind of trick of mind and he is born with it.

Graham Greene
A writer must keep anonymous in order to observe people in their daily lives and without a mask.

John D MacDonald
The writer must be a Not-I ... the observer, the questioner. That is why the writer should be wary of adopting planned eccentricities of appearance and behaviour, since, by making himself the observed rather than the observer, he dwarfs the volume of input he must have to keep his work fresh.

Albert Zuckerman
Another skill of the very best writers ... is an eye for detail. But not all details, only the most telling ones. The great storyteller has an acuity of perception as sharp as that of a visual artist and can make music in words.

... to which should be added the essential yeast of experience:

William Faulkner
A writer needs three things, experience, observation and imagination, any two of which, at times any one of which, can supply the lack of the others.

The ability to be rigorously self-critical is another requirement for those who aim to produce high-quality work:

Leo Tolstoy
In a writer there must always be two people – the writer and the critic.

Graham Greene
An author of talent is his own best critic – the ability to criticise his own work is inseparably bound up with his talent: it is his talent.

Peter Elbow
Writing calls on two skills that are so different that they usually conflict with each other: creating and criticising. In other words, writing calls on the ability to create words and ideals out of yourself, but it also calls on the ability to criticise them in order to decide which ones to use.

E B White
I do think the ability to evaluate one's own stuff with reasonable accuracy is a helpful piece of equipment.

Shirley Hazzard
A writer's ability to develop, and even to continue to produce at all, to a large measure depends on a capacity for self-questioning ... The strength to persevere with the process ... of self-enquiry is, I believe, in many cases closely related to the quality of a novelist's later work.

Harlan Ellison
Don't believe any of that flapdoodle about a writer being unable to estimate his own work; if he's anywhere near talented, he knows better than anyone else.

G K Chesterton
My real judgement of my own work is that I have spoilt a number of jolly good ideas in my time.

And then there are all the other useful talents ...

E B White
I'm not at all sure what the 'necessary equipment' is for a writer – it seems to vary greatly with the individual. Some writers are equipped with extra-sensory perception. Some have a good ear ... Some are equipped with humour – although not nearly as many as think they are. Some are equipped with a massive intellect ... Some are prodigious.

Isaac Bashevis Singer
When I was a little boy they called me a liar but now that I am grown up they call me a writer.

Ernest Hemingway
It is not *unnatural* that the best writers are liars. A major part of their trade is to lie or invent ... They often lie unconsciously and then remember their lies with deep remorse.

William Trevor
I believe in not quite knowing. A writer needs to be doubtful, questioning. I write out of curiosity and bewilderment.

William Saroyan
It is necessary to remember and necessary to forget, but it is better for a writer to remember.

James Dickey
In my own work the quality I esteem is a very frank, male tenderness. Men don't set enough store in that. Men think they have to be like John Wayne – to suppress the best things in themselves.

Ernest Hemingway
A writer without a sense of justice and of injustice would be better off editing the Year Book of a school for exceptional children than writing novels.

Irwin Shaw
An absolutely necessary part of a writer's equipment, almost as necessary as talent, is the ability to stand up under punishment, both the punishment the world hands out and the punishment he inflicts upon himself.

Roald Dahl
I mistrust clergymen and priests – like I mistrust scientists; they're the priesthood of today. In fact I'm against intellectuals. No real writer is an intellectual.

Ray Bradbury
Too often the intellectual is unpopular in this world because he's a spoil sport. Wide tastes, foolish and lovely and happy and silly tastes make the complete human and the complete writer.

Santha Rama Rau
Really, in the end, the only thing that can make you a writer is the person that you are, the intensity of your feeling, the honesty of your vision, the unsentimental acknowledgment of the endless interest of the life around you and within you.

Colin Wilson
Precision is less important to a writer than a clear knowledge of what he wants to achieve.

Hilary Mantel
On the whole I would guess that writers are ruthless people, though their saving grace is that they are ruthless with themselves.

Samuel Johnson
The two most engaging powers of an author are to make new things familiar, and familiar things new.

John Barth
There are writers whose gift is to make terribly complicated things simple. But I know my gift is the reverse: to take relatively simple things and complicate them to the point of madness.

Mary Shelley
Invention ... does not consist in creating out of void, but out of chaos.

Friedrich Nietzsche
One must still have chaos in oneself to be able to give birth to a dancing star.

... including those famous writers' aids:

Graham Greene
Every writer needs a splinter of ice in the heart.

Ernest Hemingway
The most essential gift for a good writer is a built-in, shock-proof shit detector. This is the writer's radar and all great writers have had it.

Last words on necessary qualities for a writer:

Lawrence Durrell
It doesn't really matter whether you're first rate, second rate, or third rate, but it's of vital importance that the water finds its own level and that you do the very best you can with the powers that are given you.

Clive James
For a writer to stay true to his gift, providing he has one, is not as hard as writers are fond of making out.

Robert Benchley
It took me fifteen years to discover I had no talent for writing, but I couldn't give it up because by that time I was too famous.

· Influences ·

'There are writers that awaken'

Writers are generally uncomfortable about discussing who or what has influenced them, for fear of being accused of a gamut of failings running from lack of originality to plagiarism. There are exceptions, though:

John Fowles
It's the toughest job in the world; you must manage to free yourself from everyone and everything that wants to influence you. That's the existential hell that all writers have to go through.

William Faulkner
A man cannot tell what influences him the most. Everything he has ever touched, read, tasted, smelled, heard or done since infancy influences him in some degree, and that is all reflected in the work which that man does. It is no more possible to isolate any single influence than it is to count the polliwogs in a Mississippi swamp.

John Burroughs
Thoreau's quality is very penetrating and contagious; reading him is like eating onions – one must look out or the flavour will reach his own page.

Jay McInerney
The myth of Hemingway is very powerful. I think it's hard to be an American male writer, even now, and not feel the shadow of Hemingway. The myth shapes one's concept of the nobility of the calling. I also learned a great deal about storytelling because Hemingway's work is so clean and stark.

Graham Greene
What one reads doesn't influence one as much as where one is. Still, a great many writers have had their effect on me. The serious ones, I guess, were Ford Madox Ford, Joseph Conrad and Henry James. He was my idol, but to say he influenced me is a bit absurd – like saying a mountain influenced a mouse.

Ben Okri
There are writers that awaken, and that's what's important. Talking about influences makes people lazy; instead of just reading the book they do so through the filter of the so-called influences.

Robert Browning
I had no other direction than my parents' taste for whatever was highest and best in literature; but I found out for myself many forgotten fields which proved the richest of pastures.

Pat Conroy
It is [my mother's] voice that I feel I speak in. It is the power of her voice that moves me to write, moves me to feel. She told me, 'Never write anything you cannot feel, never write anything without emotion, never write anything without passion.'

Doris Lessing
Any writer would be influenced by others. You have to read the great and the good to get a sense of value. I am influenced by them all. Sometimes I recognise flashes of myself in others' work. So what?

Inspiration

'Inspiration is a sort of spontaneous combustion – the oily rags of the head and the heart'

Inspiration is defined in various dictionaries as 'a creative influence or stimulus', 'a sudden happy idea' and 'a brain-wave', but these definitions pale beside the quantum leap of the blinding flash and the satisfaction that comes with nurturing a spark into a crackling log fire.

Writers derive their inspiration from widely disparate sources. There are the pragmatic ...

Anonymous
Inspiration is the act of drawing up a chair to the writing desk.

Anthony Trollope
I was once told that the surest aid to the writing of a book was a piece of cobbler's wax on my chair. I certainly believe in the cobbler's wax, much more than the inspiration.

Peter de Vries
I write when I'm inspired, and I see to it that I'm inspired at nine o'clock every morning.

Christopher A Bohialian
Writing ... is as much discipline as it is desire. Set time aside each day, or select days each week, and write. Don't wait until you're inspired, because if you do, you'll never finish anything.

Peter Essex
I don't believe in inspiration. When I'm writing and only when I'm writing does inspiration come. It doesn't come when you're sitting and hoping, it comes while you're working.

Alberto Moravia
When I sit at my table to write, I never know what it's going to be till I'm under way. I trust in inspiration, which sometimes comes and sometimes doesn't. But I don't sit back waiting for it. I work every day.

Madeleine L'Engle
You can't sit and wait for an inspiration. The inspiration comes while you're working, during the time at the typewriter.

Anthony Burgess
Inspiration comes out of the act of making an artifact, a work of craft.

Leonard Bernstein
Inspiration is wonderful when it happens, but the writer must develop an approach for the rest of the time. The approach must involve getting something down on the page: something good, mediocre or even bad.

Doris Lessing
I've always disliked words like inspiration. Writing is probably like a scientist thinking about some scientific problem, or an engineer about an engineering problem.

Katherine Anne Porter
It just takes a ... tiny seed. Then it takes root, and it grows.

Ned Rorem
Divine fires do not blaze each day, but an artist functions in their afterglow, hoping for their recurrence.

Jean Cocteau
It is not inspiration; it is expiration.

... and there are those who credit the physical:

Stanley Elkin
Inspiration is a sort of spontaneous combustion – the oily rags of the head and heart.

Harlan Ellison
When I was younger I was wont to say, rather melodramatically, that I wrote from the gut ... Since then I've tempered my semantics and relocated the source of my work. It comes from the heart and the soul and the head and the index fingers of my right and left hands which are the only ones (poor slobs) that ever learned to type.

Byron
Gin-and-water is the source of all my inspiration.

André Gide
Only those things are beautiful which are inspired by madness and written by reason.

The flash of enlightenment usually comes when the inspiree is alone:

Wolfgang Amadeus Mozart
When I am ... completely myself, entirely alone ... or during the night when I cannot sleep, it is on such occasions that my ideas flow best and most abundantly. Whence and how these come I know not, nor can I force them.

Leo Tolstoy
The best thoughts most often come in the morning after waking, while still in bed or during the walk.

George Moore
If you would hear the Muse you must prepare silent hours for her and not be disappointed if she breaks the appointment you have made with her.

And the subconscious plays a leading role:

Tennessee Williams
All you have to do is close your eyes and wait for the symbols.

William Faulkner
I listen to the voices.

Anthony Burgess
The unconscious mind has a habit of asserting itself in the afternoon.

Last words on inspiration to:

Anatole France
A writer is rarely so well inspired as when he talks about himself.

Ralph Waldo Emerson
All writing comes by the grace of God.

Nathaniel Hawthorne
The devil himself always seems to get into my inkstand, and I can only exorcise him by pensful at a time.

William Faulkner
I don't know anything about inspiration because I don't know what inspiration is – I've heard about it, but I never saw it.

Why do writers write?

'If I don't write, I'll die'

Some writers have the simplest motives:

Harlan Ellison
I have to write.

T S Eliot
The only good reason for writing is that one has to write.

Philip Larkin
The short answer is that you write because you have to.

Catherine Cookson
All I know is if you want to write, you'll write.

Leo Rosten
The only reason for being a professional writer is that you just can't help it.

James T Farrell
If I don't write, I'll die.

Es'kia Mphahlele
I write out of an inner compulsion – I've got to do it or I go berserk.

Geoffrey Jenkins
Writing is not a logical, intellectual process. It is emotional ... I write because I love writing.

Eudora Welty
At the time of writing, I don't write for my friends or myself, either; I write for *it*, for the pleasure of *it*.

H L Mencken
I wrote what I wrote because it was my nature to do so, and for no other reason.

Gore Vidal
A writer is someone who writes, that's all. You can't stop it; you can't make yourself do anything else but that.

Barbara Tuchman
I have always been in a condition in which I cannot not write.

Gillian Slovo
I've written, I suppose, out of my own interests and my own passions – to be honest to myself.

Doris Lessing
I became a writer because of frustration, the way I think many writers do.

E M Forster
How do I know what I think until I see what I say?

Edward Albee
I write to find out what I'm talking about.

Elie Wiesel
I write to understand as much as to be understood.

Cecil Day-Lewis
We do not write in order to be understood; we write in order to understand.

James Baldwin
When you're writing, you're trying to find out something which you don't know.

Rebecca West
I really write to find out what I know about something and what is to be known about something.

William Styron
You write because you want to be read.

Alfred Kazin
One writes to make a home for oneself, on paper, in time and in others' minds.

Mickey Spillane
I want to entertain people by the millions.

Maeve Binchy
I want to talk to people about the experiences women have, feelings, emotions, hopes and dreams.

Evelyn Waugh
I wanted to be a man of the world and I took to writing as I might have taken to archaeology or diplomacy or any other profession, as a means of coming to terms with the world. Now I see it as an end in itself.

John Updike
The itch to make dark marks on paper is shared by writers and artists.

Frank O'Connor
From the time I was nine or ten, it was a toss-up whether I was going to be a writer or a painter, and I discovered by the time I was sixteen or seventeen that paints cost too much money, so I became a writer because you could be a writer with a pencil and a penny notebook.

Mary Stewart
I have the creative temperament. I am restless, unfulfilled and unhappy if I'm not doing or making something.

Irving Wallace
The big motivation for me was the desire to be independent, to get up when you want, write what you want and work where you want.

Some writers are vague about their motives:

John Ashbery
I am often asked why I write, and I don't know really – I just want to.

Joan Didion
On the whole, I don't want to think too much about why I write what I write. If I know what I'm doing ... I can't do it.

William Golding
A book is produced by the whole man, who is more complicated than any other single object in the universe, and its motivation is therefore just as mysterious and ineluctable.

Jean Rhys
All my life I've tried to escape from writing. I'm too lazy for it and it's a lonely, beastly business and sometimes ugly, too; but always I have been dragged back to it, not once but over and over; and sometimes I've thought I have escaped at times but I haven't.

Some are waspish:

Kingsley Amis
If you can't annoy somebody, there is little point in writing.

Toni Morrison
I never wanted to grow up to be a writer, I just wanted to grow up to be an adult.

F Scott Fitzgerald
You don't write because you want to say something; you write because you've got something to say.

George Bernard Shaw
If you do not write for publication, there is little point in writing at all.

John Adams
The universal object and idol of men of letters is reputation.

Others wax portentous:

Archibald MacLeish
Of course you want to be admired ... but ... that's irrelevant. What's really going to come out of your work is something else. If you have succeeded at all you have become a part – however small a part – of the consciousness of your time.

Somerset Maugham
It did not seem enough merely to write. I wanted to make a pattern of my life, in which writing would be an essential element, but which would include all the other activities proper to man.

Peter Porter
I am sceptical of the idea that people write because they have a message for the world. People write partly to discover things in themselves, and the process of writing is still the same process as that whereby you examine your thoughts and feelings, which are natural-born abilities.

Some write because it makes them feel alive, or to cheat mortality:

Quentin Crisp
I'm not one of those writers you'll hear say, 'When you are a writer, you never retire, you go on writing – that's your life.' Living is my life. I write in order to stay alive.

Françoise Sagan
I shall live badly if I do not write, and I shall write badly if I do not live.

Emile Zola
If you ask me what I came to do in this world, I, an artist, I will answer you: I am here to live out loud.

Carlos Fuentes
Death is the great angel of writing. You must write because you are not going to live any more.

Jack Kerouac
I wrote the book because we're all gonna die.

Umberto Eco
I write a book, not to have a success now but with the hope that in the next millennium, it will be still at least in a bibliography or in a footnote. And if I like the success now, it's because probably it helps the book to survive.

Kenneth Atchity
From the beginning, writers have been accused of justifying their art as the search for immortality. But no writer I know would feel for an instant that being remembered after one's death is adequate compensation for dying, much less an efficient motivation for the wilful madness of artistic discipline.

Many have mixed motives for becoming writers:

Jonathan Raban
I've written out of compulsion, for love, and I've needed the money.

Anthony Cheetham
There are two sorts of writers. Those who write to make money and those who write because that is what they want to do. The second lot shouldn't complain about money.

E M Forster
I write for two reasons: partly to make money and partly to win the respect of people whom I respect.

Alan Paton
The writer may have several motives, and the two purest of these is the wish to express something of oneself, and to communicate this something to others. There are at least two others, the need or desire to make money or a living, and the desire to win fame.

Quentin Crisp
There are three reasons for becoming a writer: the first is that you need the money; the second, that you have something to say that you think the world should know; the third is that you can't think what to do with the long winter evenings.

Molière
Writing is like prostitution: first you do it for the love of it, then you do it for a few friends, and finally you do it for the money.

Nathaniel Hawthorne
The only sensible ends of literature are, first, the pleasurable toil of writing; second, the gratification of one's family and friends; and lastly, the solid cash.

Louis Untermeyer
Write out of love; write out of instinct; write out of reason. But always write for money.

Frederick Forsyth
There are four reasons to write. Compulsion – I don't have that. Fame and glory – I couldn't give a toss. A message for humanity – usually it is pure pretension. And money. I write for money; that is why I will never get the Booker Prize.

Anthony Burgess
One goes on writing partly because it is the only available way of earning a living ... There is also a privier reason for pushing on, and that is the hopeless hope that some day that intractable enemy language will yield to the struggle to control it.

H L Mencken
The impulse to create beauty is rather rare in literary men ... Far ahead of it comes the yearning to make money. And after the yearning to make money comes the yearning to make a noise.

Understandably, the motive that looms largest for most writers is the necessity of earning a living:

Doris Lessing
What motivates me to keep on writing is that I have earned my living from it for the past forty years. I'm a work animal. When they bury me, I will probably be scribbling. That's my epitaph.

Jimmy Breslin
The number one reason why any professional writer writes is to pay the bills. This isn't the Lawn Tennis Association where you play just for the thrill of it.

A A Milne
Almost anybody can be an author; the business is to collect money and fame from this state of being.

Dorothy Parker
I'd like to have money. And I'd like to be a good writer. These two can come together, and I hope they will, but if that's too adorable, I'd rather have money.

Jack London
I write for no other purpose than to add to the beauty that now belongs to me. I write a book for no other reason than to add three or four hundred acres to my magnificent estate.

Samuel Johnson
No man but a blockhead ever wrote, except for money.

Coventry Patmore
A man who thinks he has got anything to say should always write for money ... Modesty is preserved by the money-motive. Besides, the subtlest truths are like the remoter stars: you cannot see them unless you look a little on one side of them. You are likely to say your say the better for having your direct gaze fixed upon the five, ten or twenty pound note which your prophecy is to bring you.

Mickey Spillane
I only write when I need the money. I hate to work. If I got enough money, I don't write. What's the sense of making it if you can't spend it?

Louis-Ferdinand Céline
If I had money I'd never write.

Norman Mailer *wants it both ways. He has said on different occasions:*
- I always start a book for money. If you've married five times you have to.
- I've never written a book because there's going to be a lot of money in it, because I know that's the surest way to take five years off your life.

Many writers, specially those of yore, profess to be horrified by the very idea that filthy lucre could be an incentive:

Fyodor Dostoyevsky
I simply don't know how anyone can write at great speed, and only for the money's sake.

Gustave Flaubert
To practise art in order to earn money, flatter the public, spin facetious or dismal yarns for reputation or cash – that is the most ignoble of professions.

Lady Mary Wortley Montagu
A person of quality should never turn author ... one of the most distinguished prerogatives of mankind, writing, when duly executed does honour to human nature. If done for the purpose of making money it is contemptible.

Karl Marx
The writer must earn money in order to be able to live and to write, but he must by no means live and write for the purpose of making money.

William Faulkner
The writer doesn't need economic freedom. All he needs is a pencil and some paper. I've never known anything good in writing to come from having accepted any free gift of money. The good writer never applies to a foundation. He's too busy writing something.

Mary Lee Settle
If you set out to write for money and fame, as Freud said writers did, then you should sell junk bonds or shoot somebody instead. It's easier.

And then there are the realists:

Edna O'Brien
I have never written anything in order to make money. A story comes to me, is given me, as it were, and I write it. But perhaps the need to earn a living and my need to write coincided.

Dorothy Parker
Being in a garret doesn't do you any good unless you're some sort of Keats ... The art of the country so immeasurably adds to its prestige that if you want the country to have writers and artists – persons who live precariously in our country – the state must help.

Frank O'Connor
A student of mine had this thing about you mustn't live on your father and I argued with him. I explained that a European writer would live on anybody, would live on a prostitute if he had to – it didn't matter – the great thing was to get the job done.

George Gissing
Innumerable are the men and women now writing for bread, who have not the least chance of finding in such work a permanent livelihood. They took to writing because they knew not what else to do, or because the literary calling tempted them by its independence and its dazzling prizes. They will hang on to the squalid profession, their earnings eked out by begging and borrowing, until it is too late for them to do anything else – and what then?

The 'dazzling prizes' are another reason for writing, though writers, being contrary individualists, generally deny this and many heap scorn on their industry's honours:

T S Eliot
The Nobel is a ticket to one's own funeral. No one has ever done anything after he got it.

George Seferis
I should from the beginning tell you quite bluntly ... that the Nobel Prize is an accident ... which one has to try and forget as soon as possible. Otherwise, if you are over-dazzled by that sort of thing, you get lost and founder.

André Gide
Nothing is so silly as the expression of a man who is being complimented.

There are those who write for reasons that have to do with themselves and their relationships with others:

Truman Capote
I think the only person a writer has an obligation to is himself.

Mary Stewart
I try simply to satisfy myself and I have to go on and on trying, though I never satisfy myself wholly.

Jorge Luis Borges
I write for myself and my friends and I write to ease the passing of time.

Eldridge Cleaver
After I returned to prison, I took a long look at myself and for the first time in my life admitted that I was wrong, that I had gone astray – astray not so much from the white man's law as from being human, civilised. My pride as a man dissolved and my whole fragile structure seemed to collapse, completely shattered. That is why I started to write. To save myself.

John D MacDonald
My purpose is to entertain myself first and other people secondly.

Richard Bach
Write to please yourself. As you do, you'll reflect on your pages the thoughts and values of the people who share your own strange view of the world, and you'll remind them that they're not mad or alone.

Sidney Sheldon
Every good writer that I know writes to please himself, not to please others. He starts with an idea that excites him, develops characters that interest him, and then writes his story as skilfully as he knows how.

Doris Lessing
You should write, first of all, to please yourself. You shouldn't care a damn about anybody else at all. But writing can't be a way of life; the important part of writing is living. You have to live in such a way that your writing emerges from it.

Though **Blaise Pascal** disagrees:
Anything that is written to please the author is worthless.

Aldous Huxley
Writers write to influence their readers, their preachers, their auditors, but always, at bottom, to be more themselves.

John Steinbeck
I can say now that one of the big reasons was this: I instinctively recognised an opportunity to transcend some of my personal failings – things about myself I didn't particularly like and wanted to change but didn't know how to.

Alfred Kazin
In a very real sense, the writer writes in order to teach himself, to understand himself, to satisfy himself; the publishing of his ideas, though it brings gratification, is a curious anticlimax.

Archibald MacLeish
Writers, if they are worthy of that jealous designation, do not write for other writers. They write to give reality to experience.

For many, writing is a passionate business:

Elizabeth Hardwick
This passion has given me much joy, it has given me friends who care for the same things, it has given me employment, escape from boredom, everything.

Katherine Anne Porter
I started out with nothing in the world but a kind of passion, a driving desire. I don't know where it came from, and I do not know why – or why I have been so stubborn about it that nothing could deflect me. But this thing between me and my writing is the strongest bond I have ever had.

William Burroughs
Unless I can reach a point where my writing has the danger and immediate urgency of bull-fighting, it is nowhere.

William Sansom
A writer lives, at best, in a state of astonishment. Beneath any feeling he has of the good or evil of the world lies a deeper one of wonder at it all. To transmit that feeling, he writes.

Others write out of a sense of alienation:

Brian Aldiss
Why had I become a writer in the first place? Because I wasn't fit for society; I didn't fit into the system.

James Baldwin
My father said I was the ugliest child he had ever seen. He told me that all his life and I believed him. And I'd accepted that nobody would ever love me. But ... nobody cares what a writer looks like ... For me, writing was an act of love. It was an attempt ... to be loved.

Some write the sort of books they would want to read themselves:

Toni Morrison *has said on different occasions:*
- I wrote my first novel because I wanted to read it.
- If there's a book you really want to read but it hasn't been written yet, then you must write it.

Thornton Wilder
I think I write in order to discover on my shelf a new book which I would enjoy reading.

Some write out of a need to vent or flaunt the ideas fermenting inside them:

H L Mencken
I write in order to attain that feeling of tension relieved and function achieved which a cow enjoys on giving milk.

T S Eliot
What stimulates me to write a poem is that I have got something inside me that I want to get rid of – it is almost a kind of defecation.

John Dos Passos
You get a great deal off your chest – emotions, impressions, opinions. Curiosity urges you on – the driving force. What is collected must be got rid of. That's one thing to be said about writing. There is a great sense of relief in a fat volume.

James Jones
I do think that the quality which makes a man want to write and be read is essentially a desire for self-exposure and is masochistic. Like one of those guys who has a compulsion to take his thing out and show it on the street.

Joseph Heller
People don't write books to benefit humanity; they're doing it to satisfy, I believe, an exhibitionist.

George Orwell
All writers are vain, selfish, and lazy, and at the very bottom of their motives there lies a mystery. Writing a book is a horrible, exhausting struggle, like a long bout of some painful illness. One would never undertake such a thing if one were not driven on by some demon.

Dylan Thomas
I hold a beast, an angel and a madman in me, and my enquiry is as to their working, and my problem is their subjugation and victory, downthrow and upheaval, and my effort is their self expression.

And then there are all the other reasons:

Wilson Mizner
I wrote a short story because I wanted to see something of mine in print, other than my fingers.

Ray Bradbury
You write because it's an adventure to watch it come out of your hands.

William Faulkner
I discovered that my own little postage stamp of native soil was worth writing about and that I would never live long enough to exhaust it.

Doris Lessing
People become writers because they've had a very pressured childhood, and that doesn't necessarily mean a bad childhood. I don't think an unhappy childhood makes a writer; I think a child who has been forced to become conscious of what's going on very early often becomes a writer.

Marion Halligan
If you said to me, 'Why do you write? What are you about when you're writing?' I would say that I am trying to put the world as I see it into words. That's how everything starts off.

Nadine Gordimer
I see all my books as one book. They are an attempt to encompass the life around me; they reflect the changes in our society and the impingement of politics on the consciousness of people.

S J Perelman
I revel in the prospect of being able to torture a phrase once more.

Katherine Mansfield
Better to write twaddle, anything, than nothing at all.

H L Mencken
The physical business of writing is unpleasant to me, but the psychic satisfaction of discharging bad ideas in worse English makes me forget it.

D H Lawrence
I like to write when I feel spiteful: it's like having a good sneeze.

William Gass
Getting even is one reason for writing ... I write because I hate. A lot. Hard.

Anita Brookner
I started writing because of a terrible feeling of powerlessness: I felt I was drifting and obscure, and I rebelled against that ... I wanted to control rather than be controlled, to ordain rather than be ordained, and to relegate rather than be relegated.

Judith Krantz
I'm writing to have fun and for my readers to have fun. I do the best work I can do.

Clive Cussler
My work is geared strictly to provide a few hours of enjoyable escape ... Some writers prefer to be called novelists, some storytellers, others spokesmen for the masses. Me: I'm an entertainer, no more, no less.

Frank O'Connor
That's the reason you do it, because you enjoy it ... You don't write it because it's a serious moral responsibility. You do it for exactly the same reason that you paint pictures or play with the kids. It's a creative activity.

And to end with, here is some vintage ...

Roald Dahl
A person is a fool to become a writer. His only compensation is absolute freedom. He has no master except his own soul, and that, I am sure, is why he does it.

Edmund White
I don't think most people write because they must; perhaps economically they must, but spiritually? I wonder. I think many writers would be perfectly happy to lay down their pens and never write again if they could maintain their prestige, professorship, and PEN membership.

Basil Boothroyd
People who don't write books ... feel a mysterious awe for people who do. People who do like this. And it may well be the reason why they keep on.

Rainer Maria Rilke
Nobody can advise and help you, nobody. There is only one single means. Go inside yourself. Discover the motive that bids you write; examine whether it sends its roots down to the deepest places of your heart, confess to yourself whether you would have to die if writing were denied you. This before all: ask yourself in the quietest hour of your night: must I write? Dig down into yourself for a deep answer. And if this should be in the affirmative, if you may meet this solemn question with a strong and simple, I must, then build your life according to this necessity.

Chapter Three

Writers' Concerns

· Writers' intentions ·

'I want the reader to turn the page and keep turning to the end'

Writers love talking about their aims and aspirations, which range from the obvious – a need to communicate, explain, explore or simply entertain – via a thirst to dominate the reader, to a grandiose yearning to change the world:

Ernest Hemingway
When you write, your object is to convey every sight, feeling, emotion to the reader.

Barbara Kingsolver
I have a commitment to accessibility. I believe in plot. I want an English professor to understand the symbolism while at the same time I want one of my relatives – who's never read anything but the Sears catalogue – to read my books.

Barbara Tuchman
I want the reader to turn the page and keep turning to the end.

Will Carleton
My purpose in writing is to connect all classes of people with one common bond of sympathy; to picture all grades of life in such a way that all grades will read, under-

stand, and feel it, thus learning about each other and themselves ... to touch and draw out that vein of poetry and feeling which exists somewhere in every human nature.

Joseph Conrad
My task which I am trying to achieve is by the power of the written word to make you hear, to make you feel – it is, before all, to make you see! That – and no more; and it is everything! If I succeed you shall find there ... perhaps also that glimpse of truth for which you have forgotten to ask.

Doris Lessing
Our function as writers, I maintain, is to express what other people feel. If we're any good, it's because we're like other people and can express it.

Friedrich Nietszche
It is my ambition to say in ten sentences what other men say in whole books – what other men do not say in whole books.

William Faulkner
It is his [the poet's, the writer's] privilege to help man endure by lifting his heart, by reminding him of the courage and honour and hope and pride and compassion and pity and sacrifice which have been the glory of his past.

Albert Camus
Meaning of my work: So many men lack grace. How can one live without grace?

Alice Munro
I want to write the story that will zero in and give you intense, but not connected, moments of experience.

Christopher Fry
In my plays I want to look at life – at the commonplace of existence – as if we had just turned a corner and run into it for the first time.

James Dickey
My primary consideration is to change ... To still keep that openness, that chance taking-ness as part of the work. Not to be afraid to make a mistake, even if it's a long and costly mistake.

David Bradley
Writing is my religion ... I do believe that somehow, no matter what the writing task ... if I search my soul and my heart I will find a way to capture some kind of energy, to somehow bring down a little fire to change my readers and change myself.

John Steinbeck
Now the purpose of a book I suppose is to amuse, interest, instruct, but its warmer purpose is just to associate with the reader. You use symbols he can understand so that the two of you can be together.

Philip Roth
What I want is to possess my readers while they are reading my book – if I can, to possess them in ways that other writers don't.

Josephine Hart
That is my ambition when writing. To make it impossible for the reader to escape.

Robert Stone
I am trying ... to crowd people out of their own minds and occupy their space. I want them to stop being themselves for the moment. I want them to stop thinking, and I want to occupy their heads. I want to use language and I want the language to reverberate.

Danielle Steel
I want people to feel good about life. I hate to walk away from a book or movie feeling that life isn't worth a damn. People don't need that. I think, maybe most of all, they get hope from my books.

Samuel Johnson
The only end of writing is to enable the reader better to enjoy life, or better to endure it.

Judith Krantz
You buy my books as a treat, a really personal treat, and I'm not going to let you down. But they're not going to make you a better person.

William Zinsser
What I want to do is make people laugh so they'll see things seriously.

Maya Angelou
I intend to become America's black female Proust.

Karl Kraus
Word and substance – that is the only connection I have striven for in my life.

Ernest Hemingway
For a true writer each book should be a new beginning where he tries again for something that is beyond attainment. He should always try for something that has never been done or that others have tried and failed. Then sometimes, with great luck, he will succeed.

Norman Mailer
The sour truth is that I am imprisoned with a perception which will settle for nothing less than making a revolution in the consciousness of our time.

Frank Kermode
The natural ambition of a writer is to achieve a recognisable splendour that is inseparable from a certain power – a power over language, over inherited forms – and so alter the mood and the mind of society.

William Faulkner
A writer strives to express a universal truth in the best possible way he can: in the way that rings the most bells in the shortest amount of time ... It is almost like trying to write the Lord's Prayer on the head of a pin.

Lillian Hellman
The writer's intention hasn't anything to do with what he achieves. The intent to earn money or the intent to be famous or the intent to be great doesn't matter in the end. Just what comes out.

A striving for perfection seems endemic:

Campbell Armstrong
Everything I write is imperfect. It's lovely in my mind. It's just gorgeous when I think about it, but as soon as I put the first sentence down ... It's like chess – perfect before the first move.

Noël Coward
I am now more of a perfectionist than I used to be; I take pride in being a professional.

Sidney Sheldon
There is no way for you to escape from the agonies and despair of creation, for you will find that what you write will never be good enough to satisfy you. You will always be striving to reach that impossible perfection.

And for the really ambitious, posterity is important:

F Scott Fitzgerald
An author ought to write for the youth of his own generation, the critics of the next, and schoolmasters of ever after.

Arthur Koestler
A writer's ambition should be to trade a hundred contemporary readers for ten readers in ten years' time and for one reader in a hundred years' time.

Samuel Butler
When a man is in doubt about this or that in his writing, it will often guide him if he asks himself how it will tell a hundred years hence.

William Faulkner
The aim of every artist is to arrest motion, which is life, by artificial means and hold it fixed so that a hundred years later, when a stranger looks at it, it moves again since it is life.

Jorge Luis Borges
When writers die they become books, which is, after all, not too bad an incarnation ... A writer should have another lifetime to see whether he is appreciated.

Hilaire Belloc
When I am dead, I hope it may be said:
'His sins were scarlet, but his books were read.'

Damon Runyon's *last words:*
You can keep the things of bronze and stone and give me one man to remember me just once a year.

Kurt Weill
I don't care about posterity: I'm writing for today.

A writer's tasks & duties

'The job of a writer is to make people feel uncomfortable'

Established writers love to enumerate the duties of writers, though they don't agree what they are:

Thomas Mann
The task of a writer consists in being able to make something out of an idea.

E B White
A writer has the duty to be good, not lousy; true, not false; lively, not dull; accurate, not full of error. He should tend to lift people up, not lower them down. Writers do not merely reflect and interpret life, they inform and shape life.

Mary Renault
I think the writer has no other duty than to address himself to the individual and to display to the individual the standards he thinks he ought to have.

William Styron
The writer's duty is to keep on writing ... reflecting disorder, defeat, should that be all he sees at the moment, but ever searching for the elusive love, joy, and hope – qualities which, as in the act of life itself, are best when they have to be struggled for, and are not commonly come by with much ease.

E L Doctorow
I think the ultimate responsibility of the writer ... is to the idea of witness: This is what I see, this is what I feel, this is the way I think things are. Writers have the responsibility not to corrupt that point of view and not to be fearful of it, not to self-censor it.

Marcel Proust
I perceived that to ... write that essential book, which is the only true one, a great writer does not, in the current meaning of the word, invent it, but, since it exists already in each one of us, interprets it. The duty and the task of a writer are those of an interpreter.

Albert Camus
The nobility of our calling will always be rooted in two commitments difficult to observe: refusal to lie about what we know, and resistance to oppression.

Isabel Allende
Write to register history ... Write what should not be forgotten ... The writer of good will carries a lamp to illuminate the dark corners. Only that, nothing more – a tiny beam of light to show some hidden aspect of reality, to help decipher and understand it and thus to initiate, if possible, a change in the conscience of some readers.

W B Yeats
It is not a writer's business to hold opinions.

Somerset Maugham
The writer is more concerned to know than to judge.

Ernest Hemingway
As a man you know who is right and who is wrong. You have to make decisions and enforce them. As a writer you should not judge. You should understand.

Alberto Moravia
People expect from a writer what they once expected from a priest. They want spiritual and moral guidance, some of the greatest needs in the modern world.

Joseph Conrad
Some kind of moral discovery should be the object of every tale.

Though O Henry disagrees:
A story with a moral appended is like the bite of a mosquito. It bores you, and then injects a stinging drop to irritate your conscience.

Gabriel Garcia Marquez
The best way a writer can serve a revolution is to write as well as he can.

Graham Greene
If we enlarge the bounds of sympathy in our readers we succeed in making the work of the state a degree more difficult. That is a genuine duty we owe society, to be a piece of grit in the state machinery.

Brendan Behan
An author's first duty is to let down his country.

Aldous Huxley
The fact that many people should be shocked by what he writes practically imposes it as a duty upon the writer to go on shocking them.

Frederic Raphael
The job of a writer is to make people feel uncomfortable and to question the world. It's not to make money for the publisher, or to give anybody an easy time.

Doris Lessing
I think a writer's job is to provoke questions. I like to think that if someone's read a book of mine they've had ... the literary equivalent of a shower. Something that would start them thinking in a slightly different way perhaps.

Bernard Malamud
It seems to me that the writer's most important task ... is to recapture his image as human being as each of us in his secret heart knows it to be, and as history and literature have from the beginning revealed it.

J B Priestley
No matter how piercing and appalling his insights, the desolation creeping over his outer world, the lurid insights and shadows of his inner world, the writer must live with hope, work in faith.

Norman Mailer
At best you affect the consciousness of your time, and so indirectly you affect the history of the time which succeeds you.

Last words on the subject of writers' duties:

Anaïs Nin
The role of the writer is not to say what we can all say, but what we are unable to say.

Susan Howatch
A writer's first duty to his reader is to be readable.

Joseph Brodsky
A writer should care about one thing – the language. To write well: that is his duty. That is his only duty.

Cyril Connolly
The true function of a writer is to produce a masterpiece and ... no other task is of any consequence.

Athol Fugard
You can't impose from outside a duty or an obligation on a writer. That is something that can only come from within himself or herself.

Being individual

'Every writer has his own voice'

All the best writers are singular, which is defined as remarkable, unique, unusual – one of a kind:

Albert Zuckerman
One precious quality in the best authors, which I believe is largely innate but is sometimes slowly acquired over time, is what editors and critics call 'a voice'.

Marjorie Franco
Every writer has his own voice, and it is up to him to find it and use it with authority. That voice comes through as male or female, child or adult, humorous or serious, but behind it, within it, is the author's brooding presence, his vision of life. He describes the world from his point of view.

E L Doctorow
No matter what elevated state of inspiration you might find for yourself, you can't write the book until you find the voice for it. As it happens, there is just one voice and one voice only for a given book and you must ventriloquise until you find it.

James Kelman
I feel the business of finding a voice is something that should be examined more. For me the thing is to find the voice of your community, of your culture.

Melvin Maddocks
It is one test of a fully developed writer that he reminds us of no one but himself.

Being original

'He who can be imitated by none'

Writers try to be original though all too few succeed:

Ezra Pound
Make it new.

Goethe
The most original authors of modern times are so, not because they create anything new, but only because they are able to say things in a manner as if they had never been said before.

Edmund Wilson
The writer must always find expression for something which has never yet been expressed, must master a new set of phenomena which has never yet been mastered.

Robertson Davies
The most original thing a writer can do is write like himself. It is also his most difficult task.

J F Stephen
Originality does not consist in saying what no one has ever said before, but in saying exactly what you think yourself.

George Bernard Shaw
I owe all my originality, such as it is, to my determination not to be a literary man. Instead of belonging to a literary club I belong to a municipal council. Instead of drinking and discussing authors and reviews, I sit on committees with capable practical greengrocers and bootmakers ... Keep away from books and from men who get their ideas from books, and your own books will always be fresh.

Simone de Beauvoir
The original writer, as long as he isn't dead, is always scandalous.

Jamaica Kincaid
I personally would do everything I can not to be a mainstream writer. I loathe the mainstream.

Some say that there's no such thing:

Henry Miller
Who is original? Everything that we are doing, everything that we think, exists already, and we are only intermediaries, that's all, who make use of what is in the air.

Voltaire
Originality is nothing but judicious imitation. The most original writers borrowed from one another.

Being professional

'The professional guts a book through'

Professional writers stand very much upon their dignity and scorn 'amateur' or part-time scribblers, but it is an attitude that smacks of hypocrisy since writing is a profession where – except in America, which is pragmatic about the business of nurturing writers – qualifications are actively scorned:

Graham Watson
How does one define the 'professional' writer ...? Obviously the term ... would exclude the very large number of writers competent enough to get their books published but whose writing is a relaxation, a hobby, a means of making a modest contribution to their income.

Rayne Kruger
English genius is anti-professional; its affinities are with amateurs.

Seon Manley & Susan Belcher
Every writer, man or woman, must cope with the depressions, emotional upheavals, lassitude ... the false elation and the letdown. Professionalism is the ability to sustain such emotions for a long period of time; genius, on the other hand, is as demonic as Emily Brontë's landscape.

Paul Johnson
A professional writer ... is usually credited with singular good fortune: there is nothing – is there not – to rival the pleasure he gets from his job? This may be true, provided one accepts that pleasure and misery are inseparably linked companions.

Being serious

'... a hawk or a buzzard or even a popinjay ...'

Unless they are humorists all writers like to be taken seriously, though there are those who mock the attendant self-importance:

William Kennedy
You can't go around saying you're a writer if no one will take you seriously.

Anthony Powell
In this country [England] it is rare for anyone, let alone a publisher, to take writers seriously.

Ernest Hemingway
A serious writer is not to be confounded with a solemn writer. A serious writer may be a hawk or a buzzard or even a popinjay, but a solemn writer is always a bloody owl.

William Saroyan
How can you take anything terribly seriously? The writer who today may seem to be grand, tomorrow may be trash. We write for a human race that is constantly changing.

Output

'I have not written as much as I'd like to'

Authors' output varies from Harper Lee's single masterpiece, *To Kill A Mockingbird*, to the plethora of sexually prim romances dictated to her secretary by Barbara Cartland from the depths of her hot pink chaise longue – 623 at the last count.

Sydney Smith
Some men have only one book in them; others, a library.

Mickey Spillane
I'm a commercial writer, not an 'author'. Margaret Mitchell was an author. She wrote one book.

Isaac D'Israeli
Beware the man of one book.

T S Eliot
There are only two ways in which a writer can become important – to write a great deal, and have his writings appear everywhere, or to write very little. It is a question of temperament. I write very little.

E M Forster
I have not written as much as I'd like to.

Somerset Maugham
A writer is not made by one book, but by a body of work.

Mordecai Richler
Everybody writes a book too many.

The paradox of writers talking

'Books must be written, not talked'

Writing is a laborious process of committing thoughts to paper, so writers are seldom good public speakers – though they seem to enjoy talking about their craft:

Ernest Hemingway
A writer should write what he has to say and not speak it.

Jerzy Kosinski
A writer's true calling is not about speaking, but about being 'mute', about writing.

Daphne du Maurier
Writers should be read – but neither seen nor heard.

Edna Ferber
There is no denying the fact that writers should be read but not seen. Rarely are they a winsome sight.

John Barth
You shouldn't pay very much attention to anything writers say. They don't know why they do what they do. They're like good tennis players or good painters, who are just full of nonsense, pompous and embarrassing, or merely mistaken, when they open their mouths.

Lillian Hellman
They're fancy talkers about themselves, writers.

John Jakes
Too many amateur writers (too many professionals, I might add) are basically insecure people; this inclines them toward conversation almost exclusively centred around themselves and their work. I dislike socialising with most writers because their talk tends to be little more than a tiresome variation on one theme: 'I'.

Benjamin Disraeli
An author who speaks about his own books is almost as bad as a mother who talks about her own children.

Albert Camus
A writer should not talk about his doubts about his creation. It would be too easy to reply to him: 'Who forces you to create? If it is so continuous an anguish, why do you bear it?' Our doubts are the most personal things we have.

Philip Larkin
I can't understand these chaps who go around American universities explaining how they write poems: it's like going round explaining how you sleep with your wife.

Frank Muir
Another widely held fallacy was that authors talked and looked like the characters in their books ...Visitors to literary luncheons should not be too hopeful.

Sinclair Lewis
When audiences come to see us authors lecture, it is largely in the hope that we'll be funnier to look at than to read.

Ursula le Guin
Writers get asked to make speeches ... Being a writer but not a speaker, I have to write out what I'm going to say, if it's longer than eight words.

Mary Stewart
I can never think of clever things to say. I think a writer should write and not talk. I don't talk well because afterwards I always feel I'd have liked to say it in a different way. Writing, I can be as slow as I like.

Aeschylus
There are a lot of things that I could say but an ox sits on my tongue.

Kurt Vonnegut
Most writers are not quick-witted when they talk. Novelists, in particular, drag themselves around in society like gut-shot bears.

Isaac Asimov
If there is a category of human being for whom his work ought to speak for itself, it is the writer.

Despite their predilection for maundering on about themselves, most writers are coy about discussing work in progress and future projects. This is due to a lingering superstition that some of the creative magic could be lost:

Peter Elbow
Writers often have a great fear of *talking about* something they are writing or planning to write. It's as though talking will put a jinx on it ... If you invest yourself deeply in something as mysterious as writing, it's hard to avoid magical thinking.

A N Wilson
I don't care to talk about a novel I'm doing because if I communicate the magic spell, even in an abbreviated form, it loses its force for me. Once you have talked, the act of communication has been made.

Shirley Hazzard
I have a superstition that if I talk about a plot, it's like letting sand out of a hole in the bottom of a bag.

Ernest Hemingway
Never talk about a story you are working on. If you tell it, you never write it. You spoil the freshness, you mouth it up and get rid of it in the telling instead of the writing. Writers should work alone, then talk.

Norman Mailer
I think what [Hemingway] meant ... is that if you keep an experience and you don't talk about it and it's a crystal experience, it's still very close to you. You can beam a light through it from many an angle, get many a story, many a chapter of a novel ... Writers are like squirrels. We collect these things.

Mailer has also said:
I just think it's bad to talk about one's present work, for it spoils something at the root of the creative act. It discharges the tension.

David Wallechinsky
Don't tell anybody what your book is about and don't show it until it's finished. It's not that anybody will steal your idea but that all that energy that goes into the writing of your story will be dissipated.

Wilbur Smith
I never discuss any idea with anybody ... Whatever they say is going to affect your vision of the book; it'll lose spontaneity. There'll be some remark that affects you. It's like somebody letting off a firecracker in the middle of your golf swing.

Ray Bradbury
Writing is like sex. You have to save your love for the love object. If you go around spouting about your idea, when it comes time to go to bed with that idea, there'll be no 'charge' left. You can't father children that way.

Laurens van der Post
In beginning any new enterprise which comes to one's imagination, one must not share it with the world until it has grown strong enough to stand and contain itself.

F Scott Fitzgerald
I think it's a pretty good rule not to tell what a thing is about until it's finished. If you do you always seem to lose some of it. It never quite belongs to you so much again.

William Maxwell
More often than not the writer who talks about something he's working on talks it right out of existence.

Morris West
In a longish life as a professional writer, I have heard a thousand masterpieces talked out over bars, restaurant tables and love seats. I have never seen one of them in print. Books must be written, not talked.

Pamela Frankau
I have to renew my vows of silence. In the rising excitement, with the dream unrolling in my head, it is too easy to talk. And talking is fatal.

Maeve Brennan
The fewer writers you know the better, and if you're working on anything, don't tell them.

On the other hand:

Aldous Huxley
I've never discussed my writing with others much, but I don't believe it can do any harm. I don't think that there's any risk that ideas or materials will evaporate.

John Steinbeck
I really talk too much about my work and to anyone who will listen. If I would limit my talk to inventions and keep my big mouth shut about work, there would probably be a good deal more work done.

Most writers hate being asked to explain their books, reasoning that the books should speak for themselves:

Friedrich Nietzsche
The author should keep his mouth shut when his work begins to speak.

Eugène Ionesco
Why do people always expect authors to answer questions? I am an author because I want to ask questions. If I had answers I'd be a politician.

Ernest Hemingway
It is hard enough to write books and stories without being asked to explain them as well.

Kurt Vonnegut
You don't ask writers to explain their books. The writer has already explained as best as he can what the book is about.

Bernard Malamud
I want the books to speak for themselves. You can read? All right, tell me what my books mean. Astonish me.

J M Coetzee
The writer is simply another reader when it is a matter of discussing the books he has already written. They don't belong to him any more and he has nothing privileged to say about them, while the book he is engaged in writing is far too private and important a matter to be talked about.

And being interviewed is anathema:

Frederick Forsyth
In a perfect world, I'd like to write books and be anonymous. I hate being interviewed. That's why I'm smoking quite a lot.

Robertson Davies
If the interviewer is a skilled hand, the interview becomes an agreeable conversation. But such interviewers – informed, friendly, acquainted with the author's work – are not met with everywhere, and too often the interview becomes an hour-long interrogation, sinking to unanswerable queries such as, 'Where do you get your ideas from?' ... The interrogation of a bad interviewer is comparable to that of the secret police.

Frank Kermode
The interview is not a medium that is natural to writers; it requires of the script-bound a venture into naked orality.

Anyway, writers can talk a lot of bull, can't they?

John Barth
You shouldn't pay very much attention to anything writers say. They don't know why they do what they do ... I have never heard much that any writer has said about writing that didn't embarrass me, including the things I say about it.

Writers' failings

'I think writers are dreadfully selfish people'

Writers are as prone to have feet of clay as any icon of the arts:

James Baldwin
The writer's greed is appalling. He wants, or seems to want, everything and practically everybody; in another sense, and at the same time, he needs no one at all.

Jean Rhys
I think writers are dreadfully selfish people. But you have to be.

George Bernard Shaw
Never believe anything a writer tells you about himself. A man comes to believe in the end the lies he tells himself about himself.

Susceptibility to flattery is a common failing:

Frank Moore Colby
Writers become idiotic under flattery sooner than any other set of people in the world.

Maurice Baring
There is no amount of praise which a man and an author cannot bear with equanimity. Some authors can even stand flattery.

Oliver Wendell Holmes
I never saw an author in my life, saving perhaps one, that did not purr as audibly as a full-grown domestic cat on having his fur smoothed the right way by a skilful hand.

And it seems that unpleasantness is endemic:

Henry Edward Fox
How odious all authors are, and how doubly so to each other!

Graham Greene
It isn't easy for an author to remain a pleasant human being: both success and failure are usually of a crippling kind. There are so many opportunities for histrionics, hysterics, waywardness, self-importance; within very wide limits a writer can do what he likes and go where he likes.

Renata Adler
The writer has a grudge against society, which he documents with accounts of unsatisfying sex, unrealised ambition, unmitigated loneliness, and a sense of local and global distress.

William Faulkner
The writer's only responsibility is to his art. He will be completely ruthless if he is a good one. He has a dream. It anguishes him so much he must get rid of it. He has no peace until then. Everything goes by the board: honour, pride, decency, security, happiness, all, to get the book written.

Delmore Schwartz
Writers are self-indulgent, full of self-pity, forever seeking reassurance, constantly occupied with what they consider the proper conditions of work, and the next thing to invalids in their demands on life.

Walter Savage Landor
It is dangerous to have intercourse or dealing with small authors. They are as troublesome to handle, as easy to discourage, as difficult to pacify, and leave as unpleasant marks on you, as small children.

Malcolm Cowley
Authors are sometimes like tomcats: they distrust all the other toms, but they are kind to kittens.

Though many would call vanity the successful writer's besetting sin:

Lawrence Durrell
My problem is intense vanity and narcissism. I've always had such a good physique and such intense charm that it's difficult to be true to myself.

Logan Pearsall Smith
Every author, however modest, keeps a most outrageous vanity chained like a madman in the padded cell of his breast.

W H Auden
There is no end to the vanity of our calling.

Martin Luther
The multitude of books is a great evil. There is no measure or limit to this fever of writing; everyone must be an author; some out of vanity to acquire celebrity; others for the sake of lucre and gain.

H L Mencken
An author, like any other so-called artist, is a man in whom the normal vanity of all men is so vastly exaggerated that he finds it a sheer impossibility to hold it in. His overpowering impulse is to gyrate before his fellow men, flapping his wings and emitting defiant yells.

David Lodge
There is a vanity and a paranoia about writers – which makes them excellent dramatic material – but which also makes me question the nature of writing.

Norman Mailer
Every writer thinks he is capable of anything. Scratch a Faulkner or a Hemingway and you'll find a man who thinks he can run the world.

Lawrence Durrell
All the Jungian guilt about the importance of one's message and all that sort of thing – well, you get a nice corpulent ego standing in the way there, telling you that you're so damn clever that you're almost afraid to write it down, it's so wonderful.

Coulson Kernahan
There are two literary maladies – writer's cramp and swelled head. The worst of writer's cramp is that it is never cured; the worst of swelled head is that it never kills.

Sloan Wilson
A writer must be an egotist, but a good writer is too egotistical and too skilful to allow himself to appear that way on paper. The writer's false cloak of charming modesty is one deceit that is permitted!

Writers' problems

'If I write this paragraph, then there is the next and then the next …'

Writers moan a good deal about their problems:

Joseph Heller
Every writer I know has trouble writing.

Ernest Hemingway
A writer's problem does not change … It is always how to write truly and having found what is true, to project it in such a way that it becomes part of the experience of the person who reads it.

Julien Green
Thought flies and words go on foot. Therein lies all the drama of a writer.

Horace
I struggle to be brief and become obscure.

Gabriel Garcia Marquez
The problem for every writer is credibility. Anybody can write anything so long as it's believed.

Isaac Bashevis Singer
Every creator painfully experiences the chasm between his inner vision and its ultimate expression. The chasm is never completely bridged. We all have the conviction, perhaps illusory, that we have much more to say than appears on the paper.

Niki Daly
It is worrying to do work bordering on the personal rather than the general, asking people to accept you. One is just trotting out one's own values. There is a danger of repeating past successes – safe passages are the kiss of death.

E L Doctorow
Whenever citizens are seen routinely as enemies of their own government, writers are routinely seen to be the most dangerous enemies.

Joseph Conrad
There is nothing more dreadful to an author than neglect, compared with which reproach, hatred and opposition are names of happiness.

Katherine Mansfield
I have discovered that I cannot burn the candle at one end and write a book with the other.

Norman Mailer
Booze, pot, too much sex, too much failure in one's private life, too much attrition, too much recognition, too little recognition, frustration. Nearly everything ... works to dull a first-rate talent. But the worst probably is cowardice – as one gets older, one becomes aware of one's cowardice ... And finally there's apathy.

Henry Miller
Many writers have what you might call a demonic nature. They are always in trouble ... and not only while they're writing or because they're writing, but in every aspect of their lives, with marriage, love, business, money, everything. It's all tied together, all part and parcel of the same thing. It's an aspect of the creative personality.

Joseph Conrad
Sometimes it takes all my resolution and power of self-control to refrain from butting my head against the wall.

Katherine Anne Porter
I've only spent about ten per cent of my energies on writing. The other ninety per cent went to keeping my head above water.

Anton Chekhov (letter to Maria Kiseleva, 1886):
For one thing, it's a gloomy life. Work from morning to night, and not much sense to it ... Money – as scarce as hen's teeth ... My place is smoky and cold ... And impossible cigarettes! They are tough and damp, like little sausages. Before smoking I turn up the lamp wick, dry the cigarette over it and only then light it; while the lamp sputters and reeks, the cigarette cracks and darkens, and I scorch my fingers ... You feel that death might be a welcome release.

John Gardner
The typewriter keeps hissing at you and shooting sparks, and the paper keeps wrinkling and the lamp goes off and nothing else works ...

Anthony Burgess
The financial rewards just don't make up for the expenditure of energy, the damage to health caused by stimulants and narcotics, the fear that one's work isn't good enough. I think, if I had enough money, I'd give up writing tomorrow.

But the next three writers, typically, have practical solutions:

F Scott Fitzgerald
Sometimes you can lick an especially hard problem by facing it always the very first thing in the morning with the very freshest part of your mind. This has so often worked with me that I have an uncanny faith in it.

Isaac Asimov
When I feel difficulty coming on, I switch to another book I'm writing. When I get back to the problem, my unconscious has solved it.

H G Wells
If you are in difficulties with a book, try the element of surprise: attack it at the hour when it isn't expecting it.

· Specific problems ·
· Booze and other stimulants ·

Writers frequently drink too much, and have many excuses for doing so. These range from needing a drop to get started, through the necessity for stimulants to keep going during long hours of solitary work, to the fundamental right of every scribbler to a relaxing drink after all the mental toil:

James Thurber
Some American writers who have known each other for years, have never met in the daytime or when both were sober.

Anthony Burgess
American writers drink a lot when they're 'blocked' and drunkenness – being a kind of substitute for art – makes the block worse.

Malcolm Cowley
One of the reasons why ... many writers turn into alcoholics is that early in their lives they find that getting drunk is part of the creative process, that it opens up visions. It's a terrible sort of creative device, because three out of four who involve themselves in it become alcoholics. But it does open up doors in the beginning.

Kingsley Amis
Quaking, you sit down at the typewriter. And that's when a glass of Scotch can be very useful as a sort of artistic icebreaker ... artificial infusion of a little bit of confidence which is necessary in order to begin at all ... So alcohol in moderate amounts and at a fairly leisurely speed is valuable to me.

J G Ballard
Actually, there's no secret. One simply pulls the cork out of the bottle, waits three minutes, and two thousand or more years of Scottish craftsmanship does the rest.

Tennessee Williams
I can't write without wine.

William Styron
I like to stay up late at night and get drunk and sleep late. I wish I could break the habit but I can't. The afternoon is the only time I have left and I try to use it to the best advantage, with a hangover.

Truman Capote
I am a completely horizontal author ... I can't think unless I'm lying down, either in bed or stretched on a couch and with a cigarette and coffee handy. I've got to be puffing and sipping. As the afternoon wears on, I shift from coffee to mint tea to sherry to martinis.

Irwin Shaw
I never drink while I'm working, but after a few glasses, I get ideas that would never have occurred to me dead sober. And some of the ideas turn out to be valuable the next day. Some not.

W H Auden
I never write when I'm drunk.

James Jones
Boozing does not necessarily have to go hand in hand with being a writer, as seems to be the concept in America. I therefore solemnly declare to all young men trying to become writers that they do not actually have to become drunkards first.

James Merrill
Liquor, in my parents' world, was always your reward at the end of a hard day – or an easy day, for that matter – and I like to observe that old family tradition. But I've never drunk for inspiration. Quite the contrary – it's like the wet sponge on the blackboard.

Then there are all the other stimulants:

W H Auden
LSD? Nothing much happened, but I did get the distinct impression that some birds were trying to communicate with me.

Conrad Aiken
I've tried it [taking drugs] long ago, with hashish and peyote. This, as we find in alcohol, is an escape from awareness, a cheat, a momentary substitution, and in the end a destruction of it. With luck, someone might have a fragmentary Kubla Khan vision. But with no meaning. And with the steady destruction of the observing and remembering mind.

William Burroughs
The hallucinogens produce visionary states, sort of, but morphine and its derivatives decrease awareness of inner processes, thoughts, and feelings. They are pain killers, pure and simple. They are absolutely contra-indicated for creative work, and I include in the lot alcohol, morphine, barbiturates, tranquillisers – the whole spectrum of sedative drugs.

Margaret Drabble
I drink very strong coffee and very weak tea. Scenery can be a violent stimulant ... I love it. But rather like Wordsworth, I think too much of isn't good for you.

· Depression ·

Many writers suffer from the black dog of melancholia which ranges from despondency to abject despair:

John Hall Wheelock
Most writers are in a state of gloom a good deal of the time; they need perpetual reassurance.

E M Cioran
I write preferably in a state of semi-depression. There has to be something that's not right. When one is in a neutral mood, why write? Why declare things?

Georges Simenon
Writing is not a profession but a vocation of unhappiness. I don't think an artist can ever be happy.

Fannie Hurst
I'm not happy when I'm writing, but I'm more unhappy when I'm not.

Nelson Algren
There is no way of being a creative writer in America without being a loser.

Peter Carey
I get really depressed: is it going to work? What am I doing? What is this about? ... The whole business of writing is to live with doubt.

Paul Johnson
Every day in a writer's professional life is a complete cycle, from desperate beginnings to triumphant conclusion (or despairing admission of failure).

Susan Sontag
You have to sink way down to a level of hopelessness and desperation to find the book that you can write ... I am profoundly uncertain about how to write. I know what I love or what I like, because it's a direct, passionate response. But ... I'm very uncertain whether it's good enough. That is, of course, the writer's agony.

Though there is a powerful dissenting voice here:

Doris Lessing
I believe that the pleasurable luxury of despair, the acceptance of disgust, is as much a betrayal of what a writer should be as the acceptance of the simple economic view of man; both are aspects of cowardice, both fallings-away from a central vision, the two easy escapes of our time into false innocence.

Mary Wesley
My husband used to tell me I could write, but I thought it was just because he loved me. After he died, I was unhappy, very poor. Writing purged me of the destructive desperation.

Gustave Flaubert

Sometimes, when I find myself empty, when expression won't come, when, after scribbling long pages, I find I haven't written a sentence, then I fall on the couch and lie there, stupefied in an inward slough of despond. I hate myself, and blame myself, for this frenzy of pride which makes me pant for mere imaginings. A quarter of an hour later, everything has altered; my heart is pounding for joy.

· Drying up ·

This is more dramatically called 'writer's block', and is considered a traumatic condition by writers who are understandably terrified of running out of things to say:

Sloan Wilson

Writers do dry up, but lack of personal experience is not the reason. The loss of excitement about life can strike any writer dead.

Paul Johnson

When authors come to me complaining of writer's block it means that they are too lazy to work out a structure either in their lives or in their work.

William Goyen

This happens to writers when there are dead spells. We die sometimes. And it's as though we're in a tomb; it's a death. That's what we all fear, and that's why so many of us become alcoholics or suicides or insane – or just no-good philanderers. It's amazing that we survive.

B J Chute

The worst of times are when the words will not come at all, and the writer feels as if he were floundering in a swamp or gasping for air in a desert. This can be really frightening, and it is here – in swamp or desert – that the quality of patience will spell the difference between disaster and survival.

Heinrich Böll

Inhibitions or blocks have recently become second nature with me. It has to do with the situation on earth. I live in a country which has the greatest concentration of atomic weapons on earth … That can take away your breath, and your enjoyment of life, and give you pause about whether writing makes any sense.

Joan Didion
There is always a point in the writing of a piece when I sit in a room literally papered with false starts and cannot put one word after another and imagine that I have suffered a small stroke, leaving me apparently undamaged but actually aphasic.

Virginia Woolf
All desire to practise the art of a writer has completely left me … It's not the writing but the architecting that strains. If I write this paragraph, then there is the next and then the next.

There are remedies, however:

Erskine Caldwell
You can always write something. You write limericks. You write a love letter. You do something to get you in the habit of writing again, to bring back the desire.

John Steinbeck *(on the inhibiting effect of having to write for publication)*:
The simplest way to overcome this is to write it to someone, like me. Write it as a letter aimed at one person. This removes the vague terror of addressing the large and faceless audience and it also, you will find, will give a sense of freedom and a lack of self-consciousness.

Joanna Trollope
Very rarely, perhaps three or four times a year, I just have to give up and go and dig some spuds to release the log-jam.

Jim Harrison
I wonder, when a writer's blocked and doesn't have any resources to pull himself out of it, why doesn't he jump in his car and drive around the USA? I went last winter for 7 000 miles and it was lovely.

· *Exhaustion* ·

Two voices speak from opposite ends of our cultural epoch:

Ecclesiastes
Of making books there is no end; and much study is a weariness of the flesh.

Tennessee Williams
Nobody but a writer knows how exhausting it is to write. Nobody except perhaps a writer's wife. She knows what hell he goes through and how little he is paid for his efforts. I can write only three or four hours a day. After that I'm emotionally worn out.

· Exposure ·

This is a major problem for all but the most gregarious writers. Baring your soul in print is hard enough; more agonising still is the blast of promotional publicity after months of quiet writing. Few are able to afford the luxury of being as reclusive as J D Salinger, or as anonymous as Trevanian:

Edna St Vincent Millay
A person who publishes a book wilfully appears before the public with his pants down.

Jack Kerouac
Notoriety and public confession in literary form is a frazzler of the heart you were born with, believe me.

Henry James
The greatest of all literary quarrels is the eternal dispute between the public and the private, between curiosity and delicacy.

George Eliot
Whatever may be the success of my stories, I shall be resolute in preserving my incognito, having observed that a *nom de plume* secures all the advantages without the disagreeables of reputation.

Emily Brontë
If I could I would always work in silence and obscurity, and let my efforts be known by their results.

Igor Stravinsky
A plague on eminence! I hardly dare cross the street any more without a convoy, and I am stared at wherever I go like an idiot member of a royal family or an animal in a zoo.

Mary Stewart
I can't see the point of [being interviewed]. The kind of person I am apart from my books doesn't matter: that's not ME. My books are me and if you want to know about me, read them. Everything's there. It is with every writer.

David Malouf
All writing gives you away. You are always consciously giving things away that the reader doesn't recognise, and all the things he does recognise are things in which you may be unconsciously giving yourself away.

Francine du Plessix Gray
Here's a major point of tension in most writers' lives: How can we rub enough with the world to nourish our writing, while keeping the world enough at bay to safeguard our creative energies?

Len Deighton
I like to be able to listen to conversations without people turning around to look at me over their shoulders. I want to be the man behind you in the fish shop.

Mary Wesley
I feel very overexposed. It's a creepy feeling because I'm used to observing others and now I'm being observed.

· Failure ·

This grim spectre which haunts us all is particularly dreaded by writers, since their ability to create is necessarily bolstered by the belief that someone will want to read what they write:

Katherine Mansfield
For the last two weeks I have written scarcely anything. I have been idle; I have failed.

James Dickey
What I want is to be willing to fail, even if it costs in reputation, rather than stagnate.

Geoffrey Jenkins
There are hundreds of authors out there, all of whom are very good, and the competition is intense. My next book could fall flat on its face.

There is an up-side to failure, however, and pragmatic writers have ways of dealing with it:

William Carlos Williams
What can any of us do with his talent but try to develop his vision, so that through frequent failures we may learn better what we have missed in the past.

John Steinbeck
When I face the desolate impossibility of writing five hundred pages, a sick sense of failure falls on me and I know I can never do it. This happens every time. Then I ... write one page and then another. One day's work is all I can permit myself to contemplate and I eliminate the possibility of ever finishing.

Irwin Shaw
Failure is inevitable for the writer ... There's the kind of running failure that dogs a writer all his life – ideas that only get half-written, false beginnings, first drafts that suddenly go dead and have to be thrown away, even crucial paragraphs that stiffen under your hand and refuse to be revived ... Failure is apt to produce self-pity and it's been my experience that self-pity can be very productive.

· Fear ·

Writers' fears range from trepidation to dread to abject terror. Tennessee Williams called it 'the terror of the white page in the typewriter':

Aldous Huxley
I'm afraid of losing my obscurity. Genuineness only thrives in the dark. Like celery.

Paul Sayer
If you're smart, if you want to survive, you'll mention nothing of the sweat, the dread, not even the fleeting joy, that lies behind this writing game.

Malcolm Lowry
Fear ringed by doubt is my eternal moon.

Paul Johnson
The greatest of writers can find the act of creating a terrifying labour, whose pangs do not diminish – they may quite likely increase – with experience, success, fame, honours ... Show me a writer of quality, and you show me a deeply worried man.

Arthur Koestler
If I stop working and just try to enjoy myself, I get very neurotic and guilt-ridden. Orwell was the same. Like the man who, if he stops running, becomes afraid. Or the shark which must move to breathe.

Sara Paretsky
I am a shy and private person, and I experience a kind of fragmentation. The more successful I am, the more terrifying it is. Sometimes I feel I don't really know how to write at all.

Fran Lebowitz
Writing is the diametric opposite of having fun. All of life, as far as I'm concerned, is an excuse not to write. I just write when fear overtakes me. It causes paralytic terror. It's really scary just getting to the desk … My mouth gets dry, my heart beats fast. I react psychologically the way other people react when the plane loses an engine.

Bernard Malamud
Take chances. 'Dare to do,' Eudora Welty says. She's right. One drags around a bag of fears he has to throw to the winds every so often if he expects to take off in his writing.

· Hardship ·

Hell is the word generally used by writers to describe their hardships:

William Styron
Let's face it, writing is hell.

Jessamyn West
Writing is so difficult that I often feel that writers, having had their hell on earth, will escape all punishment hereafter.

Roald Dahl
The life of a writer is absolute hell compared with the life of a businessman. The writer has to force himself to work. He has to make his own hours and if he doesn't go to his desk at all there is nobody to scold him.

Though there are other torments too:

John Mortimer
I don't think a writer's life is a happy one. There are moments of great relief when something is finished but it's torment really.

Walker Percy
Being a writer in the South has its special miseries, which include isolation, madness, tics, amnesia, alcoholism, lust, and loss of ordinary powers of speech. One may go for days without saying a word.

Tennessee Williams
I have learned that the heart of man, his body and his brain are forged in a white-hot furnace for the purpose of the conflict. That struggle for me is creation. Luxury is a wolf at the door and its fangs are the vanities and conceits germinated by success. When an artist learns this, he knows where the dangers lie. Without deprivation and struggle, there is no salvation and I am just a sword cutting daisies.

· Health ·

It is generally agreed that writers need good health as well as stamina to withstand the hardships of the profession (see above) ...

Ralph Waldo Emerson
The writer, like the priest, must be exempted from secular labour. His work needs a frolic health; he must be at the top of his condition.

Gabriel Garcia Marquez
To be a good writer you have to be absolutely lucid at every moment of writing and in good health ... I think you have to be in a very good emotional and physical state.

... but the act of sitting at a desk (or standing, in the case of Hemingway) and writing is not particularly conducive to it:

Jane Gardam
The complexion of a novelist is seldom rosy ... We are engaged in indoor activity, haemorrhoidal, prone to chilblains, poor of circulation.

Jilly Cooper
The broad hips and big thighs are writer's bum, I think; sitting all day writing you just spread.

A contrary view is held by:

Cyril Connolly
The health of a writer should not be too good, and perfect only in those periods of convalescence when he is not writing.

· Insecurity ·

Even the best writers worry constantly. The tormenting questions they ask themselves as they sit down to begin a new project include: Can I still do it? Am I getting better or worse? Will I be able to keep going?

Ellen Goodman
We're all insecure. Insecurity is the mainstream of every writer. You write two bad columns in a row and you think: 'Well that's it, folks. I've lost it.'

Nadine Gordimer
With each book, I go through a long time when I know what I want to do and I'm held back and puzzled and appalled because I don't know before I begin to write how I'm going to do it, and I always fear that I can't do it.

Mary Stewart
Always when I'm in the middle of a new book I think it's rubbish. It is never as I planned it or as good as I'd hoped it would be.

Lillian Hellman
Nothing you write, if you hope to be good, will ever come out as you first hoped.

John Cheever
Any memory of pain is deeply buried, and there is nothing more painful for a writer than an inability to work.

Marianne Moore
I never knew anyone who had a passion for words who had as much difficulty in saying things as I do. I very seldom say them in a manner I like. If I do it's because I don't know I'm trying.

Tom Wolfe
You go to bed every night thinking that you've written the most brilliant passage ever done which somehow the next day you realise is sheer drivel. Sometimes it's six months later that it dawns on you that it doesn't work. It's a constant hazard.

· *Loneliness* ·

This is a major issue for writers, most of whom treasure their solitude, though there are those who positively hate it:

Ernest Hemingway
Writing, at its best, is a lonely life.

Lawrence Clark Powell
Writing is a solitary occupation. Family, friends, and society are the natural enemies of the writer. He must be alone, uninterrupted, and slightly savage if he is to sustain and complete an undertaking.

Rémy de Goncourt
The man of letters loves not only to be read but to be seen. Happy to be by himself, he would be happier still if people knew that he was happy to be by himself, working in solitude at night under his lamp.

Mary Stewart
I'm a solitary beast by nature. I always was, even as a child ... Probably my happiest times are when I'm entirely alone and getting on with the job and it's going well.

Minette Walters
It's lonely insofar as you have to be extraordinarily single-minded, but I like that. Even if I wasn't writing, I would probably be sitting reading and that's a rather single-minded occupation. I love to be entertained on my own.

Graham Greene
It's lonely work, writing ... One has to be alone and one has to appreciate loneliness.

William Styron
Loneliness is your companion for life. If you don't want to be lonely, you get into TV.

Rumer Godden
A writer's life is, necessarily, such a lonely one, so uncertain, that we flourish on praise.

Brooks Atkinson
Writing is an artificial activity. It is a lonely and private substitute for conversation.

Joseph Heller
I have to be alone ... Often when I am very tired, just before going to bed, while washing my face and brushing my teeth, my mind gets very clear ... and produces a line for the next day's work, or some idea way ahead.

Walter de la Mare
Again and again [the writer] must stand back from the press of habit and convention. He must keep on capturing solitude.

François Mauriac
A writer is essentially a man who does not resign himself to loneliness.

John K Hutchens
A writer and nothing else: a man alone in a room with the English language, trying to get human feelings right.

H L Mencken
My belief is that all authors are essentially lonely men. Every one of them has to do his work in a room alone, and he inevitably gets very tired of himself.

Dick Francis
When you're writing, that's when you're lonely ... There are hours and hours of silence.

Clare Boylan
What has often struck me most is the loneliness of the writer – not the solitude, which is a blessing – but the self-doubt, the rejection, the small financial return, the boredom of being confined with a frequently narcoleptic set of characters.

Robertson Davies
To be a writer, striving to write as best he can, is not a jolly, high-hearted occupation. Indeed it is lonely work and the introspection it demands is fatiguing to body and mind.

Nadine Gordimer
The fact is that I lead a rather solitary life when I'm writing ... The solitude of writing is also quite frightening. It's quite close sometimes to madness; one just disappears for a day and loses touch.

William Saroyan
When the going is good a writer knows very little, if any loneliness. When it is bad he believes he knows nothing else.

Richard Condon
Writers are too self-centred to be lonely.

Jean Rhys
[Writers are] sad, beastly and lonely but I don't see how you can be otherwise, because the words go away. I'm damned if I know how you can write about deep things and what's happened to you, if you're not alone.

· Madness ·

This is not only a favourite theme for writers – it's a positive hazard of the profession:

John Fowles
The role of a writer is that of shaman: those who suffer and go mad for society's sake.

Joseph Heller
When a writer is between books, he needs responsibility to keep him from making a fool of himself. Authors go through a period of craziness between books. Some invest in uranium stock, others change wives and agents. Some commit suicide. It's worse when you're young.

Thomas Sanchez
I used to greet each morning spitting blood in the washbasin, having the night before gnashed the inside of my mouth while dreaming I had misplaced a comma ... Years later a dentist asked me if I had a history of mental illness, because the mentally ill often exhibit advanced molar grindings.

Carlos Fuentes
In the Soviet Union a writer who is critical, as we know, is taken to a lunatic asylum. In the United States, he's taken to a talk show.

Kurt Vonnegut
Writers can treat their mental illnesses every day.

André Gide
Only those things are beautiful which are inspired by madness and written by reason.

· Noise ·

The noise level is a major problem for anyone trying to commit thoughts to paper:

Edna O'Brien
If the doorbell or the telephone rings I see it as an advancing enemy. I hate noise. Many writers hate noise. This is not simply tetchiness, it is something to do with trying to enter or indeed linger in that inside space with those inner voices.

William Styron
The actual process of writing ... demands complete, noiseless privacy, without even music; a baby howling two blocks away will drive me nuts.

Paul Theroux
The best job for a writer, a job with the fewest hours, is in the tropics. But books are hard to write in the tropics. It is not only the heat; it is the lack of privacy, the open windows, the noise.

Peter Høeg
Authors are paid by society to be marginalised. We see things that it may be difficult to see when you are drowning in noise.

Colin Thubron
I hate noise when I'm thinking.

Geoffrey Jenkins
The telephone is a bind. It interrupts a creative line of thought.

Raymond Carver
When I'm working, I put the phone on the answering machine and unplug the phone upstairs, so if it rings downstairs, I can't hear it ring. I can check it in the evening to see if there are any messages.

Paul Theroux
It is hard to see clearly or to think straight in the company of other people. Not only do I feel self-conscious, but the perceptions that are necessary to writing are difficult to manage when someone close by is thinking out loud.

On the other hand:

Isaac Asimov
Nothing interferes with my concentration. You could put on an orgy in my office and I wouldn't look up – well, maybe once.

Anita Brookner
I need noise and interruptions and irritation: irritation and discomfort are a great starter. The loneliness of doing it any other way would kill me.

· *Partners* ·

Marriage is frequently regarded as secondary to their work by male writers, even those whose majestic solitude is only made possible by their wives. Ask any woman writer what would make her life easier, however, and her heartfelt answer is nearly always, 'A wife.'

John Mortimer
A writer primarily cares more about writing than anything else, which is bad luck on the person who happens to be married to him. You're always slightly detached, your life is the material you use for writing, which can be very disconcerting for those you live with.

Burton Rascoe
What no wife of a writer can ever understand is that a writer is working when he's staring out the window.

William Trevor
'Why,' someone said to me, 'do you always dedicate your novels to your wife?' And I said it was because it's my wife, more than my children or my friends, who has to put up with it all.

Lorrie Moore
One should ... live with someone who can cook and who will both be with one and leave one alone.

· Photographs ·

Being published (oh glorious prospect!) necessitates having an author photograph taken for the dust jacket: preferably moody with strong intimations of intelligence simmering under the glamour:

Maureen Freely
In the beginning ... authors could look plain and middle-aged so long as they also looked intelligent ... All that has changed. Over the past decade, author photographs have become bigger, glossier and more significant. The future belongs to the brand image.

Blake Morrison
Any extreme will do. If you're not beautiful you can look intellectually severe. But if you're one of the poor sods in the middle, you're in trouble. You need the looks to cook the books. Some publishers won't consider a manuscript unless it's accompanied by a photo.

Rhoda Koenig
You can't judge a book by its cover, the proverb tells us, but that doesn't stop book buyers and reviewers from trying. Cover photographs of authors do help people judge whether a book is worth their money and time.

Though **Robert Winder** *says:*
In the case of a novelist you've never heard of, the photograph has next to no influence compared to the first two paragraphs.

Penny Perrick
A lot of authors look like they wouldn't know how to cross the road. They look as if they wouldn't know anything about the business of living, and why would you want to read a novel by someone like that?

Miriam Gross
If I see a gormless face, I think the person's probably written a gormless book. Also, no men with beards. There are exceptions, but they are Russian or dead.

Plagiarism

This is a surprisingly prevalent problem, as can be seen by the number of quotes — many of them quite brazen — in this section. Some writers are brutally honest:

Lawrence Durrell
I pinch.

Jules Feiffer
Good swiping is an art in itself.

Thornton Wilder
I do borrow from other writers, shamelessly! I can only say in my defence, like the woman brought before the judge on a charge of kleptomania, 'I do steal; but, Your Honour, only from the very best stores.'

John Gardner
I get great pleasure out of stealing other people's writings. Actually, I do that at least partly because of a peculiar and unfortunate quality of my mind: I remember things. Word for word. I'm not always aware of it.

Byron
I am taxed with being a plagiarist, when I am least conscious of being one; but I am not very scrupulous, I own, when I have a good idea, how I came into possession of it.

Anatole France
When a thing has been said and well said, have no scruple; take it and copy it. Give references? Why should you? Either your readers know where you have taken the passage and the precaution is needless, or they do not know and you humiliate them.

Robert Benchley
Great literature must spring from an upheaval in the author's soul. If that upheaval is not present, then it must come from the works of any other author which happen to be handy and easily adapted.

Bruce Chatwin
There are books you read for pleasure and books you read for plunder. Every writer is a cutpurse.

William Zinsser
Don't ever hesitate to imitate another writer – every artist learning his craft needs some models. Eventually you will find your own voice and shed the skin of the writer you imitated. But pick only the best models.

Some writers make heavy jokes about it:

Augustus Montague Toplady
Keep your hands from literary picking and stealing. But if you cannot refrain from this kind of stealth, abstain from murdering what you steal.

Samuel Taylor Coleridge
The Eighth Commandment was not made for bards.

Marshall McLuhan
A successful book cannot afford to be more than ten percent new.

Don Marquis
A sequel is an admission that you've been reduced to imitating yourself.

Some are scathing:

Robert Burton
They lard their lean books with the fat of others' works.

Stanley Unwin
Another illusion, seldom entertained by competent authors, is that the publisher's readers and others are waiting to plagiarise their work. I think it may be said that the more worthless the manuscript, the greater the fear of plagiarism.

Samuel Taylor Coleridge
Plagiarists are always suspicious of being stolen from – as pickpockets are observed commonly to walk with their hands in their breeches' pockets.

Samuel Johnson
No man ever yet became great by imitation.

Generally, however, the consensus is that since one cannot copyright ideas, a certain amount of plagiarism is unavoidable and a writer may steal with care. Even the best writers, it seems, 'borrow':

William Blake
The difference between a bad artist and a good one is: The bad artist seems to copy a great deal; the good one really does.

T S Eliot
The mediocre borrow, the brilliant steal.

Lionel Trilling
The immature artist imitates. Mature artists steal.

Ralph Waldo Emerson
It has come to be practically a sort of rule in literature, that a man, having once shown himself capable of original writing, is entitled thenceforth to steal from the writings of others at discretion.

And one author considers that his 'borrowing' is simply a matter of being aware of other voices:

D M Thomas
It's obviously true that my work is drenched in a sense of other voices. But it's usually been regarded as a virtue to be aware of other voices. The 18th century did this in a strong way. Other references are enriching, as long as you have your own original vision in the work as a whole.

The consensus is that nothing is sacred:

Ralph Waldo Emerson
Every man is a borrower and mimic, life is theatrical and literature a quotation.

Michel de Montaigne
Truth and reason are common to all and no more belong to him that spoke them heretofore than unto him that shall speak them hereafter.

Writers should, however, heed these words of warning:

Hunter S Thompson
There is probably some long-standing 'rule' among writers, journalists, and other word-mongers that says: 'When you start stealing from your own work you're in bad trouble.' And it may be true.

· Repetition ·

Writers complain that their readers expect them to go on doing the same thing book after book – which of course many of them do:

Doris Lessing
The main problem of some writers is that most reviewers and readers want you to go on writing the same book.

John P Marquand
If you have one strong idea, you can't help repeating it and embroidering it. Sometimes I think that authors should write one book and then be put in a gas chamber.

· Sacrifices ·

Writers will sacrifice anything for a few hours of peace and quiet in which to work:

Peter Essex
Writers would sell their wives and daughters to stay at their desks.

Muriel Spark
I'd give up anything for my work. Otherwise I don't care about my goods ... I'm careless about material things really. I don't care what I spend or what I do provided it's in favour of me getting down to write.

William Faulkner
If you have a piece of serious writing, a universal truth that you feel must be told, you will find some way to tell it ... The urge will eventually become so strong that a man will desert his wife or poison his grandmother, if need be, to get it told.

· *Sickness & suffering* ·

Some writers see their occupation as a kind of sickness:

George Orwell
Writing a book is a horrible, exhausting struggle, like a long bout of some painful illness.

Montesquieu
I suffer from the disease of writing books and being ashamed of them when they are finished.

Anthony Burgess
I don't get writing blocks except from the stationer, but I do feel so sickened by what I write that I don't want to go on.

Lawrence Durrell
I suffer from terrible nausea about my own work ... By the time the thing is in typescript, it is really with physical nausea that I regard it. When the proofs come back I have to take an aspirin before I can bring myself to read it through.

Others stress their suffering:

Samuel Beckett
Suffering is the main condition of the artistic experience.

Susan Sontag
For the modern consciousness, the artist (replacing the saint) is the exemplary sufferer. And among artists, the writer, the man of words, is the person to whom we look to be able best to express his suffering.

Though **James Michener** *pooh-poohs the whole notion:*
I've never been big on the agony of writing. I see no evidence that Tolstoy suffered from writer's block.

Time

Time has its own peculiar problems for writers:

Gloria Katz
How can you write anything topical when it takes three years to make [a book]?

Paul Tabori
The thieves of time are greater enemies of a writer than even plagiarists or pirates. For they are stealing his irreplaceable and most precious possession, his very life.

Last words on writers' problems

One of the main things that writers have to come to terms with is their unusual – sometimes verging on frankly dull – lifestyle:

Beryl Bainbridge
When I am working I don't dress or wash or anything. It's not a normal sort of life at all.

Raymond Carver
I don't watch much TV ... and I go to bed fairly early. It's a pretty quiet life, generally.

Gustave Flaubert
Be regular and ordinary in your life, like a bourgeois, so that you can be violent and original in your works.

Alice Walker
Deliver me from writers who say the way they live doesn't matter.

One problem that defies categorisation is that of:

Joseph Heller
I think I sometimes move my lips, not only when I'm writing, but when I'm thinking of what I'm going to be having for dinner.

And there is a ready remedy for all the others:

Joseph Conrad
Facing it – always facing it – that's the way to get through it! Face it!

Plus a crumb of consolation:

Lorrie Moore
The only happiness you have is writing something new, in the middle of the night, armpits damp, heart pounding, something no one has yet seen. You have only those brief, fragile, untested moments of exhilaration when you know: you are a genius.

· *Writers' issues* ·

· *Freedom* ·

Writers demand the freedom to write as they choose – though they don't always get it:

James Kelman
One of the few remaining freedoms we have is the blank page. No one can prescribe how we should fill it.

Alice Walker
I write what I want, and when I finish I deliver it. I don't care what anyone thinks in terms of what I'm going to do ... I would do what I did, write what I did, no matter what. I'm not worried about how many books I sell.

Annie Dillard
Your freedom as a writer is not freedom in the sense of wild blurting; you may not let rip. It is life at its most free, if you are fortunate enough to be able to try it, because you select your materials, invent your task, and pace yourself.

Nadine Gordimer
I must take my freedom as a writer to show human beings as they are. If you do not, you become a propagandist. They are necessary, but I'm not one. As a writer I'm too selfish to put what talent I have [at the disposal of] any cause.

Carlos Fuentes
In a way we are all involved in the same adventure: to know what you are going to say, to have control over your material, and at the same time to have that margin of freedom which is discovery, amazement, and a precondition of the freedom of the reader.

Vernon Watkins
I hate conferences, manifestos, groups, movements ... I feel that people write best when they write independent of groups.

S J Perelman
The dubious privilege of a freelance writer is he's given the freedom to starve anywhere.

Jean-Paul Sartre *(on declining the Nobel Prize for Literature)*:
A writer must refuse to allow himself to be transformed into an institution.

Many writers believe that there is a conflict between real life and their writing:

Sylvia Plath
My writing is a hollow and failing substitute for real life, real feeling.

Henry Miller
No man would set a word down on paper if he had the courage to live out what he believed in.

W B Yeats
Neither Christ nor Buddha nor Socrates wrote a book, for to do that is to exchange life for a logical process.

William Wantling
> Consonance and assonance and inner
> rhyme won't make up for the fact
> that I can't figure out how to get
> down on paper the real or the true
> which we call life.

Though **Edna Ferber** *has a more bracing attitude:*
Life cannot defeat a writer who is in love with writing – for life itself is a writer's lover until death.

Thomas Bailey Aldrich *is cynical:*
Between the reputation of the author living and the same author dead there is ever a wide discrepancy.

And **Tennessee Williams** *has a kind word for the Grim Reaper:*
I think it's good for a writer to think he's dying; he works harder.

· Work ·

Writers' feelings about their work vary from dislike to mystification:

Lillian Hellman
I don't think many writers like their best known piece of work, particularly when it was written a long time ago.

William Saroyan
All writers are discontented with their work as it's being made. That's because they're aware of a potential, and believe they're not reaching it. But the reader is not aware of the potential, so it makes no difference to him.

Sidney Sheldon
The trick is to do your best. It is an unfortunate fact of life that too many writers – like too many people in other fields – are satisfied with less than their best.

Norman Mailer
The love-hate relationship comes when the book is just treating you like a bitch. The book reveals herself to you one day and hides herself the next. And you're just running around and you don't know what your relation is to the book.

Truman Capote
If what I write doesn't fulfill something in me, if I don't honestly feel it's the best I can do, then I'm miserable. In fact, I just don't publish it.

Mary Stewart
The writer is the worst judge of his work, at least until some time after ... Sometimes I think I've written something brilliantly, and that's fatal. I tend to fall in love with a phrase and ... these are the phrases I'm ashamed of two years later.

Henry Miller
The author's ... idea of the significance of his own work is lost in the welter of other voices. Does he know his own work as well as he imagines? I rather think not. He's like a medium who, when he comes out of his trance, is amazed at what he's said and done.

John Steinbeck
We work in our own darkness a great deal with little real knowledge of what we are doing.

Tennessee Williams
Because it's so important, if my work is interrupted I'm like a raging tiger.

· Gnomic utterances ·

(According to the dictionary, 'gnomic' means of or like an aphorism, which is a pithy saying, but one can't avoid a mind picture of a puzzled old white-bearded dwarf in a pointy red hat.)

Since writers are much given to Deep Thinking, they tend to make occasional statements which the general reader may find disconcertingly gnomic. Here is a small collection which you should only tackle when you are feeling mentally strong and chipper:

Jorge Luis Borges
Every writer creates his own precursors.

E M Forster
Creative writers are always greater than the causes that they represent.

Jean-Paul Sartre
The writer has a place in his age. Each word has an echo. So does each silence.

Samuel Taylor Coleridge
Until you understand a writer's ignorance, presume yourself ignorant of his understanding.

Albert Camus
It is from the moment when I shall no longer be more than a writer that I shall cease to write.

Herman Melville
So far as I am individually concerned, and independent of my pocket, it is my earnest desire to write those sort of books which are said to 'fail'.

David Malouf
Your writings are very personal to you, but how they are related to your actual vision is not visible, or clear. It is imponderable and may be so even to yourself.

Jorge Luis Borges
The opinions of an author are wrought by the superficial accidents of circumstances.

Gore Vidal
Having no talent is no longer enough.

· A few last words on writers ·

Oliver Edwards
Literature would be altogether tense if it were written solely by immortal authors. We must take writers as they are, and not expect them all to last.

Charles Jackson
[The writer] must essentially draw from life as he sees it, lives it, overhears it or steals it, and the truer the writer, perhaps the bigger the blackguard. He lives by biting the hand that feeds him.

François Mauriac
Of all the compliments that can be paid to a writer, there is one especially that will make him glow with pleasure, namely: 'You are admired so much among the younger generation.'

Graham Greene
I am my books.

Marguerite Duras
All my books refer to all my books.

Baltasar Gracian
Even monarchs have need of authors, and fear their pens more than an ugly woman the painter's pencil.

Samuel Johnson
The chief story of every people arises from its authors.

James Michener
Many people who want to be writers don't really want to be writers. They want to have been writers. They wish they had a book in print.

Clive Barnes
This may be the last generation of writers; in the future, everything may be taped.

Bennett Cerf
Coleridge was a drug addict. Poe was an alcoholic. Marlowe was killed by a man whom he was treacherously trying to stab. Pope took money to keep a woman's name out of a satire then wrote a piece so that she could still be recognised anyhow. Chatterton killed himself. Byron was accused of incest. Do you still want to be a writer – and if so, why?

More Quotes

Chapter Four

Writing

'Writing is the hardest way of earning a living, with the possible exception of wrestling alligators'

Every writer has a different definition of the activity that is usually conducted at a desk behind closed doors, in silence and solitude, sometimes with the help of a tape recorder or typewriter or computer, but as often as not with a simple pen or pencil.

Writing is ...

... just having a sheet of paper, a pen and not a shadow of an idea of what you are going to say. **Françoise Sagan**

... simply the writer and the reader on opposite ends of a pencil; they should be as close together as that. **Jay R Gould**

... thinking. It is more than living, for it is being conscious of living. **Anne Morrow Lindbergh**

... practically the only activity a person can do that is not competitive. **Paul Theroux**

... like a contact sport, like football ... You can get hurt, but you enjoy it. **Irwin Shaw**

... the only profession where no one considers you ridiculous if you earn no money. **Jules Renard**

... one of the few professions left where you take all the responsibility for what you do. **Erica Jong**

... the most seductive, the most deceiving, the most dangerous of professions. **John Morley**

> ... not a profession but a vocation of unhappiness. **Georges Simenon**
>
> ... less a profession than a professing – a way of stimulating, organising and affirming thoughts to give meaning to some slice of life. **William Safire**
>
> ... the hardest way of earning a living, with the possible exception of wrestling alligators. **Olin Miller**
>
> ... an affair of yearning for great voyages and hauling on frayed ropes. **Israel Shenker**
>
> ... the science of the various blisses of language. **Roland Barthes**
>
> ... an art like all other forms and it should not be pipelined or squeezed in a water-tight channel. **Miriam Tlali**
>
> ... a yoga that invokes Lord mind. **Allen Ginsberg**
>
> ... an exploration. You start from nothing and learn as you go. **E L Doctorow**
>
> ... the loneliest job in the world. **Bill Adler**
>
> ... a suspension of life in order to re-create life. **John McPhee**
>
> ... a dog's life, but the only life worth living. **Gustave Flaubert**
>
> ... pretty crummy on the nerves. **Paul Theroux**
>
> ... oblivion. **Peter Høeg**

Perhaps the most comprehensive definition is that of:

Rod McKuen

Writing is a privilege. A joy. A pain in the ass. The easiest thing in the world to do. The most difficult feat to pull off. It is profound. It is ridiculous. Better than making love. Akin to dying. More trouble than it's worth. Like rolling down a hill. Like scaling the Alps. Whatever it is – and it's all of the above – it's not for amateurs. You really have to want to write, to write.

Then there are the jokers:

Gene Fowler
Writing is easy, all you do is sit staring at a blank sheet of paper until the drops of blood form on your forehead.

Red Smith
There's nothing to writing. All you do is sit down at a typewriter and open a vein.

John Steinbeck
The profession of book-writing makes horse racing seem like a solid, stable business.

John Updike
Writing doesn't require drive. It's like saying a chicken has to have drive to lay an egg.

Fay Weldon
If you're me you write first, think later … Beginners, alas, have to think first, write next. Poor beginners!

Levity aside, writing is considered by most of its practitioners to be a deeply meaningful occupation:

Gabriel Garcia Marquez
There is no more splendid act of individual liberty than to sit down to invent the world before a typewriter.

Jean Malaquais
The only time I know that something is true is at the moment I discover it in the act of writing.

Breyten Breytenbach
Writing is a transcription of the real; in other words, a spinning out of the known or of that which has been experienced. But writing also explores the unknown nooks and crannies of our mental surroundings, and in so doing it modifies our expectations. By identification it invents the real.

For some, writing has elements of magic and mystery:

Bernard Malamud
Wrestling with illusion is part of writing.

Elizabeth Jolley
There are lots of things that the writer does that the writer doesn't understand. If I did understand I probably wouldn't do them. One is exploring in writing all the time.

Will Blythe
Writing well remains a mysterious endeavour, resistant to blueprints and outlines (thank God) and it is reassuring to establish connection with the masters, even if the link is as slender as a pencil.

Lorrie Moore
What writers do is workmanlike: tenacious, skilled labour. That we know. But it is also mysterious. And the mystery involved in the act of creating a narrative is attached to the mysteries of life itself, and the creation of life itself: that we are; that there is something rather than nothing.

Elizabeth Hardwick
I'm not sure I understand the process of writing. There is ... something strange about imaginative concentration. The brain slowly begins to function in a different way, to make mysterious connections. Say, it is Monday, and you write a very bad draft, but if you keep on trying, on Friday, words, phrases, appear almost unexpectedly.

Gail Godwin
I believe that the writer's unconscious works always within his conscious craft. Sometimes it slows him down, even blocks him; other times it wrests his material right out of his hands and produces unexpected results. My own happiest results have been those stories in which the Uncontrolled gave energy and magic to the part I could control.

John McGahern
It is true that there can be times of intense happiness ... when all the words seem, magically, to find their true place, and several hours turn into a single moment; but these occurrences are so rare that they are, I suspect, like mirages in desert fables, to encourage and torment the half-deluded traveller.

Isabel Allende
Writing is a long process of introspection; it is a voyage toward the darkest caverns of consciousness, a long, slow meditation. I write feeling my way in silence, and along the way discover particles of truth, small crystals that fit in the palm of one hand and justify my passage through this world.

Allende has also said:
In the slow and silent process of writing, I enter a different state of consciousness.

David Malouf
One of the things that writing, or everything that claims to be art, wants to deal with, is what is mysterious, what is not capable of being answered yet, or known, the inexpressible. What hasn't been expressed, and what maybe can't be expressed, is precisely what tempts you each time.

William Saroyan
[The Presence] is known and recognised pretty much by all writers. After you've taken your chair and have written a while – perhaps an hour or so – it comes along, and you start to move ahead strongly. It appears to be a very deep order of energy. Psychiatrists say you're drawing on the collective memory in the Jungian sense.

Jean Cocteau
I feel myself inhabited by a force or being – very little known to me. It gives the orders; I follow.

Doris Lessing
Every writer feels when he, she, hits a different level. A certain kind of writing or emotion comes from it. But you don't know who it is who lives there. It is very frightening to write a story soaked in emotions that you don't recognise as your own.

Jane Gardam
Whoever the writer, wherever he or she comes from, finding the way in to the source of invention, the well in the forest, is always peculiar and appears – discs, notes or not – to be haphazard. To write, there are times when you must hang about. You must loiter and dream.

John Hersey
When the writing is really working, I think there is something like dreaming going on ... It remains mysterious; and it's probably a good thing that it does. It may be that the mystery is among the things that attract those of us who write.

*O*ther writers see writing as a logical progression of ideas committed to paper:

Francis Bacon
Reading maketh a full man, conference a ready man and writing an exact man.

Clive James
Writing is essentially a matter of saying things in the right order.

Nadine Gordimer
Writing is making sense of life. You work your whole life and perhaps you've made sense of one small area ... It's seeking that thread of order and logic in the disorder, and the incredible waste and marvellous profligate character of life.

R V Cassill
Writing is a way of coming to terms with the world and with oneself. The whole spirit of writing is to overcome narrowness and fear by giving order, measure, and significance to the flux of experience constantly dinning into our lives.

Stephen Spender
Writing is the gradual revelation of a wholeness already felt.

Laurence Sterne
Writing, when properly managed (as you may be sure I think mine is), is but a different name for conversation.

*T*hough music and dance and oral poetry and rock paintings were earlier arts, the practice of making meaningful marks on a smooth surface goes back a good five millenniums, to the cuneiform squiggles of the Sumerians:

Frank Muir
When writing was first developed it was used to make civic records, royal inventories and similar documents, not to record stories, but eventually the songs and myth-poems sung by wandering poets were put down on papyrus by scribes ... It was many centuries later that the Greeks began recording prose.

*W*riting falls into two categories, prose and poetry, though there is a lot of blurring at the edges, specially now that poetry has put on hippy raiment and doesn't have to scan or rhyme any more:

Samuel Taylor Coleridge
I wish our clever young poets would remember my homely definitions of prose and poetry, that is, prose – words in their best order; poetry – the best words in their best order.

Henrik Ibsen
Verse is for visions, prose for ideas.

Ursula le Guin
The borderline between prose and poetry is one of those fog-shrouded literary minefields where the wary explorer gets blown to bits before ever seeing anything clearly. It is full of barbed wire and the stumps of dead opinions.

Edward Arlington Robinson
There are too many words in prose, and they take up altogether too much room.

Henry Green
Prose is not to be read aloud but to oneself at night, and it is not as quick as poetry, but rather a gathering web of insinuations ... Prose should be a long intimacy between strangers ... It should slowly appeal to feelings unexpressed, it should in the end draw tears out of the stone.

Winston Churchill
Men will forgive a man anything except bad prose.

*A*nd writers' perspectives on their writing vary as sharply as their divergent personalities:

Agostinho Neto
If writing is one of the conditions of your being alive, you create that condition.

Christopher Isherwood
I am a camera with its shutter open, quite passive, recording, not thinking.

Tennessee Williams
When I write, everything is visual, as brilliantly as if it were on a lit stage.

Marina Warner
If the writing is going well, I can feel I'm racing to transcribe in words a picture scrolling in front of my eyes.

William Hazlitt
The more a man writes, the more he can write.

Carlos Fuentes
In a way [controversy] goes with the territory because it is not natural to write. We are created to run and hunt and swim and make love but not to sit hunched with a piece of paper and some ink scribbling hieroglyphs. And when we do it, it is an act of rebellion against God himself.

Alfred Kazin
To write is in some way to cut the seemingly automatic pattern of violence, destructiveness and death wish. To write is to put the seeming insignificance of human existence into a different perspective. It is the need, the wish, and please God, the ability, to reorder our physical faith.

Edward Albee
No writer who's any good at all would sit down and put a sheet of paper in a typewriter and start typing ... unless he knew what he was writing about. But at the same time, writing has got to be an act of discovery. Finding out things about what one is writing about.

Joan Didion
I think of writing anything at all as a kind of high-wire act. The minute you start putting words on paper you're eliminating possibilities.

Mary Wallace
The art of writing goes beyond the rules into an area where nothing is fixed and absolute; where we must find our way by instinct, by ear, by some subtle awareness of what makes one word or group of words better than another for the expression of what we want to say.

Sara Paretsky
I think writing is like singing. Singers talk about having a line; you can tell when you're in your line and when you're not – and you can certainly tell when you're listening to someone. That's my image for writing.

John Mortimer
The hours spent writing are like giving a performance on the page, a prolonged one-man show which will grip the audience's attention and keep the customers laughing and crying or being alarmed and continually wondering what is going to happen next.

Ursula le Guin
Writing ... is trying to get all the patterns of sounds, syntax, imagery, ideas, emotions, working together in one process ... [Writers] are trying to get the reader to go along helplessly, putty in their hands, seeing, hearing, feeling, believing the story, laughing at it, crying at it.

Chenjerai Hove
For me, writing involves disturbing the peace so that people can never think that the society in which we live is okay, as the politicians want us to believe. We need to be able to locate ourselves as the skies shift.

Doris Lessing
The whole process of writing is a setting at a distance. That is the value of it – to the writer, and to the people who read the results of this process, which takes the raw, the individual, the uncriticised, the unexamined, into the realm of the general.

Clive James
My trick, or condition, of being able to compartmentalise my life allows me to be active in several fields at once ... I could write during the day, go on stage at night, and each activity would benefit from the other.

Ray Bradbury
By lecturing I fill out the other half of my creative life. Writing is a living process, dynamic. Lecturing is an explaining process, analytical.

Sholem Asch
It has always been like writing a cheque ... It is easy to write a cheque if you have enough money in the bank, and writing comes more easily if you have something to say.

Jerome Bruner
There is something antic about creating, although the enterprise be serious. And there is a matching antic spirit that goes with writing about it, for if ever there was a silent process, it is the creative one. Antic and serious and silent.

Jay McInerney
The only sensible approach is not to take it too seriously. What counts is the writing.

Don Marquis:
> i never think at all when i write
> nobody can do two things at the same time
> and do them both well.

Most successful writers love their profession and wouldn't do anything else:

David Hare
I wasn't born until I started to write.

John Gardner
It's as if God put me on earth to write.

James Dickey
I love to write. Writing is an obsession with me.

Jean Grenier
To write is to put one's obsessions in order.

John Irving
I am compulsive about writing, I need to do it the way I need sleep and exercise and food and sex; I can go without it for a while, but then I need it.

Susan Hill
Heady stuff. Writing is. Gets more so.

Muriel Spark
Writing is a driving force. You get up in the middle of the night and write if you have to. My writing has got that frightful first claim on me ... I can't imagine ever not writing. I think I would just die there and then.

William Goyen
I can't imagine *not* writing. Writing simply is a way of life for me. The older I get the more a way of life it is ... Writing is something I cannot imagine living without, nor scarcely would want to. Not to live daily as a writing person is inconceivable.

André Brink
I can't not write. Since I was nine, I knew I had to be a writer.

Doris Lessing
I am a writing animal and I can't imagine myself not writing; I literally get quite ill if I don't write a bit.

P G Wodehouse
I love writing. I never feel really comfortable unless I am either actually writing or have a story going. I could not stop writing.

Firdaus Kanga
I like writing better than anything in the world. I have had a little life but in writing you can use everything. Nothing is wasted.

Sherwood Anderson
I think the whole glory of writing lies in the fact that it forces us out of ourselves and into the lives of others.

Evan Hunter
The nice thing about writing, unlike public speaking, is that you can correct all your mistakes later.

Diane Case
It's nice to write. It's comforting. You don't always get people who understand what you have to say or who have the time to listen to you. When you write you can express it anyway. You are never alone if you write.

Terry Pratchett
I can't think of anything I'd rather do [than write books], but it is hard. It ought to be hard. It's much more enjoyable if it is.

Joseph Heller
Writing's a respectable occupation, and for me, it's the best form of occupation to have. Very few people do the work they want to do. I'm one of the fortunate ones. I'm doing the work I want to do.

Robert Stone
The wonderful thing about writing is that you're constantly having to ask yourself questions. It makes you function morally. It makes you function intellectually. That's the great pleasure and great reward of writing.

Harlan Ellison
I'm nothing. Nothing at all without writing. Without truth, my truth, the only truth I know, it's all a gambol in the pasture without rhythm or sense.

Dennis Potter
I've always had this passion for writing. It is an antique word, and it's one that's easily scoffed at, but I do have a sense of vocation, and I will have it to the last ounce of my life, the last second.

Gabriel Garcia Marquez
Torture for me would be to stop writing.

*O*thers are ambivalent:

Mary Stewart
I suppose I love writing and hate writing. Like every writer. You always hope the agony of getting through the difficult bits will grow easier as the years go by, but it's just the same except that you've learned from experience the thing will come out if you stick at it.

Octavio Paz
Writing is a painful process that requires huge effort and sleepless nights. In addition to the threat of writer's block, there is always the sensation that failure is inevitable. Nothing we write is what we wish we could write. Writing is a curse. The worst part of it is the anguish that precedes the act of writing – the hours, days or months when we search in vain for the phrase that turns the spigot that makes the water flow. Once that first phrase is written, everything changes: the process is enthralling, vital, and enriching, no matter what the final result is. Writing is a blessing!

Mary Wesley
Writing for me is a compulsion. It's companionship, but it's not always enjoyable. It can be painful and frustrating like a dog digging at a rabbit hole, when the rabbit is long gone.

Robert Stone
It's goddamn hard. Nobody really cares whether you do it or not. You have to make yourself do it. I'm very lazy and I suffer as a result. Of course, when it's going well there's nothing in the world like it. But it's also very lonely.

Beryl Bainbridge
Most of the time I wonder what it's all for. It's a mug's game. It's no way for a normal person to live.

Many complain that writing is hard work and induces a high level of angst, though the mental anguish is bravely borne:

Jean Auel
Some people have this funny idea about writing. That you just sit at the machine and it just flows out of your body. Even if you're an organic writer, it doesn't work that way. Writing is damned hard work.

Judith Krantz
People think it's so easy, writing, and it isn't, it's terribly hard.

Richard Nixon
Writing a book is the most intensive exercise anyone can give his brain.

Laurence Olivier
Writing is not a glamorous occupation, as anyone who has attempted it will know; it requires hard work and self-discipline. It is lonely, it can be depressing; it creates an unwelcome feeling of vulnerability ... It is not romantic ... a daily grind, and anyone who succeeds in filling up a page is a hero.

Peter Dobereiner
About 99 per cent of the population regardless of age, is incapable of equating writing with work, not real work.

Honoré de Balzac
It is as easy to dream a book as it is hard to write one.

Peter Høeg
There is nothing else in the world that involves two years of constantly packing energy into this small brick – [he slaps his hand on a copy of his novel] – which then waits to explode between the eyes of the reader.

Josephine Hart
For most of my adult life I resisted writing. I fought an 'internal battle' with the words, characters and lives that inhabited my mind, and at times threatened to devour it ... In the summer of 1989 I finally collapsed on to the page. As though insane with relief, the words poured from their prison.

Joseph Heller
Writing ... is the agony of putting down what I think are good ideas and finding the words for them and the paragraph forms for them ... a laborious process.

J M Coetzee
I don't like writing, so I have to push myself. It's bad if I write but worse if I don't.

Hilary Mantel
Line by line, writing's not so hard ... It's when you allow yourself to think of the totality of what you have to do, of the task which faces you with each book, that you feel it's hard, even terrifying. In my daily work, minimizing the terror is my object.

Morris West
Like a sentence of death, the mere act of writing concentrates the mind most wondrously.

Kingsley Amis
I find writing very nervous work.

Rebecca West
It's a nauseous process.

Angela Carter
Writing certainly doesn't make better people, nor do writers lead happier lives.

While for others, writing is just plain hell:

George Orwell
Writing a book is a horrible, exhausting struggle, like a long bout of some painful illness.

Edna O'Brien
When a writer, or an artist, has the feeling that he can't do it anymore, he descends into hell.

Jessamyn West
Writing is so difficult that I often feel that writers, having had their hell on earth, will escape all punishment hereafter.

Marika Cobbold
Writing is absolute hell ... Pulling teeth is preferable.

William Styron
Let's face it, writing is hell.

Writers often invoke the language of the senses when talking about their writing, likening it to love, marriage and sex:

Adam Small
My writing has always been writing of a passionate, emotional kind.

Marcel Proust
Our passions shape our books; repose writes them in the intervals.

Eileen Jensen
Writing, like making love, is more fun when you know what you're doing.

Morris West
Writing is like making love. You have to practise to be good at it. Like the best love-making, it has to be done in private and with great consideration for your partner in the enterprise, who in this case is the reader.

Mario Vargas Llosa
Writing is at first a very vague excitement, something that takes only part of your life, then it becomes very dominant, very absorbing, then there is a climax, where you know you have produced, you have arrived. Then there is a cooling-off, a depression.

Iris Murdoch
Writing is like getting married. One should never commit oneself until one is amazed at one's luck.

Lorrie Moore
You will read somewhere that all writing has to do with one's genitals. Don't dwell on this. It will make you nervous.

What does writing demand of the serious practitioner?

Albert Camus
The nobility of our calling will always be rooted in two commitments difficult to observe: refusal to lie about what we know, and resistance to oppression.

Carlos Fuentes
Writing requires the concentration of the writer, demands that nothing else be done except that.

Muriel Spark
I have to be totally honest because I couldn't write otherwise; the pen just wouldn't write.

T S Eliot
To look into one's heart and write is not enough. One has to look in the cerebral cortex and the digestive tract.

John Peale Bishop
All authentic writing comes from an individual; but a final judgement of it will depend, not on how much individuality it contains, but how much of common humanity.

J M Coetzee
Writing is not carried out in a vacuum. The book is what you are about to become, or have become, or used to be.

· Good & bad writing ·

'Good writing excites me'

Good writing is …

… a kind of skating which carries off the performer where he would not go.
Ralph Waldo Emerson

… supposed to evoke sensation in the reader – not the fact that it's raining, but the feel of being rained upon. **E L Doctorow**

… true writing. If a man is making a story up it will be true in proportion to the amount of knowledge of life that he has had and how conscientious he is.
Ernest Hemingway

Somerset Maugham
It has been said that good prose should resemble the conversation of a well-bred man.

F Scott Fitzgerald
All good writing is swimming under water and holding your breath.

We all know what we like in a book, but how does one tell good writing from the mediocre or positively bad? Some define good writing by their reaction to it ...

Harold Pinter
Good writing excites me, and makes life worth living.

Ernest Hemingway
All good books ... are truer than if they had really happened ... and afterwards it all belongs to you; the good and the bad, the ecstasy, the remorse and sorrow, the people and the places and how the weather was.

Lord Chesterfield
The easiest books are generally the best; for, whatever author is obscure and difficult in his own language, certainly does not think clearly.

Reginald Hill
A good read is not about original ideas or exciting experiences; it's about good writing.

... and some by comparison with bad writing:

C S Lewis
We can never know that a piece of writing is bad unless we have begun by trying to read it as if it was very good and ended by discovering that we were paying the author an undeserved compliment.

Glenway Wescott
Bad writing is in fact a rank feverish unnecessary slough. Good writing is a dyke, in which there is a leak for every one of our weary hands.

Elizabeth Young
There is a persistent belief nowadays that writing which is very popular cannot be any good. Very often ... it's not very good – much populist fiction is conventional, predictable and unimaginative – but there are notable exceptions, just as Dickens and Mark Twain were popular exceptions to the tides of late Victorian dross.

Peter Wilhelm
One tires of ... polished, eerily empty products of over-cultivation. One almost feels nostalgic for bad, rough, honest writing.

What qualities are necessary to produce good writing?

Georges-Louis Leclerc de Buffon
To write well is at once to think well, to feel rightly, and to render properly! It is to have, at the same time, mind, soul, taste.

Horace
The secret of all good writing is sound judgement ... Knowledge is the foundation and source.

Somerset Maugham
To write good prose is an affair of good manners. It is, unlike verse, a civil art.

Gabriel Josipovici
In the end good writing has little to do with dictionaries and much to do with a writer's active ear and imagination.

Edna Ferber
I think that to write really well and convincingly, one must be somewhat poisoned by emotion. Dislike, displeasure, resentment, fault-finding, imagination, passionate remonstrance, a sense of injustice – they all make fine fuel.

William Styron
The good writing of any age has always been the product of *someone's* neurosis, and we'd have a mighty dull literature if all the writers that came along were a bunch of happy chuckleheads.

Jessamyn West
There is no royal path to good writing, and such paths as do exist do not lead through neat critical gardens, various as they are, but through the jungles of self, the world, and of craft.

Gabriel Garcia Marquez
You write better in good health. You write better without [unhappy] pre-occupations. You write better when you have love in your life. There is a romantic idea that suffering and adversity are very useful to the writer. I don't agree at all.

Jean de la Bruyère
The same common sense which makes an author write good things, makes him dread they are not good enough to deserve reading.

How should one set about writing to the best of one's ability?

Isaac Asimov
It's the writing that teaches you. It's the rotten stories that make it possible for you to write the good stories eventually.

Ray Bradbury
If you write a hundred short stories and they're all bad, that doesn't mean you've failed. You fail only if you stop writing.

Richard Harding Davis
The secret of good writing is to say an old thing a new way or to say a new thing an old way.

William Faulkner
[Good writing] is the result of sweat, hard work and a belief in truth; truth as a condition of the human heart, not the individual human heart but the composite heart of man. A writer uses what material he can to present truth in the best possible way.

George Orwell
It is also true that one can write nothing readable unless one constantly struggles to efface one's own personality. Good prose is like a windowpane.

Mary Stewart
Good writing should be unobtrusive and the reader shouldn't ever have to stop and think, 'That's a fine phrase.' The good writer curbs his natural impulse to show off. He has to get through with a whang to his reader's heart, without the reader even noticing how he's done it.

Florence King
Good writing obeys the dictum of Horace: 'Remember always never to bring a tame in union with a savage thing.' – Meaning, among other things, don't distract a mystery reader with a romantic subplot.

Patrick Lee
I have learnt that good writing is undeliberated: you work best when you simply conduct the current and don't create noise with rational analysis.

And there are compensations if you don't make it into the top echelon:

George Eliot
Bad writing of the sort called amusing is spiritual gin.

Jean de la Bruyère
A mediocre mind thinks it writes divinely; a good mind thinks it writes reasonably.

Horace Walpole
I am persuaded that foolish writers and readers are created for each other; and that Fortune provides readers as she does mates for ugly women.

Ralph Waldo Emerson
People do not deserve to have good writing, they are so pleased with bad.

Jonathan Raban
For someone in love with the idea of writing, the joy of writing something hasty, derivative and bad goes as deep as the joy of writing something genuinely original.

Aldous Huxley
A bad book is as much a labour to write as a good one; it comes as sincerely from the author's soul.

Hilaire Belloc
The truth is missed by people who say that good writing has no market. That is not the point. Good writing sometimes has a market, and very bad writing sometimes has a market. Useful writing sometimes has a market, and writing of no use whatsoever, even as recreation, sometimes has a market. Writing the most ridiculous errors and false judgments sometimes has a market. The point is that the market has nothing to do with the qualities attached to writing. It never had and it never will.

William Saroyan
As a kid I used to throw things out, saying, 'This isn't great.' It didn't occur to me that it didn't have to be *great*. Then some of the things that I thought were useless ... took on more and more meaning. This was because I was not straining for greatness.

Jeremy Gordin
To be sure, a book must be well wrought. But that is only the first step. The second and more important step, and this is why we sometimes love books that are clearly badly written, is for a piece of writing to have that certain *je ne sais quoi*.

Last words on the subject of good writing:

Ernest Gowers
Let us therefore agree ... that a reasonably good standard of writing is a mark not of preciosity but of good sense, not of prissiness but of efficiency; that such a standard can be attained by anyone with a little effort; that the effort will be worth-while ...; that it requires ... a willingness to acquire good habits; and, finally, that a writer with good habits may be allowed to make an occasional slip ... without incurring eternal damnation.

· The craft of writing ·

'The hardest trade in the world'

Most writers agree that writing is a craft, but their high-minded tone generally implies that in the hands of a master, craft becomes art.

Archibald MacLeish
The first discipline is the realisation that there is a discipline – that all art begins and ends with discipline, that any art is first and foremost a craft.

Geoffrey Chaucer
The lyf so short, the craft so long to lerne.

Katherine Anne Porter
Most people won't realise that writing is a craft. You have to take your apprenticeship in it like anything else.

Anthony Burgess
When I hear a journalist like Malcolm Muggeridge praising God because he has mastered the craft of writing, I feel a powerful nausea. It is not a thing to be said. Mastery never comes, and one serves a lifelong apprenticeship. The writer cannot retire from the battle; he dies fighting.

Ernest Hemingway
We are all apprentices in a craft where no one ever becomes a master.

Paul Claudel
The literary beauty of my work has no other significance for me than that found by a workman who is aware of having performed his task well; I simply did my best; but, had I been a carpenter, I should have been just as conscientious in planing a plank properly.

Anatole France
Word-carpentry is like any other kind of carpentry: you must join your sentences smoothly.

George Bussy
Literature's like carpentry – a matter of dovetailing at the right spot.

Gabriel Garcia Marquez
Ultimately, literature is nothing but carpentry ... Both are very hard work. Writing something is almost as hard as making a table. With both you are working with reality, a material just as hard as wood. Both are full of tricks and techniques.

Kaatje Hurlbut
The body of words which carries your story into the world is the work of the craftsman, and the craftsman's labour is as conscious, as canny, and as practical as that of the bricklayer.

Kurt Tucholsky
Writing prose is like laying a mosaic.

William Faulkner
The craft is too fluid for any set pattern. One day you can do a certain thing and the next you need a complete change of pace.

Frederick Forsyth
My approach is to be reasonable, commonsensical, practical, not intellectual. I'm a mechanic when I write. I put together a car. It may not be a Rolls-Royce or a Grand Prix racer but it runs.

Roald Dahl
I mistrust clergymen and priests – like I mistrust scientists; they're the priesthood of today. In fact I'm against intellectuals. No real writer is an intellectual ... I'm a jolly hardworking and pretty successful craftsman; I refuse to *analyse* everything.

Though (as usual) there is a dissenting voice:

Robert Lowell
I'm sure that writing isn't a craft, that is, something for which you learn the skills and go on turning out. It must come from some deep impulse, deep inspiration.

In a wider sense, writers see themselves as involved in a difficult and complex trade:

Simone de Beauvoir
Writing is a trade ... which is learned by writing.

Ernest Hemingway
The hardest trade in the world is the writing of straight, honest prose about human beings.

Jean de la Bruyère
To make a book is as much a trade as to make a clock; something more than intelligence is required to become an author.

Agatha Christie
It's no good starting out by thinking one is a heaven-born genius – some people are, but very few. No, one is a tradesman – a tradesman in a good honest trade. You must learn the technical skills, and then, within that trade, you can apply your own creative ideas.

Jonathan Raban
When the first galley proofs arrived, they gave off a faint whiff of old clothes, as if the rags from which their paper had been manufactured had been stripped from the backs of tramps. It was the authentic smell of writing as a trade, a trade secret.

George Bernard Shaw
Literature is like any other trade; you will never sell anything unless you go to the right shop.

Erica Jong
I don't regard writing as just a trade, but really as a calling. I feel that I was meant to be a writer, and I consider myself a success in having found the thing that I was put on this earth to do.

Hilaire Belloc
Of all fatiguing, futile, empty trades, the worst, I suppose, is writing about writing.

And it's important to follow the rules:

Hector Bolitho
Good writing involves certain fixed laws of craftsmanship. Without those laws a writer's art will perish in confusion.

Arthur Kopit
Start with fundamentals. A writer has to master his craft and learn the rules before he tries to break them. It's much more than just feeling that you have something to say. You have to learn how to say it.

Ellery Queen
There are no rules of technique or taboos of subject matter which cannot be broken by a talented craftsman – indeed … the only true value of 'don'ts' is that they give the really creative writer the challenge to 'do'.

George Jean Nathan
Experiment is a valuable thing, but before indulging yourself in it you must have a thorough grounding in the established principles of your craft.

Phyllis Whitney
Like any other artist you must learn your craft – then you can add all the genius you like.

Can writing be taught?

'If the natural talent is there, it can be improved'

Can the art of writing be taught, or are schools of creative writing a waste of time?

Arguments for and against seem to be about equal. Those who are pro-teaching argue that if would-be writers have the necessary talent, they can be helped in three ways: with instruction in basic techniques, by providing the enrichment of structured reading and exchanged ideas, and through informed criticism and support:

John Jakes
Writing is in part a skill, and certain technical aspects of it can be learned by any reasonably intelligent person.

John Gardner
I discovered very quickly that it's fairly easy to transform an eager, intelligent student to a publishing creative writer. Anyone has stories he can tell, and, once you've shown him a little technique, can tell them relatively well.

Russell Celyn-Jones
If people accept that you can be taught music or painting, why do they not accept that you can be taught writing?

Raymond Carver
Everybody, whether it's a conductor or composer or microbiologist or mathematician – they've all learned their business from older practitioners; the idea of the maestro–apprentice relationship is an old and distinguished [one].

Rumer Godden
No one can teach anyone else how to write but one can teach them basic technique, give them a firm grounding.

John Barth
There's some justification for having courses in so-called creative writing. I know from happy experience with young writers that the muses make no distinction between undergraduates and graduate students. The muses know only expert writers and less expert writers.

Nicolette Jones
The British, on the whole, mistrust creative writing courses. There is a feeling here that ... writers are born, not made, and writing cannot be learned like a craft, let alone marked like an exam ... All the evidence is that such attitudes sabotage our own chances of nurturing talent.

Truman Capote
If I were a young writer and convinced of my talent, I could do a lot worse than to attend a really good college workshop – for one reason only. Any writer, and especially the talented writer, needs an audience. The more immediate that audience is, the better for him because it stimulates him in his work; he gets a better view of himself and running criticism. Young writers couldn't get this even if they were publishing stories all the time. You publish a story and there's no particular reaction. It's as though you shot an arrow into the dark ... But if you are working in close quarters with others who are also interested in writing, and you've got an instructor with a good critical sense, there's a vast stimulation.

Jay McInerney
One of the great advantages of creative writing programmes is that you're in an environment of support, and you're with people engaged in the same enterprise.

Robert Stone
A creative writing class can at least be good for morale. When I teach writing, I do things like take classes to bars and race tracks to listen to dialogue.

Malcolm Bradbury
[Writing] is teachable, if you have whatever else it takes – very powerful motivation, that thing which drives them obsessively to be writers ... This is the difference between the person who has one story in them and the one who has that range of talent and lasting drive to write.

Caryl Phillips
I'm not attempting to impose style, but we talk about the basic decisions a writer has to make, about tense, point of view, dialogue and characterisation. The main thing is that students should discover their own strengths. They have to find the most comfortable way for them.

Elizabeth Jolley
If you are teaching creative writing, you will find you can't teach people to have imagination. You can teach them techniques and you can teach them how to be aware of things by keeping a journal and really notice, observe, but you can't teach them to be imaginative.

Frank Kermode
Bernard Malamud ... argues that teaching writing is teaching literature; occasionally the instructor may help a genuine writer, but the real justification is not that; it is that one adds to the number of people who have some skill in recognising good writing.

John Gardner
When you teach creative writing, you teach people, among other things, how to plot. You explain the principles, how it is that fiction thinks.

Richard Wilbur
I think the best part of teaching from the point of view of the teacher-writer, writer-teacher, is that it makes you read a good deal and makes you be articulate about what you read.

Joseph Wambaugh
I think that I did learn a lot in my formal education, going to college part-time as a policeman ... I don't think I was necessarily born with the ability to put down a hundred and forty thousand words between two hard covers. I needed the schooling, the formal education.

Donald Barthelme
I've just read an article that strongly implies that teaching writing is a dismal racket, an impoverishing fraud ... but I'd hate this to be taken as generally true ... Where I teach a graduate workshop, the writing students are fully the equals in seriousness and accomplishment of the other graduate students.

Kurt Vonnegut
In a creative writing class of twenty people anywhere in this country, six students will be startlingly talented. Two of those might actually publish something by and by. They will have something other than literature itself on their minds. They will probably be hustlers too.

Raymond Carver
Once you're out there in the world, on your own, nobody cares.

Somerset Maugham
A writer does well to place himself in such conditions that he may experience as many as possible of the vicissitudes which occur to men. He need do nothing very much, but he should do everything a little. I would have him be in turns tinker, tailor, soldier, sailor; I would have him love and lose, go hungry and get drunk, play poker with rough-necks in San Francisco, bet with racing touts at Newmarket, philander with duchesses in Paris and argue with philosophers in Bonn, ride with bullfighters in Seville and swim with Kanakas in the South Seas. No man is not worth the writer's knowing: every occurrence is grist to his mill.

Those who are against the teaching of creative writing argue that writers are born, not made; that talent will out, and that education is either unnecessary or positively harmful:

Elie Wiesel
I never taught creative writing courses. I believe in creative reading.

Harlan Ellison
If you're a writer, you know it when they drag you squawking out of the womb. You may be able to fake it by attending writing classes, but you haven't got it here.

Christopher Hope
It's impossible to teach people how to be writers. They can only be encouraged, or better still, discouraged. I don't know what to say to people who say they want to write. I head for the door.

Doris Lessing
I started to write all on my own ... I never learned to write, and I am still persuaded, moreover, that literature is not learned. One simply encounters, in that realm, people or books which suddenly speak to you, show you what you have needed to hear or see. And you go on, pragmatically, by trial and error.

Jane Gardam
I am wary of those who think all can be rationalised and made smooth by instruction. I am particularly wary of creative writing classes ... They cannot teach the spirit of light that wakes the imagination – kick-starts it like an electric charge. This blast of pleasure has to happen by itself.

Hugh MacDiarmid
Our principal writers have nearly all been fortunate in escaping regular education.

E M Cioran
For a writer the university is death.

Vera Brittain
The idea that it is necessary to go to a university in order to become a successful writer or even a man or woman of letters (which is by no means the same thing) is one of those phantasies that surround authorship.

Catherine Cookson
Steel yourself to look that ... dear friend straight in the eye when he casually remarks that without a suitable education, by which he means university, your chance of landing on the literary planet is on a par with that of your being selected to orbit the moon.

Stanley Elkin
To a large extent, contemporary literature is shaped by writing programmes in universities. It's not that the writing programmes harm people. But an awful lot of people influence people who shouldn't be influencing people ... Today the kids are standing on the shoulders of midgets.

Gore Vidal
Teaching has ruined more American novelists than drink.

Kurt Vonnegut
A lot of creative writing courses teach you how to counterfeit concern, how to counterfeit energy, sincerity and involvement. It's a little like going to modelling school to learn how to put on your make-up and always be beautiful.

Fran Lebowitz
I think you can't learn to write, and people who spend money on writing courses would do much better to send the money to me, and I'll introduce them to the author.

This writer's feeling is that it's all very well for established authors to say that writing talent will thrust up out of life's compost like a healthy mushroom — but what about the talented writers who never make it because they don't get a decent chance? How many works of genius have been lost to posterity because their would-be writers have not been encouraged and helped by knowledgeable mentors when they most needed it? Pitifully few writers make it entirely on their own.

Perhaps the most balanced views are those of:

Tim Heald
I am not saying that you can't teach writing, nor that any writer worth reading is not learning all the time. What I am saying is that you cannot teach anyone to write.

Rod McKuen
Writing can't be taught, but if the natural talent is there, it can be improved. A grasp of language never hurt anyone. Writing courses are fine as long as they don't take away individuality. The best thing about workshops is that they are supportive. The young writer needs encouragement, especially from a successful peer.

Clare Boylan
I would agree with the view of many fiction writers that creative writing, coming as it does out of one's own centre, cannot be imparted to another. I would, however, disagree completely that one ought not to advise and guide and share something of what one knows on the basis that there are already enough works of fiction in the world. This is simply not true.

John Matshikiza
It is a difficult craft. People can help you and guide you, but nobody can teach you … I think once you reach a certain level of skill, the important thing is to be bold.

Malcolm Bradbury
The ill-balanced relationship between contemporary writing and contemporary criticism has been, for me, one among many reasons for believing that creative writing has a significant place in the modern department of English or literature … I think those universities that have also taken an interest have added to the stock of serious contemporary writing in Britain.

Francine du Plessix Gray
Teaching offers me a form of human contact which I find deeply satisfying yet less draining than most other social engagements. Listening to students' problems, inciting them to read Plato or Colette, the heatedness and fun of class discussions – that's one of the most nourishing and inspiring things I know.

James Baldwin
If you are going to be a writer there is nothing I can say to stop you; if you're not going to be a writer nothing I can say will help you. What you really need at the beginning is somebody to let you know that the effort is real.

Summing up

To sum up the subject of writing, here are some ideas to ponder:

Stephen King
A lot of what this business is about is faith and confidence.

Winston Churchill
Writing a book is an adventure: it begins as an amusement, then it becomes a mistress, then a master, and finally a tyrant. The last phase is that just as you are about to be reconciled to your servitude, you kill the monster, and fling him to the public.

Somerset Maugham
Though very good writers have led narrow lives they have written well in spite of their circumstances rather than on account of them.

Isabel Allende
We should continue to write in spite of the bruises and the vast silence that frequently surrounds us. A book is not an end in itself, it is only a way to touch someone … and sometimes it is a way of winning other people to our causes.

Elizabeth Jolley
Perhaps the writer in writing can close the spaces, can console and heal others and in this heal himself.

John Matshikiza
Everybody says that writing doesn't get easier, but I think it does as you get less self-indulgent.

Albert Camus
To write is to become disinterested. There is a certain renunciation in art.

Ernest Hemingway
In writing you are limited by what has already been done satisfactorily. So I have tried to learn to do something else.

Dietrich Schwanitz
Like the German Romantics, a lot of our contemporary writers still believe that all you have to do is listen to some inner demon and divine words will flow. They don't realise that you also have to know how to write.

Henry David Thoreau
Nothing goes by luck in composition. It allows of no tricks. The best you can write will be the best you are.

Benjamin Disraeli
There is a moment when a heavenly light rises over the dim world you have been so long creating, and bathes it with life and beauty. Accept this omen that your work is good, and revel in the sunshine of composition.

John Steinbeck
I have written a great many stories and I still don't know how to go about it except to write it and take my chances.

Flannery O'Connor
There is only one answer ... and that is that one writes what one can.

Colette
When one can read, can penetrate the enchanted realm of books, why write?

Gore Vidal
The most interesting thing about writing is the way that it obliterates time. Three hours seem like three minutes. Then there is the business of surprise. I never know what is coming next. The phrase that sounds in the head changes when it appears on the page. Then I start probing it with a pen, finding new meanings. Sometimes I burst out laughing at what is happening as I twist and turn sentences. Strange business, all in all. One never gets to the end of it. That's why I go on, I suppose. To see what the next sentences I write will be.

Chapter Five
The Nuts & Bolts of Language

This chapter covers the construction materials used by writers – words, sentences, grammar, punctuation, language, imagery, metaphors, symbols – as well as the more sophisticated aspects of the verbal edifice: pace, tone and technique.

· Words ·

'In the beginning was the word … '

Nadine Gordimer
Man became man not by the tool but by the Word. It is not walking upright and using a stick to dig for food or strike a blow that makes a human being, it is speech.

Words are ...

... weapons. **George Santayana**

... loaded pistols. **Jean-Paul Sartre**

... the small change of thought. **Jules Renard**

... pegs to hang ideas on. **Henry Ward Beecher**

... great foes of reality. **Joseph Conrad**

... of course, the most powerful drug used by mankind. **Rudyard Kipling**

... the only things that last forever. **William Hazlitt**

... all we have. **Samuel Beckett**

Words are a writer's basic building blocks, and the greater the variety you can command, the more subtle and detailed your edifice will be. Words should be to writers as gold is to misers — treasure to be collected and gloated over:

Maya Angelou
Words. Words. I have always loved them. I love words spoken and I love words sung, and I even love to see words sitting primly on pages ... It was fitting that I would become a writer.

Norman Mailer
We are in love with the word. We are proud of it ... The word comes to us from every avatar of human existence. As writers, we are obliged more than others to keep our lives attached to the primitive power of the word.

Dylan Thomas
I fell in love ... at once, and am still at the mercy of words, though sometimes now, knowing a little of their behaviour very well, I think I can influence them slightly and have even learned to beat them now and then, which they appear to enjoy.

James Dickey
I have a plain-and-simple fascination with words. There are so many combinations of possibilities that can be done. I love the sound of words.

Shena Mackay
The look of words, the way they affect one another, the reactive colours of individual letters and numbers, the characters of characters have always fascinated me.

Evelyn Waugh
Words should be an intense pleasure to a writer just as leather should be to a shoemaker.

Alexander Smith
I have ear for no other harmony than the harmony of words.

Words possess their own magic ...

Godfrey Smith *(in a letter to a new grandchild):*
In a world full of audio visual marvels, may words matter to you and be full of magic.

David Malouf
Words are ... used in some way magically.

Peggy Noonan
Poetry has everything to do with speeches – cadence, rhythm, imagery, sweep, a knowledge that words are magic; that words, like children, have this power to make dance the dullest beanbag of a heart.

... though not everyone sees them through a rosy haze:

Susan Hill
I have heard writers declare that they are in love with words. I do not understand what they mean. Words are tools, like bricks.

Charles Péguy
A word is not the same with one writer as with another. One tears it from his guts. The other pulls it out of his overcoat pocket.

May Sarton
The more articulate one is, the more dangerous words become.

William Shakespeare
Zounds! I was never so bethumped with words.

Learning how to assemble words to the best possible effect is the writer's trade. David Profumo put it very well when he praised Norman Maclean's stories in A River Runs Through It *for 'the discreet curl of their words':*

André Breton
Words make love with one another.

Norman Cousins
Words have to be crafted, not sprayed. They need to be fitted together with infinite care.

James Earl Jones
Living in silence taught me to listen, to appreciate good language, never to be glib. Words could not just be haphazard things. They had to be carefully chosen to strike a chord in the hearer.

Aldous Huxley
Words form the thread on which we string our experiences.

John Milton
His words ... like so many nimble and airy servitors trip about him at command.

John McGahern
Words had been physical presences for me for a long time ... each word with its own weight, colour, shape, relationship, extending out into a word without end. Change any word in a single sentence and immediately all the other words demand to be rearranged.

And storing them up for future use is the work of a lifetime ...

John D MacDonald
Vocabulary ... can only come from constant omnivorous reading, beginning very early in life.

Jacques Barzun
The price of learning to use words is the development of an acute self-consciousness ... You must attend to words when you read, when you speak, when others speak. Words must become ever present in your waking life, an incessant concern.

Evelyn Waugh
One forgets words as one forgets names. One's vocabulary needs constant fertilisation or it will die.

... aided and abetted by dictionaries:

Oliver Wendell Holmes
When I feel inclined to read poetry I take down my Dictionary. The poetry of words is quite as beautiful as that of sentences. The author may arrange the gems effectively, but their shape and lustre have been given by the attrition of ages.

Arthur Scargill
My father still reads the dictionary every day. He says your life depends on your power to master words.

Paul Johnson
Hemingway paid particular attention to exactitude of expression and ransacked dictionaries for words.

C S Lewis
One understands a word much better if one has met it alive, in its native habitat. So far as is possible our knowledge should be checked and supplemented, not derived, from the dictionary.

Ambrose Bierce
Dictionary, n. A malevolent literary device for cramping the growth of a language and making it hard and elastic.

The power of words is a common theme:

Laurens van der Post
The word has power. In World War II, what else but words did Churchill have to save his people from total ruin?

Marion Halligan
That's what a book is. Words on a page. It's the most miraculous thing. Little black marks on a page. Words. And they have power. Look at my passion for lists. Lists are charms and chants. To list is to possess things.

F Scott Fitzgerald
You can stroke people with words.

On the other hand:

Samuel Beckett
Every word is like an unnecessary strain on silence and nothingness.

Shena Mackay
The ability to work with words sometimes seems like a torment as well as a gift.

Joy Williams
Words are an albatross to a writer – heavy, hopeless, fateful things. One writes to make words mean something new.

William Burroughs
I think that words are an around-the-world, ox-cart way of doing things, awkward instruments, and they will be laid aside eventually, probably sooner than we think.

T S Eliot
It's strange that words are so inadequate.

Doris Lessing
Words, it seems, can no longer be used simply and naturally. All the great words like love, hate; life, death; loyalty, treachery; contain their opposite meanings and half a dozen shades of dubious implication.

Joseph Joubert
Words, like glass, obscure when they do not aid vision.

John Ray
He that uses many words for the explaining of any subject, doth, like the cuttle fish, hide himself for the most part in his own ink.

Henry David Thoreau
Some men have a peculiar taste for bad words. They will pick you out of a thousand the still-born words, the falsettos, the wing-clipped and lame words, as if only the false notes caught their ears.

Aldous Huxley
Thanks to words, we have been able to rise above the brutes; and thanks to words, we have often sunk to the level of the demons.

Many believe that our thoughts are shaped by words:

Osbert Sitwell
The word itself, of which our works of art are fashioned, is the first art-form, older than the roughest shaping of clay or stone. A word is the carving and colouring of a thought, and gives to it permanence.

Ugo Betti
Thought itself needs words. It runs on them like a long wire. And if it loses the habit of words, little by little it becomes shapeless, sombre.

Evelyn Waugh
There are always words going round in my head; some people think in pictures, some in ideas. I think entirely in words.

Martin H Fischer
Whenever ideas fail, men invent words.

And the process of turning thoughts into words is not easy:

Thomas Hood
A moment's thinking is an hour in words.

Maurice Maeterlinck
How strangely do we diminish a thing as soon as we try to express it in words.

T S Eliot:
> Words strain,
> Crack and sometimes break, under the burden,
> Under the tension, slip, slide, perish,
> Decay with imprecision, will not stay in place,
> Will not stay still.

Ursula le Guin
A rarer kind of failure is the story in which the words go careering around bellowing and plunging and kicking up a lot of dust and when the dust settles you find they never got out of the corral. They got nowhere, because they didn't know where they were going. Feeling, idea, image, just got dragged into the stampede, and no story happened.

But nearly everyone agrees that words must be exactly used:

Dylan Thomas
There is always one right word; use it, despite its foul or merely ludicrous associations.

Mark Twain
Use the right word and not its second cousin ... The difference between the almost-right word and the right word is ... the difference between the lightning-bug and the lightning.

Gustave Flaubert
Whatever the thing you wish to say, there is but one word to express it, but one word to give it movement, but one adjective to qualify it; you must seek until you find this noun, this verb, this adjective.

Catherine Drinker Bowen
For your born writer, nothing is so healing as the realisation that he has come upon the right word.

Ken Follett
Words are our tools, and subtle distinctions are important even if readers are not consciously aware of them.

Evelyn Waugh
Words have basic inalienable meanings, departure from which is either conscious metaphor or inexcusable vulgarity.

And there is a strong preference for short, lively words ...

Winston Churchill
Short words are best and the old words when short are best of all.

Laurie Lee
In those Cotswold villages of the 'twenties ... our vocabulary was small, though naturally virile; our words ancient, round, warm from the tongue ... Such was my background, and in some ways it still rules me. I am made uneasy by any form of writing which cannot readily be spoken aloud.

John Wesley
We should constantly use the most common, little, easy words (so they are pure and proper) which our language affords.

Jorge Luis Borges
Whenever I find an out-of-the-way word ... then I strike it out and I use a common word ... If you write an uncouth word or an astonishing or an archaic word, then the rule is broken; and what is far more important, the attention of the reader is distracted by the word.

H W Fowler
Prefer the familiar word to the far-fetched. Prefer the concrete to the abstract. Prefer the single word to the circumlocution. Prefer the short word to the long.

Walter de la Mare
Until we learn the use of living words we shall continue to be waxworks inhabited by gramophones.

... used as sparingly as possible:

Anonymous
>The written word
>Should be clean as bone
>Clear as light
>Firm as stone.
>Two words are not
>As good as one.

Homer
Few were his words, but wonderfully clear.

Elmore Leonard
I don't like big books. I've got to page 30 of *Crime and Punishment* three times. Too many words.

Be warned, though:

Doris Lessing
Words appear in your mind and dance there to rhythms you consciously know nothing about ...They can jiggle or sing for days, driving you mad. They can be like invisible film ... between you and reality.

Malay proverb
Buffaloes are held by cords, man by his words.

Colin Falck
Words never let you conquer them by force.

Carl Sandburg
> Look out how you use proud words,
> When you let proud words go, it is not easy
>   to call them back,
> They wear long boots, hard boots; they walk
>   off proud; they can't hear you calling –
> Look out how you use proud words.

John Steinbeck
A writer lives in awe of words for they can be cruel or kind, and they can change their meanings right in front of you. They pick up flavours and odours like butter in a refrigerator.

Somerset Maugham
Words have weight, sound and appearance; it is only by considering these that you can write a sentence that is good to look at and good to listen to.

Noël Coward
Verbal diarrhoea is a major defect in many American writers. They have learnt assiduously too many words and they wish you to know that they know far more words than other people and, what is more, long and complicated words. This adolescent crowing becomes quite deafening sometimes and gets between them and what they are trying to say.

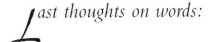

Last thoughts on words:

W B Yeats
Our words must seem inevitable.

Barry Ronge
Words, cleverly used, are the ultimate power play.

Mary Wallace
The words we use and the way we use them determine the strength or weakness, the brilliance or dullness, of what we write.

G K Chesterton
Why shouldn't we quarrel about a word? What is the good of words if they aren't important enough to quarrel over? Why do we choose one word more than another if there isn't any difference between them?

Muriel Spark
The best we can do is write words from which a kind of truth emerges.

H Allen Smith
Alexander Woollcott says good writers should never use the word 'very'. Nuts to Alexander Woollcott.

Adlai Stevenson
Man does not live by words alone, despite the fact that sometimes he has to eat them.

Sentences

'A perfectly healthy sentence is extremely rare'

> **A sentence is ...**
>
> ... not easy to define. **Ernest Gowers**
>
> ... a sound in itself on which other sounds called words may be strung. **Robert Frost**

The ability to string words together starts before the age of two, but formal study only begins at school:

Winston Churchill
By being so long in the lowest form [at Harrow] I gained an immense advantage over the cleverer boys ... I got into my bones the essential structure of the normal British sentence – which is a noble thing.

Some writers are eloquent on the pleasures of constructing sentences:

Ralph Waldo Emerson
The maker of a sentence launches out into the infinite and builds a road into Chaos and old Night, and is followed by those who hear him with something of wild, creative delight.

John Cheever
One never puts down a sentence without the feeling that it has never been put down before in such a way, and that perhaps even the substance of the sentence has never been felt. Every sentence is an innovation.

Theodore Haecker
One's astonishment, half tragic, half comic, at coming across a good sentence that one has completely forgotten having written. Poverty and wealth!

And advice is, as always, forthcoming:

Fay Weldon
Don't think because a sentence is short and looks easy it's going to be simpler to handle.

Henry David Thoreau
A sentence should read as if its author, had he held a plough instead of a pen, could have drawn a furrow deep and straight to the end.

William Gass
I am unlikely to trust a sentence that comes too easily.

Kenneth Atchity
If your writing attracts your reader's attention, your style probably needs editing. Suspect all your favourite sentences. Each sentence must serve the whole.

William Strunk Jnr
Vigorous writing is concise. A sentence should contain no unnecessary words, a paragraph no unnecessary sentences, for the same reason that a drawing should have no unnecessary lines and a machine no unnecessary parts.

Bill Scott *(on what to do when a sentence stinks):*
Change it. How? Easy. Read a stinky sentence over. Figure out what it means. Now ... put the sentence's meaning in your own words ... You may have to expand the sentence into two or three sentences.

Richard Lanham
Take a piece of your prose and a red pencil and draw a slash after every sentence. Two or three pages ought to make a large enough sample. If the red marks occur at regular intervals, you have ... a problem ... No rules prevail except to avoid monotony.

James J Kilpatrick
Effective writing ... has to have cadence. By that, I do not mean metronomic regularity. I certainly don't mean that we should strive for a singsong effect ... No. I suggest only that we cultivate the inner ear. Let us listen to our sentences as they break upon the mind.

Truman Capote
Call it precious and go to hell, but I believe a story can be wrecked by faulty rhythm in a sentence – especially if it occurs toward the end – or a mistake in paragraphing, even punctuation.

Though there is a dissenting voice:

Bill Stout
You don't write a sentence to get a certain rhythm. You write to say something.

Writers can sometimes be surprisingly frank about their role models ...

Joan Didion
Hemingway ... taught me how sentences worked. When I was fifteen or sixteen I would type out his stories to learn how the sentences worked ... They're perfect sentences. Very direct sentences, smooth rivers, clear water over granite, no sinkholes.

Janet Suzman
Ibsen wrote in the most banal way, but his little Norwegian sentences can carry huge feelings, his words boil down to essentials.

Truman Capote
From the point of view of ear, Virginia Woolf never wrote a bad sentence.

... and equally frank about others' perceived faults:

Mark Twain
Whenever the literary German dives into a sentence, that is the last you are going to see of him till he emerges on the other side of his Atlantic with his verb in his mouth.

Last words on sentences to:

Roland Barthes
A writer is not someone who expresses his thoughts, his passion, or his imagination in sentences but someone who thinks sentences. A Sentence-Thinker.

Henry David Thoreau
Sentences which suggest far more than they say, which have an atmosphere about them, which do not merely report an old, but make a new impression, sentences which suggest as many things and are as durable as a Roman aqueduct: to frame these, that is the art of writing ... A perfectly healthy sentence is extremely rare.

Shena Mackay
No sentence you can reconstruct will ever be quite as good as the original on some absconded scrap of paper.

T S Eliot
Every phrase and every sentence is an end and a beginning.

Paragraphs

'The paragraph should embrace a distinct episode'

Just four quotes here:

Winston Churchill
Just as the sentence contains one idea in all its fullness, so the paragraph should embrace a distinct episode; and as sentences should follow one another in harmonious sequence, so paragraphs must fit on to one another like the automatic couplings of railway carriages.

Thomas S Kane
No one can say how long a paragraph should be. Subject, purpose, audience, editorial fashion, and individual preference, all affect the length and complexity of paragraphs ... Numerous brief paragraphs are liable to be disjointed and underdeveloped. Great long ones fatigue readers.

V S Naipaul
My paragraphs are composed of thought, all kinds of thought. Thoughts are impressions of things seen, things felt, things related to what has gone before. A paragraph

is a little orchestration of various impressions. I just try to write as clearly as I can to let those thoughts appear on the page.

James Thurber
With sixty staring me in the face, I have developed inflammation of the sentence structure and a definite hardening of the paragraphs.

· Language ·

'Language is the archives of history'

Language is...

... the archives of history. **Ralph Waldo Emerson**

... by its very nature a communal thing; that is, it expresses never the exact thing but a compromise – that which is common to you, me, and everybody.
T E Hulme

... only a fraction of a culture. **Guy Butler**

Ursula le Guin
Written language is the greatest single technology of the storage and dissemination of knowledge, which is the primary act of human culture.

As with words, writers revel in language, often disporting themselves in its more esoteric reaches:

Tom Stoppard
My fascination is with words and language. Some writers are fascinated with the subtleties of character, but for me it's what language can do.

Ken Follett
Writers are generally fascinated by puns, word games, variant spellings, regional dialects, forms of pidgin English, new coinages and everything to do with the language they use ...You'll never be a writer if you don't love the language you use.

A S Byatt
My passions have always been language and the earth.

Tom Robbins
Language has to exist in an exalted state to awaken wonder. I'm not interested in colloquial language. If something doesn't have that rhythm, it doesn't have the radiance, the luminosity – it doesn't have the angelic intensity.

Lorrie Moore
I know the main struggle for every writer is with the dance and limitations of language – to honour the texture of it but also to make it unafraid. One must throw all that one is into language, like a Christmas tree hurled into a pool.

William Hazlitt
Language, if it throws a veil over our ideas, adds a softness and refinement to them, like that which the atmosphere gives to naked objects.

Bernard Malamud
I work with language. I love the flowers of afterthought.

Though language attracts some sour comments too:

Molière
I live on good soup and not fine language.

Gustave Flaubert
Human language is like a cracked kettle on which we beat out tunes for bears to dance to, when all the time we are longing to move the stars to pity.

Nathaniel Hawthorne
Language – human language – after all is but little better than the croak and cackle of fowls, and other utterances of a brute nature – sometimes not so adequate.

Advice on the use of language stresses efficiency and the differences between the spoken and the written:

Ezra Pound
Good writers are those who keep the language efficient. That is to say, keep it accurate, keep it clear.

Anthony Trollope
The language used should be as ready and as efficient a conductor of the mind of the writer to the mind of the reader as is the electric spark which passes from battery to battery.

Toni Morrison
The language must be careful and must appear effortless. It must not sweat. It must suggest and be provocative at the same time.

Jacques Barzun
Simple English is no one's mother tongue. It has to be worked for.

Nikki Giovanni
If you don't learn the language, you are not going to be able to pursue writing. It's just that basic. Before you take liberties with the language, you better know what liberties you're taking.

John Updike
It comes down to what is language? ... Until this age of mass literacy, language has been something spoken. In utterance there's a minimum of slowness. In trying to treat words as chisel strokes you run the risk of losing the quality of utterance, the rhythm of utterance, the happiness.

Richard A Lanham
Spelling mistakes, typos, mistakes in idiom, unfashionable usages, all these characterise you as a writer controlled by language rather than controlling it ... These revelations of self ... reveal that you have not paid attention to your own writing and invite the reader to respond in kind.

Joseph Heller
I don't think of myself as a naturally gifted writer when it comes to using language. I distrust myself. Consequently I try every which way with a sentence, then a paragraph, and finally a page, choosing words, selecting pace (I'm obsessed with that, even the pace of a sentence).

J Middleton Murry
Every work of enduring literature is not so much a triumph of language as a victory over language; a sudden injection of life-giving perceptions into a vocabulary that is, but for the energy of the creative writer, perpetually on the verge of exhaustion.

Slang has admirers as well as detractors ...

John Galsworthy
Slang is vigorous and apt. Probably most of our vital words are slang.

Carl Sandburg
Slang is the language that takes off its coat, spits on its hands, and goes to work.

Ernest Hemingway
Try and write straight English; never using slang except in dialogue and then only when unavoidable. Because all slang goes sour in a short time. I only use swear words, for example, that have lasted at least a thousand years.

Victor Hugo
Slang is nothing more nor less than a wardrobe in which language, having some bad deed to do, disguises itself. It puts on word-masks and metaphoric rags.

... as does the English language:

James Dickey
The English language is the greatest medium for communication in-depth or in any other way that has ever been devised.

George Bernard Shaw (Henry Higgins to Eliza Dolittle in Pygmalion):
Remember that you are a human being with the divine gift of articulate speech; that your native language is the language of Shakespeare and Milton and the Bible; and don't sit there crooning like a bilious pigeon.

James Thurber
Ours is a precarious language, as every writer knows, in which the merest shadow line often separates affirmation from negation, sense from nonsense, and one sex from another.

E B White
English usage is sometimes more than mere taste, judgement and education – sometimes it's sheer luck, like getting across a street.

William Safire
English is a stretch language; one size fits all. That does not mean anything goes; in most instances, anything does not go. But the language, as it changes, conforms itself to special groups and occasions. There is a time for dialect, a place for slang, an occasion for literary form.

Kole Omotoso
We may speak English at the free market bazaar, but our moral choices and the trials of our daily existence – birth, death, worship, celebration and so on – are locked up in our mother tongues.

George Eliot
Correct English is the slang of prigs who write history and essays.

There is an ongoing debate as to whether writers are hampered or blessed by knowing more than one language ...

Philip Larkin
A writer can have only one language, if language is going to mean anything to him.

Ezra Pound
The sum of human wisdom is not contained in any one language, and no single language is capable of expressing all forms and degrees of human comprehension.

Elizabeth Jolley
If the writer has the mixed blessing of a foreign language spoken in the household of childhood, there is the broken language of more than one culture to fall back on.

... and another about the value of translations:

Roy Campbell
Translations, like wives, are seldom faithful if they are in the least attractive.

James Howell
>Some hold translations not unlike to be
>The wrong side of a Turkey tapestry.

Ned Rorem
The art of translation lies less in knowing the other language than in knowing your own.

Friedrich Nietzsche
What is most difficult to render from one language into another is the tempo of its style.

As so often, the voice of reason comes from:

Isaac Bashevis Singer
We all learned our literature through translation. Most people have studied the Bible only in translation, have read Homer in translation, and all the classics.

Last words on language to:

Arundhati Roy
Language to me is just the way I think. It's a way of seeing ... I don't have a choice in my language: it's instinctive.

Cynthia Ozick
The power of language, it seems to me, is the only kind of power a writer is entitled to.

Gabriel Garcia Marquez
I try to achieve a perfection of structure and language, but also a perfection of intensity, which is just as important.

Antoine de Saint-Exupéry
To grasp the meaning of the world of today we use a language created to express the world of yesterday. The life of the past seems to us nearer our true natures, but only for the reason that it is nearer our language.

S J Perelman
Writers who pontificate about their own use of language drive me up the wall.

Grammar

'To grammar even kings bow'

Grammar is …

… common speech formulated. **Somerset Maugham**

… a piano I play by ear. All I know about grammar is its power. **Joan Didion**

… the grave of letters. **Elbert Hubbard**

We will pass quickly over the subject of grammar – that necessary foundation which older writers stress …

William Langland
Grammere, that grounde is of alle.

Molière
To grammar even kings bow.

Samuel Johnson
I have laboured to refine our language to grammatical purity, and to clear it from colloquial barbarisms, licentious idioms, and irregular combinations.

Anthony Trollope
How may an author best acquire a mode of writing which shall be agreeable and easily intelligible to the reader? He must be correct, because without correctness he can be neither agreeable nor intelligible.

Edgar Allan Poe
A man's grammar, like Caesar's wife, must not only be pure, but above suspicion of impurity.

Benjamin Disraeli
I will not go down to posterity talking bad grammar.

... though there are exceptions ...

Thomas Jefferson
When strictness of grammar does not weaken expression, it should be attended to ... But where, by small grammatical negligences, the energy of an idea is condensed, or a word stands for a sentence, I hold grammatical rigour in contempt.

Artemus Ward
Why care for grammar as long as we are good?

... and more recent writers, even the Great Fowler himself, sometimes casually dismiss:

H W Fowler
Prefer geniality to grammar.

Robert Frost
You can be a little ungrammatical if you come from the right part of the country.

Red Smith
I have known writers who paid no damned attention whatever to the rules of grammar and rhetoric and somehow made the language work for them.

Would-be writers should, however, take to heart these words of wisdom from:

Ursula le Guin
Ignorance of English vocabulary and grammar is a considerable liability to a writer of English. The best cure for it is, I believe, reading.

Beryl Bainbridge
Once the grammar has been learnt writing is simply talking on paper and in time learning what not to say.

Split infinitives (ok or not ok?)

'When I split an infinitive, god damn it, I split it so it stays split'

The pundit whom many consider to be the ultimate authority on the English language gives both an overview and a sensible approach to split infinitives:

H W Fowler
The English-speaking world may be divided into (1) those who neither know nor care what a split infinitive is; (2) those who do not know, but care very much; (3) those who know and condemn; (4) those who know and approve; and (5) those who know and distinguish. Those who neither know nor care are the vast majority and are a happy folk, to be envied by most of the minority classes ... Those upon whom the fear of infinitives splitting sits heavy, should remember that to give conclusive evidence, by distortions, of misconceiving the nature of the split infinitive, is far more damaging to their literary pretensions than an actual lapse could be.

And then there are the wisecrackers:

James Thurber
Word has somehow got around that the split infinitive is always wrong. That is apiece with the outworn notion that it is always wrong to strike a lady.

Mark Twain
A verb has a hard time enough of it in this world when it's all together. It's downright inhuman to split it up.

Jimmy Durante
I don't split 'em. When I go to work on an infinitive, I break it up in little pieces.

Raymond Chandler
When I split an infinitive, god damn it, I split it so it stays split.

Adjectives

'The adjective is the banana peel of the parts of speech'

Mark Twain *(to a schoolboy essayist):*
I notice that you use plain, simple language, short words and brief sentences. This is the way to write English – it is the modern way, and the best way. Stick to it; don't let fluff and flowers and verbosity creep in. When you catch adjectives, kill most of them – then the rest will be valuable. They weaken when they are close together; they give strength when they are wide apart. An adjective habit, or a wordy, diffuse or flowery habit, once fastened upon a person, is as hard to get rid of as any other vice.

Clifton Fadiman
The adjective is the banana peel of the parts of speech.

Ernest Hemingway
[Ezra] Pound was the man who believed in the *mot juste* – the one and only correct word to use – the man who taught me to distrust adjectives.

Gabriel Josipovici
The image of the writer as one who searches for the *mot juste* is a cliché of our world, and we can see its pernicious results in those 'sensitive novels' and travelogues which use two adjectives when one will do.

J Anthony Lukas
If the noun is good and the verb is strong, you almost never need an adjective.

Helen Garner
I spend many wonderful hours shifting clauses around and taking out adjectives and putting more in. Somebody once said to me that adjectives were the small change of language ... now I use thousands of them. I love them.

Elizabeth Jolley
I used to implore apprentice writers to avoid adjectives, until one of them snarkily pointed out that Iris Murdoch is capable of writing sixteen adjectives in a row and it works wonderfully.

Adverbs

'Using adverbs is a moral sin'

Only one trenchant voice here:

Elmore Leonard
[Using adverbs is] a moral sin. If you've developed your character adequately, the way the character speaks should be apparent. I used all my adverbs up when I was writing car catalogues for Chevrolet.

Spelling

'My spelling is Wobbly'

Those who wish to be grand call correct spelling 'orthography' …

Thorstein Veblen
English orthography satisfies all the requirements of respectability under the law of conspicuous waste. It is archaic, cumbrous, and ineffective; its acquisition consumes much time and effort; failure to acquire it is easy of detection. Therefore it is the first and readiest test of reputability in learning.

… and the rest of us struggle on with its arbitrary mysteries:

Geoffrey Grigson
In language there is a spice of spelling.

Mark Twain
They spell it Vinci and pronounce it Vinchy; foreigners always spell better than they pronounce.

A A Milne *(Winnie-the-Pooh):*
My spelling is Wobbly. It's good spelling but it Wobbles, and letters get in the wrong place.

Punctuation

'Do not be afraid of the semicolon'

Phillip Howard has said: 'Punctuation is bound to change, like the rest of language', and indeed today's schoolchildren (when they can write) scatter punctuation marks about like confetti. For clarity's sake, however, the would-be writer should not be too cavalier:

Phillip Howard
Punctuation is made for man, not man for punctuation; a good sentence should be intelligible without the help of punctuation in most cases; and, if you get in a muddle with your dots and dashes, you may need to simplify your thoughts, and shorten your sentence.

Fyodor Dostoyevsky
Every author has his own style and consequently his own grammatical rules. I put commas where I deem them necessary, and where I deem them unnecessary others must not put them! ... I never use superfluous commas.

Marion Halligan
What I work by very much is semicolons ... Semicolons are very powerful things. I don't know whether other people read them like that, whether they just skim through them and see them more or less as commas.

Ernest Gowers
Do not be afraid of the semicolon; it can be most useful.

F Scott Fitzgerald
Cut out all those exclamation marks. An exclamation mark is like laughing at your own joke.

Miles Kington
So far as good writing goes, the use of the exclamation mark is a sign of failure. It is the literary equivalent of a man holding up a card reading LAUGHTER to a studio audience.

From the style book of the **Oxford University Press**, New York:
If you take hyphens seriously you will surely go mad.

George Dennison Prentice
Many writers profess great exactness in punctuation, who never yet made a point.

Lois Gould
Life is the only sentence which doesn't end with a period.

· *Imagery* ·

'Imagery ... occurs in the reader's mind'

Images in the literary sense are the mental pictures created in the reader's mind by writers:

Ursula le Guin
Imagery takes place in 'the imagination', which I take to be the meeting place of the thinking mind with the sensing body. What is imagined isn't physically real, but *feels as if it were*: the reader sees or hears or feels what goes on in the story, is drawn into it, exists in it, among its images, in the imagination.

Ezra Pound
It is better to present one Image in a lifetime than to produce voluminous works.

Certain writers are past masters at creating images and offer excellent advice:

Dylan Thomas
I let, perhaps, one image be 'made' emotionally in me and then apply it to what intellectual and critical forces I possess – let it breed another, let that image contradict the first, make, of the third image bred out of the other two together, a fourth contradictory image, and let them all, within my imposed formal limits, conflict.

Nikki Giovanni
Follow your image as far as you can no matter how useless you think it is. Push yourself.

Judy Delton
Don't generalise. Use specific images. Avoid abstractions. Be concrete. There is one thing that makes [Sinclair Lewis's] books classics, makes them absolutely memorable. It is his imagery – his very specific images.

Tom Robbins
[The primary purpose of imagery is] to awaken in the reader his or her own sense of wonder. If you get too predictable and too symmetrical, you lull readers ... you put part of their brain to sleep. Even if they might stay physically awake and finish your book, their imagination, their sense of wonder, is asleep.

Stephen King
Too many beginning writers feel that they have to assume the entire burden of imagery; to become the reader's seeing-eye dog. That is simply not the case.

· Metaphor ·

'The metaphor is probably the most fertile power possessed by man'

Metaphors go a crucial step further than images, making comparisons between things that are not literally alike and thus creating new linkages in readers' minds — for example, 'the blood at the heart of the ruby':

Rita Mae Brown
Let others live in black and white; you must live in Technicolor ... make your reader see the blood at the heart of the ruby.

James J Kilpatrick
The intensity I am urging not only will enrich our vocabularies and induce more accurate writing, it will also ... give us images. We look intently at a caterpillar, and perhaps we see a covered wagon. We look closely at a hill of close-cropped stubble, and perhaps we see the head of a fresh-caught recruit in the US Marines.

Brigid Brophy
The pleasure we take in literature, and perhaps in any of the arts, seems ultimately always to lie in metaphor. For a reason I do not know (it may be too fundamental to be knowable), the human mind delights less in the exact evocation of one image, however beautiful, than in the lightning-flash (very like that of wit) which compares or actually fuses and assimilates two images ... This process goes, I believe, far beyond the verbal metaphors in the sentence-to-sentence texture of writing. I am fairly sure that when we say a book has 'depth' or 'universality' we mean that the author has

implied perspectives viewed down which even the book's most seemingly single and particularised images, even its characters, are metaphors of something beyond themselves.

The grand master of metaphor is:

William Shakespeare
> Taffeta phrases, silken terms precise,
> > Three-pil'd hyperboles, spruce affectation,
> Figures pedantical; these summer flies
> > Have blown me full of maggot ostentation ...
> Henceforth my wooing mind shall be express'd
> > In russet yeas and honest kersey noes.

Like imagery when carefully used, metaphors enrich the writing of fiction and are a writer's secret weapon ...

Bernard Malamud
I love metaphor. It provides two loaves where there seems to be one. Sometimes it throws in a load of fish.

William Gass
I love metaphor the way some people love junk food.

José Ortega y Gasset
The metaphor is probably the most fertile power possessed by man.

Dylan Thomas
Man be my metaphor.

... though they have their downside ...

Sheridan Baker
Beware of the metaphor. It is the spirit of good prose. It gives the reader a picture, a glimpse of what the subject really looks like to the writer. But it is dangerous, can easily get tangled and insistent, the more so when it almost works.

Somerset Maugham
I knew that I had no lyrical quality. I had a small vocabulary and no efforts that I could make to enlarge it much availed me. I had little gift of metaphor; the original and striking simile seldom occurred to me.

Thomas Carlyle
The coldest word was once a glowing new metaphor.

Arthur Koestler
Yesterday's daring metaphors are today's clichés.

... and there are warnings against excess:

Jonathan Raban
The more extravagant the similes become, the more you smell the writer's basic disengagement from the world he is describing. He is fatally engaged by the mere business of description, by that verbal manufacturing industry in which skies are always being turned into bolts of shot silk, or gunmetal, or eiderdown.

Ogden Nash
    One thing that literature would be
        greatly the better for
    Would be a more restricted employment
        by authors of simile and metaphor
    Authors of all races, be they Greeks
        Romans, Teutons or Celts,
    Can't seem just to say that anything is the
        thing it is but have to go out of their way
        to say that it is like something else.

· Symbols ·

'There's a pox of symbolist theory going the rounds'

The use of heavy symbolism in fiction writing seems to have fallen out of fashion — and about time too:

Ernest Hemingway
I suppose there are symbols since critics keep finding them ... I dislike talking about them and being questioned about them. It is hard enough to write books and stories without being asked to explain them as well. Also it deprives the explainers of work. If five or six or more good explainers can keep going why should I interfere with them?

Katherine Anne Porter
I never consciously took or adopted a symbol in my life ... There's a pox of symbolist theory going the rounds these days in American colleges in the writing courses.

Tennessee Williams
All you have to do is close your eyes and wait for the symbols.

· *Pace* ·

'*The pacing grows out of the subject matter of the book*'

Pace is the speed at which a narrative moves – which involves constant decision-making as to the relative importance of each section:

Shelly Lowenkopf
The prolific writers who have learned their craft well get to the basics fast in the first three pages.

P G Wodehouse
I always feel the thing to go for is speed. Nothing puts the reader off more than a great slab of prose at the start. I think the success of every novel – if it's a novel of action – depends on the high spots.

Jean Auel
I'm conscious of pace. It's a thing that I think about when I write.

Paul Schrader
Feel the pages under you the same way a runner feels the gravel under his feet. He can tell how fast that gravel is moving under his feet ... the same way you can tell how fast the pages are, how fast the scenes are moving ... I believe the script should read and feel fast.

Lawrence Block
Not every scene deserves full treatment ... But the more space you give to a scene and the more importance you assign to it, the greater is your obligation to make that scene pull its weight by commanding the reader's attention and keeping him interested and entertained.

Robert Graves & Alan Hodge
There should be two main objectives: ... to convey a message and to include in it nothing that will distract the reader's attention or check his habitual pace of reading – he should feel that he is seated at ease in a taxi, not riding a temperamental horse through traffic.

John Updike
In the execution there has to be a 'happiness' that can't be willed or fore-ordained. It has to sing, click, something. I try instantly to set in motion a certain forward tilt of suspense or curiosity, and at the end of the story or novel to rectify the tilt.

And then there is the speed with which the writer writes:

Jacques Barzun
I strongly recommend writing ahead full tilt, not stopping to correct. Cross out no more than the few words that will permit you to go on when you foresee a blind alley. Leave some words in blank, some sentences not complete. Keep going!

John Updike
As for a writer, if he has something to tell, he should perhaps type it almost as fast as he could talk it … There's a kind of tautness that you should feel within yourself no matter how slow or fast you're spinning out the reel.

· Tone ·

'Any tone is acceptable – but don't mix two or three'

A good definition is that of:

J A Cuddon (in A Dictionary of Literary Terms):
Tone – the reflection of a writer's attitude (especially towards his readers), manner, mood and moral outlook on his work; even, perhaps, the way his personality pervades the work.

Tone is a slippery quality, difficult to pin down. Like exercising to fitness, it is achieved with practice:

Elizabeth Hardwick
I can't write a story or an essay until I can, by revision after revision, get the opening tone right. Sometimes it seems to take forever, but when I have it I can usually go on. It's a matter of the voice, how you are going to approach the task at hand.

Gabriel Garcia Marquez
There was something missing and I was not sure what it was until one day I discovered the right tone – the one that I eventually used in *One Hundred Years Of Solitude*. It was based on the way my grandmother used to tell her stories. She told things that sounded supernatural and fantastic, but she told them with complete naturalness.

William Zinsser
Any tone is acceptable. But don't mix two or three.

· Technique ·

'Technique is only a means to an end'

Writers' opinions are (as usual) divided when it comes to technique. Most seem to see it as a somewhat pedestrian accumulation of necessary skills:

Joyce Carol Oates
Technique is only a means to an end; it is never the end itself ... Technique holds a reader from sentence to sentence, but only content will stay in his mind.

Graham Greene
The moment comes to every writer ... when he faces for the first time something which he knows he cannot do. It is the moment by which he will be judged, the moment when his individual technique will be evolved. For technique is above everything else a means of evading the personally impossible, of disguising deficiency.

Gabriel Garcia Marquez
The best advice I was given early on was that it was all right to [let myself be taken by chance] when I was young because I had a torrent of inspiration. But I was told that if I didn't learn technique, I would be in trouble later on when the inspiration had gone and the technique was needed to compensate.

John McGahern
Technique can certainly be learned, and only a fool would try to do without it, but technique for its own sake grows heartless. Unless technique can take us to that clear mirror that is called style ... then the most perfect technique is as worthless as mere egotism.

Ford Madox Ford
You must keep your eyes forever on your Reader. That alone constitutes Technique.

But there are those who gleefully pooh-pooh it:

Henry Miller
The best technique is none at all.

William Faulkner
Let the writer take up surgery or bricklaying if he is interested in technique. There is no mechanical way to get the writing done, no shortcut.

And the last comment in this chapter could apply to all the technical aspects of writing:

Raymond Chandler
Technique alone is never enough. You have to have passion. Technique alone is just an embroidered pot-holder.

More Quotes

Chapter Six
Style

> *'Style is knowing who you are, what you want to say, and not giving a damn'*

The development of a personal style is so important to writers that it has a whole chapter to itself, starting with the question: What exactly is style?

Style is ...

... character. **Norman Mailer**

... knowing who you are, what you want to say, and not giving a damn. **Gore Vidal**

... the hallmark of a temperament stamped upon the material at hand. **André Maurois**

... the saying in the best way what you have to say. **Matthew Arnold**

... the dress of thoughts. **Lord Chesterfield**

... the mind skating circles round itself as it moves forward. **Robert Frost**

... the physiognomy of the mind, and a safer index to character than the face. **Arthur Schopenhauer**

... as much under the words as in the words. **Gustave Flaubert**

... effectiveness of assertion ... He who has nothing to assert has no style and can have none. **George Bernard Shaw**

> ... not neutral; it gives moral directions. ***Martin Amis***
>
> ... a magic wand, and turns everything to gold that it touches. ***Logan Pearsall Smith***

Jonathan Swift
Proper words in proper places, make the true definition of a style.

B J Chute
In its simplest form, style in writing can be defined as the way in which a thing is said ... Style is a great preservative of writing, and no writer ought ever to think that a really good style is beyond his reach.

Julian Barnes
Style is a function of theme. Style is not imposed on subject-matter, but arises from it. Style is truth to thought. The correct word, the true phrase, the perfect sentence are always 'out there' somewhere; the writer's task is to locate them by whatever means he can.

Doris Lessing
Each novel or story has this characteristic note, or tone of voice – the style, peculiar to itself and self-consistent. But behind this must sound another note, independent of style ... It seems to me we are listening to, responding to, the essence of a writer here, a groundnote.

Aspirant writers should try not to be intimidated by the necessity of acquiring a style, since most writers and critics believe that it is intrinsic and will develop with time and practice:

E B White
I don't think [style] can be taught. Style results more from what a person is than from what he knows.

Bernard Malamud
My style flows from the fingers. The eye and ear approve or amend.

Nadine Gordimer
The big time when people influence you is when you're very young and you start to write; after that you slough off what you don't need and you painfully hammer out your own style.

Mary Wallace
Individual style ... develops from the writer's own personality ... and, to some extent, from everything absorbed in years of reading. In short, it is the writer. Consequently, there is no need to worry about it, or even to think about it, for it is bound to make its own way to the surface in good time.

François Fénelon
A man's style is nearly as much a part of him as his physiognomy, his figure, the throbbing of his pulse.

Henry Green
[The writer's] style is himself, and we are all of us changing every day – developing, we hope! We leave our marks behind us like a snail.

Truman Capote
I don't think that style is consciously arrived at. Any more than one arrives at the colour of one's eyes. After all, your style is you.

Katherine Anne Porter
The style is you ... it is one of those unarguable truths. You do not create a style. You work, and develop yourself; your style is an emanation from your own being.

V S Naipaul
I am not pleased when people tell me I have a nice style. It suggests that style is something applied. It is not. Style in itself has no value. I believe that style is thought.

Lawrence Durrell
I don't think anyone can ... develop a style consciously ... I think the writing itself grows you up, and you grow the writing up, and finally you get an amalgam of everything you have pinched with a new kind of personality which is your own.

Fay Weldon
'Style' is not something to be consciously sought after; it arrives by itself, if you ask me, at some moment between the first and final draft.

Martin Amis
Style is everything and nothing. It is not that, as is commonly supposed, you get your content and soup it up with style; style is absolutely embedded in the way you perceive.

Isaac D'Israeli
And, after all, it is style alone by which posterity will judge of a great work, for an author can have nothing truly his own but his style.

Ernest Hemingway
In stating as fully as I could how things really were, it was often very difficult and I wrote awkwardly and the awkwardness is what they called my style. All mistakes and awkwardness are easy to see, and they call it style.

Maurice Valency
A man's style is intrinsic and private with him like his voice or his gesture, partly a matter of inheritance, partly of cultivation. It is more than a pattern of expression. It is the pattern of the soul.

Havelock Ellis
The great writer finds style as the mystic finds God, in his own soul.

Vladimir Nabokov
The best part of a writer's biography is not the record of his adventures but the story of his style.

William Styron
Style comes only after long, hard practice and writing.

Kurt Vonnegut
[My style] just comes out of the typewriter. You develop a style from writing a lot. I have been writing since adolescence. The style will change from book to book, according to subject material.

Leon Edel
A style is a writer's passport to posterity.

How does one recognise a good style?

Somerset Maugham
A good style should show no sign of effort. What is written should seem a happy accident.

Nathaniel Hawthorne
The greatest possible mint of style is, of course, to make the words absolutely disappear into the thought.

Tacitus
Style, like the human body, is specially beautiful when the veins are not prominent and the bones cannot be counted.

Mary Wallace
Someone ... once said that he could no more define a gentleman than a terrier could define a rat, but that just as a terrier knows a rat when it sees one, so he knows a gentleman. For most of us, that's how it is with style.

And (more importantly perhaps) what constitutes a bad style?

J Middleton Murry
There is nothing more dangerous to the formation of a prose style than the endeavour to make it poetic.

William Hazlitt
The florid style is the reverse of the familiar. The last is employed as an unvarnished medium to convey ideas; the first is resorted to as a spangled veil to conceal the want of them.

Cyril Connolly
The Mandarin style ... is beloved by literary pundits, by those who would make the written word as unlike as possible to the spoken one.

George Orwell
The inflated style is itself a kind of euphemism. A mass of Latin words falls upon the facts like soft snow, blurring the outlines and covering up the details. The great enemy of clear language is insincerity.

Albert Camus
I am well aware that an addiction to silk underwear does not necessarily imply that one's feet are dirty. None the less, style, like sheer silk, too often hides eczema.

For the aspirant stylist, here are some useful hints on how to achieve a good style:

William Safire
Style should befit the occasion – you don't wear a black tie to a picnic.

James Michener
Where style is concerned, I would go to as many movies and plays as I could, and read the words of people who are experimenting.

Kurt Vonnegut
Find a subject you care about and which you in your heart feel others should care about. It is this genuine caring, not your games with language, which will be the most compelling and seductive element in your style.

Havelock Ellis
All progress in literary style lies in the heroic resolve to cast aside accretions and exuberances, all the conventions of a past age that were once beautiful because alive and are now false because dead.

Edmund Gosse
Let a man speak with earnestness and promptitude, have something first to communicate, and let him eliminate from his speech all that is loose, needless, and ineffective, and there is style, the pure juice of his nature.

George Bernard Shaw
It was from Handel that I learned that style consists in force of assertion. If you can say a thing with one stroke, unanswerably you have style; if not, you are at best a ... painter of fans with cupids and coquettes. Handel had power.

Thomas Hardy
The whole secret of a living style and the difference between it and a dead style, lies in not having too much style – being in fact a little careless ... Otherwise your style is like worn halfpence – all the fresh images are rounded off by rubbing, and no crispness at all.

Kurt Vonnegut
The writing style which is most natural for you is bound to echo the speech you heard when a child. English was the novelist Joseph Conrad's third language, and much that seems piquant in his use of English was no doubt coloured by his first language, which was Polish.

Norman Mailer
A really good style comes only when a man has become as good as he can be. Style is character. A good style cannot come from a bad, undisciplined character.

Alain
An abstract style is always bad. Your sentences should be full of stones, metals, chairs, tables, animals, men and women.

Karl Kraus
I have decided many a stylistic problem first by head, then by heads or tails.

Arthur Helps
Which, of all defects, has been the one most fatal to a good style? The not knowing when to come to an end.

Clarity is important to a good style:

Aristotle
A good style must, first of all, be clear. It must not be mean or above the dignity of the subject. It must be appropriate.

Matthew Arnold
People think that I can teach them style. What stuff it all is! Have something to say, and say it as clearly as you can. That is the only secret of style.

Emile Zola
The best writer will not be the one who gallops madly amid hypotheses, but rather the one who marches squarely to the middle of the truth. Actually we are rotten with lyricism; we think quite wrongly that the grand style is composed of startling sublimity, ever close to tumbling over into lunacy. The grand style is composed of logic and clarity.

Goethe
Altogether, the style of a writer is a faithful representative of his mind; therefore, if any man wish to write a clear style, let him be first clear in his thoughts; and if any man would write in a noble style, let him first possess a noble soul.

So are simplicity and conciseness:

Henry David Thoreau
As for style of writing, if one has anything to say, it drops from him simply and directly, as a stone falls to the ground.

Jean Cocteau
What is style? For many people, a very complicated way of saying very simple things. According to us, a very simple way of saying very complicated things.

Nathaniel Hawthorne
I am glad you think my style plain. I never, in any one page or paragraph, aimed at making it anything else, or giving it any other merit – and I wish people would leave off talking about its beauty.

Fay Weldon
[Style] has something to do, I think, with the proportion that exists between what the writer wishes to say, and the economy of language with which he or she manages to say it.

And there are some famous stylists to learn from:

Ben Jonson
A strict and succinct style is that where you can take away nothing without loss.

Truman Capote
Essentially I think of myself as a stylist and stylists can become notoriously obsessed with the placing of a comma, the weight of a semi-colon. Obsessions of this sort, and the time I take over them, irritate me beyond endurance.

Kurt Tucholsky *(on himself)*:
He's always been successful in hiding his lack of brains behind a graceful writing style.

Julian Barnes
Flaubert ... believed in style; more than anyone. He worked doggedly for beauty, sonority, exactness; perfection – but never the monogrammed perfection of a writer like Wilde.

Arthur Schopenhauer
Imitating another's style is like wearing a mask.

George Meredith *(on Thomas Carlyle)*:
A style resembling either early architecture or utter dilapidation, so loose and rough it seemed; a wind-in-the-orchard style, that tumbled down here and there an appreciable fruit with uncouth bluster; sentences without commencements running to abrupt endings and smoke, like waves against a sea-wall, learned dictionary words giving a hand to street-slang, and accents falling on them haphazard, like slant rays from driving clouds; all the pages in a breeze, the whole book producing a kind of electrical agitation in the mind and the joints.

Norman Mailer
For certain writers, their style is their identity. They're two and the same. We can't think about Hemingway without thinking of his style ... On the other hand, Picasso went through twenty styles and loved each one in different ways.

Karl Kraus
A good stylist should have narcissistic enjoyment as he works. He must be able to objectivise his work to such an extent that he catches himself feeling envious and has to jog his memory to find that he is himself the creator. In short, he must display that highest degree of objectivity which the world calls vanity.

Henri Troyat
If [Tolstoy] could, he would live and write like a peasant: hammer words the way you hammer wooden wedges into a shoe sole. Make them stick, make it work, make it last for generations.

John Gardner
Some writers last a long time because of their brilliance, their style; [Scott] Fitzgerald is a good example – a fine stylist. But he never quite got to the heart of things.

Plus some handy rules:

Stendhal
I know of only one rule: style cannot be too clear, too simple.

Arthur Schopenhauer
The first rule, indeed by itself virtually a sufficient condition for good style, is to have something to say.

George Polya
The first rule of style is to have something to say. The second rule of style is to control yourself when ... you have two things to say; say first one, then the other, not both at the same time.

Theodore F Munger
My own rule would be: Be something, know something, feel truly, practise, and then let the style be what it will. It will reflect the man, and that is the true end of composition.

Sydney Smith
In composing, as a general rule, run your pen through every other word you have written; you have no idea what vigour it will give your style.

E B White
There are a few hints [about style] that can be thrown out to advantage. They would be the twenty-one hints I threw out in Chapter V of *The Elements of Style*. There was

nothing new or original about them, but there they are ...:
1. Place yourself in the background
2. Write in a way that comes naturally
3. Work from a suitable design
4. Write with nouns and verbs
5. Revise and rewrite
6. Do not overwrite
7. Do not overstate
8. Avoid the use of qualifiers
9. Do not affect a breezy manner
10. Use orthodox spelling
11. Do not explain too much
12. Do not construct awkward adverbs
13. Make sure the reader knows who is speaking
14. Avoid fancy words
15. Do not use dialect unless your ear is good
16. Be clear
17. Do not inject opinions
18. Use figures of speech sparingly
19. Do not take shortcuts at the cost of clarity
20. Avoid foreign languages
21. Prefer the standard to the offbeat

Though rules are not for everyone ...

Thomas Hardy
Any studied rules I could not possibly give, for I know of none that are of practical utility. A writer's style is according to his temperament, and my impression is that if he has anything to say which is of value, and words to say it with, the style will come of itself.

Seneca
Style has not fixed laws; it is changed by the usage of the people, never the same for any length of time.

... and many writers are brusquely dismissive of style:

Isobel Burton:
I have no leisure to think of style or of polish, or to select the best language, the best English – no time to shine as an authoress. I must just think aloud, so as not to keep the public waiting.

Samuel Butler

I never took the smallest pains with my style, have never thought about it, and do not know or want to know whether it is a style at all or whether it is not; as I believe and hope, just common, simple straightforwardness. I cannot conceive how any man can take thought for his style without loss to himself and his readers.

William Faulkner

I am not a stylist. The necessity of the idea creates its own style. The material itself dictates how it should be written. A writer must express himself in the most honest, truthful manner that he can.

Tom Robbins

You can't be too concerned, too occupied, with conforming to a style when you write.

· Summing up ·

There's no need to worry about developing a style until you've discovered whether you can actually write or not, by which time it will probably have developed all on its own. Here are some final thoughts on the subject:

Robert Stone

One doesn't consider style, because style is.

John Cheever

A man's prose style is very responsive – even a glass of sherry shows in a sentence.

Oscar Wilde

In matters of grave importance, style, not sincerity, is the vital thing.

Vladimir Nabokov

Style and structure are the essence of a book; great ideas are hogwash.

Fay Weldon

All styles are different, as all handwritings are different, and the better the writer, the more recognisable the style.

Gustave Flaubert
You don't know what it is to stay a whole day with your head in your hands trying to squeeze your unfortunate brain so as to find a word ... Ah! I certainly know the agonies of style.

Frederick Buechner
The limitation of the great stylists – Henry James, say, or Hemingway – is that you remember their voices long after you've forgotten the voices of any of the people they wrote about.

William Styron
I used to spend a lot of time worrying over word order, trying to create beautiful passages. I still believe in the value of a handsome style ... But I'm not interested anymore in turning out something shimmering and impressionistic ... I just get more and more interested in people. And story.

Blaise Pascal
We are surprised and delighted when we come upon a natural style, for instead of an author we find a man.

Robert Hughes
The sense of quality, of style, of measure, is not an imposition bearing on literature from the domain of class, race or gender. All writers or artists carry in their mind an invisible tribunal of the dead ... This tribunal sits in judgement on their work. They intuit their standards from it. From its verdict there is no appeal ... If the tribunal weren't there, every first draft would be a final manuscript. You can't fool Mother Culture.

Truman Capote
There is such an animal as a nonstylist, only they're not writers – they're typists.

Geoffrey Grigson
Nobody is going to parody you if you haven't a style.

Chapter Seven
How Writers Write

'An author's routines are as propitiatory as a rain doctor's'

The first question a writer gets asked – by everyone – is: How do you write? And they want to know exact details: when, where, with what and for how long. If you're obliging and tell, the inquisition will escalate: How did you get started? Where do your ideas come from? What do you do when you get stuck? How do you sell your work when it's finished? What's the name of your agent? Right at the end comes the crunch question: Does your writing earn good money?

Here is a selection of answers from writers old and new, from literary to popular, both famous and obscure, and from the struggling majority to the best-selling few.

Many confess to being nonplussed by the intense curiosity about their work habits:

Mary Stewart
Everyone asks me how I work – but why do they want to know? It doesn't interest me one bit whether another writer scribbles with a pencil, types or dictates to a secretary.

Jonathan Raban
Strangers at parties, striking up a 'literary' conversation ... want to know whether you

use a pen or a typewriter, what time you get up in the morning, whether you keep regular working hours, whether you can really make a living from it and – the big clincher – exactly what and how you get paid.

Philip Roth
I don't ask writers about their work habits. I really don't care. Joyce Carol Oates says somewhere that when writers ask each other what time they start working and when they finish ... they're actually trying to find out 'Is he as crazy as I am?' I don't need that question answered.

Ezra Pound
I don't know about method. The what is so much more important than how.

· Writers' rites & rituals ·
'Belief in the magic of getting words to come out of one's guts'

Ritual plays a large part in the writing process ...

Peter Elbow
Many serious, professional, and otherwise rational writers dally with magic in their writing. They have to get the right pencil or chair or paper. If they get any steps wrong in the ritual dance ... they feel as though words won't come or that the wrong words will come or that the words won't be effective.

V S Naipaul
I am superstitious. When I was young I never numbered my pages for fear that it was too arrogant and that I would not come to the end. Another thing that I did was that I never wrote my own name on the finished book ... These are little acts of magic.

Isabel Allende
I always write the first line of my books on that date [8 January]. When that time comes, I try to be alone and silent for several hours; I need a lot of time to rid my mind of the noise outside and to cleanse my memory of life's confusion. I light candles to summon the muses and guardian spirits, I place flowers on my desk to intimidate tedium and the complete works of Pablo Neruda beneath the computer with the hope that they will inspire me by osmosis – if computers can be infected

with a virus, there's no reason they shouldn't be refreshed by a breath of poetry. In a secret ceremony, I prepare my mind and soul to receive the first sentence in a trance, so the door may open slightly and allow me to peer through and perceive the hazy outlines of the story waiting for me.

Will Blythe
An author's routines are as propitiatory as a rain doctor's. To read about writing habits is to realise how assiduously, how slyly the muse must be courted.

... though not all writers believe in it:

Isaac Bashevis Singer
Experience has shown me that there are no miracles in writing. The only thing that produces good writing is hard work. It's impossible to write a good story by carrying a rabbit's foot in your mouth.

Stephen King
There's nothing really magical about it. If you've done it day in and day out, the cylinders all sort of fire over. I think the best trick is experience.

· Writers' routines ·
· Daily does it ·

'The important thing is to write every day'

Most professionals claim to write every day, or at least regularly:

John Mortimer
I get up early and write every day of my life.

Philip Roth
Eight hours a day, seven days a week, 365 days a year, that's the only way I know how to do it.

Ernest Hemingway
The important thing is to work every day. No matter what has happened the day or night before, get up and bite on the nail.

Rod McKuen
I try to write every day. That way I stay in training. Developing good writing habits is a must if you're serious about your work.

Nadine Gordimer
When I am working I work every day. If I start something I will work for many months at a stretch but I never have any set stint.

Gerald Brenan
It is by sitting down to write every morning that one becomes a writer. Those who do not do this remain amateurs.

John Updike
I work every weekday morning.

Carol Smith
I write every single morning, every single day of the week, because as an agent of twenty-something years, I know all about the rules.

Mordecai Richler
I work every day – or at least I force myself into office or room. I may get nothing done, but you don't earn bonuses without putting in time. Nothing may come for three months, but you don't earn the fourth without it.

· Time of writing ·

'I see to it that I'm inspired at nine o'clock every morning'

While most writers claim to do their best work in the morning (often at the crack of dawn) and keep to set hours, a vociferous minority pour scorn on such clerk-like timekeeping:

Jacques Barzun
It is wise ... to have not simply a set time for writing ... but also a set stint for the day, based on a true, not vainglorious estimate of your powers. Then, when you come to a natural stop somewhere near the set amount, you can knock off with a clear conscience.

Leo Tolstoy
I always write in the morning. In the morning one's head is particularly fresh.

Eve Palmer
At the writing stage of a book, I like to get up early, about 3 o'clock. One does get very tired by the end of the day. I don't know how writers manage a social life – I haven't got the energy left.

Barbara Trapido
I write from 4am to breakfast time, on any form of lined paper, on every third line.

May Sarton
I do all my work before eleven in the morning. That's why I get up so early. Around five.

John le Carré
There is nothing more satisfying than getting up at five and working through until eight before breakfast. You really feel you have stolen a march on the day ... I smoke one small cigar, and drink lots of black coffee, and then I'm on a high.

Gabriel Garcia Marquez
I have one absolute rule: I spend every morning writing until lunch. I start at 5am, revising three or four pages I've left on my bedside table.

Ernest Hemingway
When I am working on a book or a story I write every morning as soon after first light as possible. There is no one to disturb you and it is cool or cold and you come to your work and warm as you write ... I work from about seven until noon.

Of Jeffrey Archer:
He rises at five and works in two-hour bursts – six to eight, ten to twelve, two to four and six to eight – seven days a week for forty days. In between, he eats simple food and goes for what he calls 'thinking walks' during which he does not speak.

Katherine Anne Porter
I prefer to get up very early in the morning and work. I don't want to speak to anybody or see anybody. Perfect silence. I work until the vein is out ... I always write a story in one sitting.

Frederick Forsyth
I start at 6.30 and, with the help of two bananas, a packet of Rothmans and a thermos of coffee, I go on until I've got twelve typewritten pages, however long that takes. That way, I turn out a chapter every second day, and a 580-page book in fifty, with the odd day off.

Raymond Carver
I get up early, somewhere between six and 6.30. I'm always at my desk by eight. If it's a good day, I'll just stay at my desk until at least eleven or twelve, when I'll break. On a good day, I can stay at my desk and do something all day.

Of Kurt Vonnegut:
He generally gets up about 7am, eats a light breakfast, and sits down at the typewriter from about 8.30 to noon. Sometimes, if the day is right, he works from five to six in the evening. If the spirit moves him at other times, he writes then too.

Stephen King
I work from about 7.30 or 8am until noon, maybe 12.30, maybe 1 o'clock.

James Michener
I get up at 7.30am, and work very diligently all morning. I quit about noon. I never work in the afternoons, almost never, and I do this seven days a week, month in and month out until the book is written.

J M Coetzee
My day is a long decline from early morning till late night, so I can really be productive only in the first hours.

Geoffrey Jenkins
It's an iron discipline, and it's been like that for many years. I work six days a week, from 8am till 12.45, take half an hour for a sandwich, and then work till 4pm.

Doris Lessing
I usually write from 8am to 1pm and 4 to 6pm. It takes me a year to write a book.

A N Wilson
I usually work from eight to two, but if it's going well I may go on to four. Only, if I do, I'm extremely exhausted. In fact, when the book is going well the only thing that stops me is sheer exhaustion.

John Dos Passos
I find it easier to get up early in the morning, and I like to get through by one or two o'clock. I don't do very much in the afternoon. I like to get out of doors then if I can.

William Maxwell
I like to work in my bathrobe and pyjamas, after breakfast, until I suddenly perceive, from what's on the page in the typewriter, that I've lost my judgement. And then I stop.

Henry Miller
I generally go to work right after breakfast. I sit right down to the machine. If I find I'm not able to write, I quit.

Carlos Fuentes
I am a morning writer; I am writing at 8.30 in longhand and I keep at it till 12.30, when I go for a swim. Then I come back, have lunch, and read in the afternoon until I take my walk for the next day's writing.

Irving Stone
My problem is not to start myself, but to stop myself. I'm a compulsive worker ... And if I am not at my desk by 8.30 in the morning every day including Saturdays, I hear my grandmother's voice over my shoulder saying, 'Irving, why aren't you at work?'

Leonard Woolf
Every morning, at about 9.30 after breakfast, each of us, as if moved by a law of unquestioned nature, went off and worked until lunch at one. It is surprising how much one can produce in a year ... if one works hard and professionally for three and a half hours every day ... That was why, despite her disabilities, Virginia was able to produce so much.

Joseph Conrad
I sit down religiously every morning. I sit down for eight hours every day – and the sitting down is all. In the course of that working day of eight hours I write three sentences which I erase before leaving the table in despair.

Sidney Sheldon
I work five or six days a week from ten in the morning to six in the evening, with a short break for lunch.

Judith Krantz
I work, when I'm writing, five, sometimes six days a week. I start at about ten, lunch for fifteen minutes and then take a yellow pad and write by hand because my brain is still working. I don't see anyone, and I work all day until the evening.

Of Roald Dahl:
Dahl's writing regime remains rigid: at 10am sharp he's ensconced in his spartan garden shed. There, an old blanket tucked over his knees and a drawing board on his lap, with six pencils plus a sheaf of paper at his side, he works through until 12.30pm. Then it's lunch ... a rest until 4pm and back to the shed until 6pm.

Scott Spencer
I work every day, from ten in the morning till I'm done with my pages. I try not to write beyond a certain point. It's my experience that if I write too much in one day it kills a couple of days' work ... I keep myself to three or four pages a day.

Etienne van Heerden
I work best in the mornings when my subconscious is still at its most active. I have a sleep in the afternoon – I'm very strict about that. Then I work from 9pm until very late.

Catherine Cookson
I like to get down a story while it is, as I call it, hot, everything vibrating inside me. I sometimes sit for as long as six to eight hours at the tape, stopping only for coffee or a snack. As the tapes are finished, my secretary takes them.

Mary Stewart
I try to work a regular stint each day. Six hours. It isn't always easy because, after all, I am a housewife, with a husband to look after and a house to run. I'd actually work best in the morning, but there's too much to do about the house.

Annie Dillard
I work mornings only ... Afternoons I play with the baby, walk with my husband, or shovel mail.

Beryl Bainbridge
I used to work from eight in the evening until three in the morning when the children were small because I could only write when they were in bed. Now I get up at 6am.

Es'kia Mphahlele
When I was younger, I'd look after the children before they went to bed, and then I'd write. In those days I was a night person. Now they've grown up and gone, I've changed.

James Baldwin
I start working when everyone has gone to bed. I've had to do that ever since I was young – I had to wait until the kids were asleep. And then I was working at various jobs during the day. I've always had to write at night.

Jon Cleary
I never work at night – I just find that's tiring. I get my quota done each day and I keep working on until my first draft is done. I work Mondays to Fridays – no weekends. I'm strictly a union man!

Graham Greene
When I was young, not even a love affair would alter my schedule. A love affair had to begin after lunch, and however late I might be in getting to bed, so long as I slept in my own bed I would read the morning's work over and sleep on it.

Henry David Thoreau
I put a piece of paper under my pillow, and when I could not sleep I wrote in the dark.

François Mauriac
I write whenever it suits me. During a creative period I write every day; a novel should not be interrupted. When I cease to be carried along, when I no longer feel as though I were taking down dictation, I stop.

Dorothy Uhnak
I frankly don't know when I work. Sometimes, I leap out of bed at six in the morning, jump into my clothes, gulp my cup of tea and hammer out scene after scene ... Then, for days at a time, I avoid the top floor, which is where I work.

Somerset Maugham
Writing is a wholetime job: no professional writer can afford only to write when he feels like it.

Samuel Johnson
A man may write at any time, if he will set himself doggedly to it.

James Russell Lowell
If one waits for the right time to come before writing, the right time never comes.

· Place ·

'In my opinion a brothel is the perfect milieu for an artist to work in'

Generally, writers prefer their own special workplace, preferably quiet and secluded, but there are some interesting variations:

John Dos Passos
All you need is a room without any particular interruptions.

Mary McCarthy
A nice peaceful place with some good light.

Erica Jong
I think the most important thing for a writer is to be locked in a study ... I usually write in my office on the third floor of the house.

Toni Morrison
I type in one place, but I write all over the house.

Gabriel Garcia Marquez
I can only work in surroundings that are familiar and have already been warmed up with my work. I cannot write in hotels or borrowed rooms or on borrowed typewriters.

Rod McKuen
I write everywhere, but I write best at home ... The greatest luxury of writing at home, in addition to familiar surroundings, is being able to leave things where they are between spells of writing. Even my animals respect my clutter.

Joyce Carol Oates
If you are a writer you locate yourself behind a wall of silence and, no matter what you are doing, driving a car or walking or doing housework ... you can still be writing, because you have that space.

P D James
I need time on my own, particularly when I am writing. I can write more or less anywhere as long as I have total privacy.

Charles Bukowski
There is only one place to write and that is *alone* at a typewriter ... When you leave your typewriter you leave your machine gun and the rats come pouring through.

Beryl Bainbridge
The top room is a tip, full of cig ash and bits of paper. I keep the word processor there out of sight, like the telly, because it is so ugly.

William Maxwell
I prefer small messy rooms that don't look out on anything interesting. I wrote [the end of my last book] beside a window looking out on a tin roof. It was perfect. The roof was so boring it instantly drove me back to my typewriter.

Laurie Lee
In a prison cell, as many writers have found, it is easy to work, for there is nothing else to do.

Edna Ferber
The ideal view for daily writing, hour on hour, is the blank brick wall of a cold storage warehouse. Failing this, a stretch of sky will do, cloudless if possible.

Blaise Cendrars
A writer should never install himself before a panorama, however grandiose it may be ... Like St Jerome, a writer should work in his cell. Turn the back. Writing is a view of the spirit ... Today, I even veil the mirrors.

Rumer Godden
I have my writing room at last with Jon's desk in the window so that as I write I can look at the view but sometimes it is so exquisite I have to turn my desk to the wall.

Edna O'Brien
Up here [in my tiny attic room] I am safe. I have no excuse but to scratch out a few words. The view is in no way distracting because it does not alter and I am saved the irkdom of human voices.

Norman Mailer
I like a room with a view, preferably a long view. I dislike looking out on gardens. I prefer looking at the sea, or ships, or anything which has a vista to it.

Vladimir Nabokov
A first-rate college library with a comfortable campus around it is a fine milieu for a writer. There is of course the problem of fellow readers.

George Bernard Shaw
Most of my recent plays were written in the train between Hatfield and King's Cross. I write anywhere, on the top of omnibuses or wherever I may be; it is all the same to me.

William Faulkner
The best job that was ever offered to me was to become a landlord in a brothel. In my opinion it's the perfect milieu for an artist to work in. It gives him perfect economic freedom; he's free of fear and hunger; he has a roof over his head and nothing whatever to do except keep a few simple accounts and to go once every month and pay off the local police. The place is quiet during the morning hours, which is the best time of the day to work. There's enough social life in the evening, if he wishes

to participate, to keep him from being bored ... So the only environment the artist needs is whatever peace, whatever solitude, and whatever pleasure he can get at not too high a cost. All the wrong environment will do is run his blood pressure up.

Paul Bowles
I don't use a typewriter. It's too heavy, too much trouble. I use a notebook, and I write in bed. Ninety-five percent of everything I've written has been done in bed.

Of *Voltaire*:
A possibly apocryphal story has it that Voltaire did at least some of his writing in bed, using his naked mistress's back as a desk.

Commercially successful writers can afford to write in ever more exotic locations:

Graham Turner
[Jeffrey] Archer normally writes his first drafts at Lyford Quay in the Bahamas, all the rest — and there are usually another thirteen — in a folly at the bottom of his Grantchester garden. Jilly Cooper has a table with metal legs in a gazebo overlooking a Cotswold valley. Jack Higgins uses the mahogany dining-table of his villa in Jersey. Wilbur Smith writes in a sarong on an island in the Seychelles.

· *Writers' tools* ·

'I am rather particular about my instruments'

The tools used by writers range from quills to pencils to pens, typewriters to dictaphones to computers:

Thomas Fuller
I like writing with a Peacock's Quill; because its Feathers are all Eyes.

Tom Robbins
I like the idea of ink flowing out of my hand and saturating the paper. There's something intimate about that. It's more like you're making something than typing is. I'm thinking of going back to raven quill. And writing in lizard blood.

George Greenfield
Many established novelists retain the eighteenth-century method of writing books in their own hand ... Novelists have often told me that they like to see the words emerging on to the paper; they feel more in control and they have a sense of achievement as one line follows another, gradually working their way down the page. Some prefer the fountain pen or the ballpoint or the felt-tip pen because it keeps them in direct contact with their medium.

John Barth
My Baltimore neighbour Anne Tyler ... made the remark that there's something about the muscular movement of putting down script on the paper that gets her imagination back in the track where it was. I feel that too, very much so ... Good old script, which connects this letter to that, and this line to that ... that's how good plots work, right?

A N Wilson
I write very easily in longhand.

Rumer Godden
I believe, as the Chinese and Japanese calligraphers believe, that there is a mystique between the brain, the hand and the tool, pen, brush or scalpel; sometimes a flow is established between them, bringing a strange power.

George Greenfield
As one writer put it: 'This may sound mystical but I do believe it's essential ... to feel that something's flowing straight from here [he tapped his head] through my right arm, my hand, my forefinger and thumb, into the pen and right on to the paper without a break ... Nothing must break that circuit.'

Graham Greene
Some authors type their works, but I cannot do that. Writing is tied up with the hand, almost with a special nerve.

Dick Francis
I write by hand. I like to see a sentence on a page, see how it flows ... I work in longhand in a children's exercise book and then put it on a word processor.

W H Auden
Most people enjoy the sight of their own handwriting as they enjoy the smell of their own farts.

Rebecca West
My memory is certainly in my hands. I can remember things only if I have a pencil and I can write with it and I can play with it. I think your hand concentrates for you.

Ernest Hemingway
Wearing down seven number two pencils is a good day's work.

John Steinbeck
Pencils must be round. A hexagonal pencil cuts my fingers after a long day.

Martin Versfeld
I write in pencil ... And you must be able to give it an individual point with a pocket knife. I can't think without writing, I can't write without a pencil and I can't use a pencil without a knife. For me to lose my penknife is for me to lose my brains.

Vladimir Nabokov
My schedule is flexible, but I am rather particular about my instruments: lined Bristol cards and well sharpened, not too hard, pencils capped with erasers.

Ursula le Guin
The one thing a writer has to have is a pencil and some paper. That's enough, so long as she knows that she and she alone is in charge of that pencil, and responsible, she and she alone, for what it writes on the paper.

Rod McKuen
I'm deadly afraid of being caught without a pencil and paper. I may start something on the back of a magazine, misplace it, and finish it years later. Once the situation or the emotion is set, it's easily recaptured if it's valid. Lots of scraps of paper get thrown away.

Phyllis McGinley
>Oh, shun, lad, the life of an author.
>>It's nothing but worry and waste.
>Avoid that utensil,
>The labouring pencil,
>>And pick up the scissors and paste.

Truman Capote
I believe more in the scissors than I do in the pencil.

Miguel de Cervantes
The pen is the tongue of the mind.

Henry Ward Beecher
The pen is the tongue of the hand, a silent utterer of words for the eye.

Petrarch
There is no lighter burden, nor more agreeable, than a pen.

John Banville
I work with a pet of a pen – a beautiful Parker which cost about £150.

George Dennison Prentice
The pen is a formidable weapon, but a man can kill himself with it a great deal more easily than he can other people.

Master Wace
It is the pen / Gives immortality to men.

William Plomer
> Scratch, scratch his pen goes
> > Day and night,
> And much inflames his
> > Itch to write.

Of **Muriel Spark**:
[She writes] unhesitatingly on to the page, seldom revising a word. This is an essential part of the Spark mystique, along with her fetishistic obsession for writing on the same spiral-bound note books from Thin's of Edinburgh, and discarding any of her fountain pens which have been touched by anybody else.

Louise Erdrich
I sort of curl up in a beat-up red easy chair and write, in longhand. I know it's old-fashioned, but at least I don't use a fountain pen any more. I used to, but I could never remember to fill it.

Jeffrey Archer
If everything is not the same, I worry. I always write on an Oxford pad, I always use black Papermate felt-tipped pens, and I always correct my work with Staedtler HB pencils.

Clare Boylan
Some writers have a personal love affair with particular pens. Others do not give a

blot what comes to hand so long as it is stick-shaped, silent, and able to make its mark … I was surprised to discover that about 70 per cent of writers still write full manuscripts by hand.

Josephine Hart
You can dominate the pen. Machines seem to me to have a mind of their own.

William Allingham
> With pen and pencil we're learning to say
> Nothing, more cleverly, every day.

Shirley Hazzard
I write in longhand and I cram the page as I'm writing. My husband said that I shouldn't be so mean with paper. He suggested that I leave spaces between the lines and at the sides, so I could just scribble in the change on that piece of paper with a green or a red biro.

Rumer Godden
My flymark handwriting is small because I am so secretive when I write books that I make it small so that no one can read it. To me the writing of books should be secretive.

Edna Ferber
The office equipment consists of one flat table, a sheaf of yellow paper and one of white. All the wheels, belts, wire, bolts, files, tools – the whole manufacturing process – has got to be contained in the space between my chin and my topmost hairpin.

Edna O'Brien
My desk is a pine kitchen table … and I am without benefit of word processor, fax machine or anything modern. An array of pens reside in a green oblong velvet box.

Mark Twain *(from his first letter written on a typewriter):*
The machine has several virtues … One may lean back in his chair and work it. It piles an awful stack of words on one page. It don't muss things or scatter ink blots around.

Molly Keane
I have never used a typewriter in my life and I rather think that at 88 it is too late to start.

Mickey Spillane
The typewriter's my carpenter box.

V S Pritchett
I have an assortment of rotting pens that have run out of ink. I type after an appalling three-fingered fashion, but all my manuscripts are done by hand ... My hand-writing is awful but my wife understands it and she does my typing.

Dorothy Parker
I wrote in longhand at first, but I've lost it. I use two fingers on the typewriter ... I know so little about the typewriter that once I bought a new one because I couldn't change the ribbon on the one I had.

Robert Benchley
The biggest obstacle to professional writing today is the necessity for changing a typewriter ribbon.

Truman Capote
I write my first version in longhand (pencil). Then I do a complete revision, also longhand ... Then I type a third draft on yellow paper ... I don't get out of bed to do this ... I balance the machine on my knees. I can manage a hundred words a minute.

Joseph Heller
I write longhand and I type and I rewrite on the typed pages.

Carlos Fuentes
First I write the book out in longhand and then when I feel I 'have' it, I let it rest. Then I correct the manuscript and type it out myself, correcting it until the last moment.

Ray Bradbury
My handwriting is so dreadful my daughters weep when I visit at school on open house night and sign my name. At fourteen I learned to type and I've grown to be a very fast typist.

Nadine Gordimer
I sit at a typewriter or have one on my knee. I have never written anything by hand. I had a little typewriter when I was very young. To me, hand-writing is for letters, personal things, not for work.

Agatha Christie
All I needed was a steady table and a typewriter ... a marble-topped bedroom wash-stand table made a good place; the dining room table between meals was also suitable.

Edmund Wilson
I believe that composing on the typewriter has probably done more than anything else to deteriorate English prose.

Doris Lessing
I use an old-fashioned typewriter for the simple reason that I've done so since sixteen. But I'm also terribly afraid of disrupting the brain process, the flow between my brain and fingers. My friends who use the word processor haven't improved.

Tom Wolfe
I use a typewriter. My wife gave me a word processor two Christmases ago which still stares at me accusingly from a desk in my office. One day I am going to be compelled to learn how to use it. But for the time being, I use a typewriter.

Frederick Forsyth
I don't use a word processor. I cannot understand electronics. I have only just finally managed to use an electric typewriter.

Anthony Burgess
Electric typewriters keep going 'mmmmmmmm – what are you waiting for?' So does the word processor. I never use a notebook but I waste a very great deal of paper as I am endlessly re-writing.

Tom Robbins
One day I painted [my typewriter] red because I couldn't stand to look at it any longer and it never worked right after that. I ended up beating it to pieces with a 2 X 4 and throwing it in a garbage can ... Part of it was the noise. Electric typewriters buzz.

Charles Wood
Electric typewriters are intelligent, warm, sexy and they hum soothingly, unlike wives.

James Russell Lowell
Typewriter quotha! ... I could never say what I would if I had to pick out my letters like a learned pig.

Raymond Carver
Up at school there's a typist who has one of those space-age typewriters, a word processor, and ... once she has it typed and I get back the fair copy, I can mark it up to my heart's content ... It's changed my life, that woman with her word processor.

Jean Auel
My biggest problem was going from a pencil to a typewriter ... But it took me a certain amount of effort to learn how to be creative at the typewriter. Once I had that, the transition from typewriter to word processor wasn't a problem.

Beryl Bainbridge
I start off ... working with pen and paper on the kitchen table ... When I am finished with my notes I carry them up to the typewriter and after they have been typed up I move to the top floor with both notes and typescripts and edit the two on to the word processor.

Gabriel Garcia Marquez
I can't bear using the same adjective twice in the same book, except in very rare cases where exactly the same effect needs to be recreated. The word processor is very useful for solving that kind of problem. But it can't handle the memory of the narrative. That's the novelist's job.

Tom Sharpe
I've spent years trying to circumvent the swine [word processors]. They give you verbal diarrhoea. And, because the process of revising is so easy, I spend all my time compulsively editing and re-editing.

Elsa Joubert
Physically [a word processor] takes the labour out of thumping a typewriter, and correcting is easier. Sometimes there's an awful moment when the screen goes blank and you lose what you're working on ... I've never lost a manuscript but I've lost the changes I've made on a file.

Catherine Cookson
I now dictate my stories on to tape. This came about after I developed a frozen shoulder, caused through years of scribbling every spare minute of the day and often far into the night.

James Thurber
I still write occasionally ... using black crayon on yellow paper and getting perhaps twenty words to the page. My usual method, though, is to spend the mornings turning over the text in my mind. Then in the afternoon, between two and five, I call in a secretary and dictate to her.

Of Edgar Wallace:
[He] had the easiest method of working. He would write a book in a day without putting pen to paper. He merely dictated everything into a dictaphone, then off to the races.

Bruce Chatwin
In France, [the notebooks I use] are known as *carnets moleskines*: 'moleskine', in this case, being its black oilcloth binding. Each time I went to Paris, I would buy a fresh supply from a *papeterie* ... The pages were squared and the end-papers held in place with an elastic band.

Isaac Bashevis Singer
The wastepaper basket is the writer's best friend.

Gabriel Garcia Marquez
With a word processor, you can have an original of the manuscript every day. So I spend my time shredding. The machine that works hardest for me is ... my shredder. My wife Mercedes forces me to hang on to the revised versions once I've produced something that hangs together.

William Faulkner
The tools I need for my work are paper, tobacco, food, and a little whiskey.

Saccai
If all the sky were paper, and all the trees pens, and all the waters of the earth ink, they would not suffice to record my wisdom.

· Giving thought ·

'I compose in my head for a long, long time'

The act of writing is naturally preceded by prolonged cogitation:

Isaac Asimov
Thinking is the activity I love best, and writing to me is simply thinking through my fingers.

E B White
I am apt to let something simmer for a while in my mind before trying to put it into words.

Lawrence Block
I write books in quite a short time, usually no more than two months, with long periods in between when I just think.

Henry Miller
Most writing ... occurs in the quiet, silent moments, while you're walking or shaving or playing a game ... or even talking to someone you're not vitally interested in. You're working, your mind is working, on this problem in the back of your head.

Nadine Gordimer
A writer doesn't only need the time when he's actually writing – he or she has got to have time to think and time just to let things work out. Nothing is worse for this than society. Nothing is worse for this than the abrasive, if enjoyable, effect of other people.

Dorothy Parker
It takes me six months to do a story. I think it out and then write it sentence by sentence – no first draft.

V S Naipaul
My early books were written in eight to twelve weeks. Now it takes me about fourteen months. It is very hard to take longer since I do nothing else but work and think on a book.

Doris Lessing
I usually spend a very long time thinking about it. Sometimes years. You know when you are able to write it. The work goes in before you start, really. You can have variations of the pattern, but the whole book must be there.

Es'kia Mphahlele
I compose in my head for a long, long time – sometimes a story is five years old by the time I get it down. I never sit down until I'm sure the whole thing is finished in my own mind.

E B White
It has never struck me as harmful to make a conscious effort to elevate one's thoughts, in the hope that by so doing one's writing will get off the ground, even if only for a few seconds (like Orville Wright) and to a low altitude.

Tennessee Williams
I get up just before daybreak, as a rule. I like being completely alone in the house in the kitchen when I have my coffee and ruminate on what I'm going to work on.

Getting started

'I always start writing with a clean piece of paper and a dirty mind'

After writers have collected their thoughts, the preparations begin:

Charles Dickens *(to his wife Catherine):*
I have frequently told you that my composition is peculiar; I never can write with effect – especially in the serious way – until I have got my steam up, or in other words until I have become so excited with my subject that I cannot leave off.

Edward Albee
There's a time to go to the typewriter. It's like a dog – the way a dog before it craps wanders around in circles ... for a long time before it squats. It's like that – figuratively circling the typewriter getting ready to write, and then finally one sits down.

John Keats
All clean and comfortable I sit down to write.

Patrick Dennis
I always start writing with a clean piece of paper and a dirty mind.

For most, getting started is a daunting prospect:

Mary Stewart
Getting started each day is the worst part. I sometimes sit for half an hour before a blank page, longing to get up, but if I write something, however rubbishy, that gets the wheels turning and I can go on. And next day it's always better than I'd thought.

Dorothy Uhnak
It must be admitted that no matter how many books I've written, how many characters created and lived with and let go, when I put the blank white paper in my machine, it is no easier for me to begin the written word than it ever has been.

Laurence Olivier
Any writer will tell you that the most depressing thing in the world to experience is

that early morning trudge to the dreaded typewriter, sitting down and then staring at the blank page of A4. There it is, this whiter than white piece of paper glaring back at you from the roller, daring you to disfigure it with filthy black type or only just legible handwriting. The brightness of the white begins to affect your eyes. You sit down, you stand up, you look the other way, hoping that when you turn again some miracle will have been performed and the page will be full. You walk, you talk to yourself, you ask how you ever got yourself into this position in the first place.

Ruth Rendell
When you first sit down, it is, however much one enjoys it, a great effort. I like writing, but I don't fall upon it with childlike enthusiasm. It's a great leap of faith just to get down that first word – and then it gets better.

Paul Johnson
A very high percentage [of writers] find it difficult to get started in the morning: each day of their writing lives they face that initial, daunting hour of lonely agony ... a threshold which often seems impossibly high. There is nothing more fearsome than a blank sheet of paper.

And many and marvellous are the stratagems writers use to get going. Some read or listen to uplifting works first:

Maya Angelou
I'll read something, maybe the Psalms ... And I'll remember how beautiful, how pliable the language is, how it will lend itself. If you pull it, it says, 'Okay.' I remember that, and I start to write.

Ken Kesey
When I want to get going I read Faulkner. It's good because you can't write like him.

Gore Vidal
I often read for an hour or two. Clearing the mind. I'm always reluctant to start work, and reluctant to stop.

May Sarton
Music. I play records, mostly eighteenth-century music ... Mozart, Bach, Albinoni ... Haydn, I love. I feel the tremendous masculine joy of Haydn. That gets me going.

Thornton Wilder
Many writers have told me that they have built up mnemonic devices to start them off on each day's writing task. Hemingway once told me he sharpened twenty pen-

cils; Willa Cather that she read a passage from the Bible ... (to get in touch with fine prose)... My springboard has always been long walks.

Bernard Malamud
The idea is to get the pencil moving quickly.

Some arrange their tools nicely:

Bruce Chatwin
I put my pencils in a tumbler and my Swiss Army knife beside them. I unpacked some exercise pads and, with the obsessive neatness that goes with the beginning of a project, I made three neat stacks of my 'Paris' notebooks.

Arthur Kopit
I put on a big eight-cup percolator of coffee and sharpen about 35 pencils and I'm all set. I have to have sharp pencils.

Some resort to a drop of Dutch courage:

Norman Mailer
I usually need a can of beer to prime me.

E B White
Before I start to write, I always treat myself to a nice dry martini. Just one, to give me the courage to get started. After that, I am on my own.

Tennessee Williams
I go to my studio. I usually have some wine there. And then I carefully go over what I wrote the day before ... I'm inclined to excesses because I drink while I'm writing, so I'll blue pencil a lot the next day. Then I sit down, and begin to write.

Others are expert at delaying tactics:

E B White
I walk around, straightening pictures on the wall, rugs on the floor, as though not until everything in the world was lined up and perfectly true could anybody reasonably expect me to set a word down on paper.

Bernard Levin
The occupational disease of this trade is a constitutional inability to get down to work a moment earlier than is absolutely necessary, and the lengths to which I will go ... sometimes make me think that they will be coming to take me to the funny-farm any day now.

Laurence Olivier
The obstacles a writer puts in front of himself before he finally gets to the study are more than in the Grand National. There are papers to read, letters to be relished, bills to be paid, cheques to be signed ... instructions to be given; the day must be set in order.

Of J B Priestley:
In one of his essays [he] delightfully describes the elaborate desk-rituals, involving paper-clips, pencil sharpeners, pipe-cleaners and so forth, which can be performed as an alternative to beginning the morning stint.

James Jones
After I get up it takes me an hour and a half of fiddling around before I can get up the courage and nerve to go to work. I smoke half a pack of cigarettes, drink six or seven cups of coffee, read over what I wrote the day before. Finally there's no further excuse ...

Irving Stone
Sometimes I can go sit down and am absolutely obtuse. I'm dense, I'm confused, I feel lousy, I wish I had another job, and for a half-hour, hour and a half, while I piddle, I read a little bit out of a book, I read the morning paper.

Bernard Levin
I calculate that I have eaten at least 7 000 tons of digestive biscuits in my time solely because the prospect of eating a digestive biscuit seemed to me more inviting than sitting down and hitting the keys of the typewriter.

But delay is not necessarily a bad thing:

E B White
Delay is natural to a writer. He is like a surfer – he bides his time, waits for the perfect wave on which to ride in. Delay is instinctive with him. He waits for the surge (of emotion? of strength? of courage?) that will carry him along.

Donald M Murray
The Law of Delay: that writing which can be delayed, will be. Teachers and writers too often consider resistance to writing evil, when, in fact, it is necessary ... There must be time for the seed of the idea to be nurtured in the mind.

And there are those who just get on without any fuss:

William Styron
If writers had to wait until their precious psyches were completely serene there wouldn't be much writing done.

Toni Morrison
I don't wait to be struck by lightning and don't need certain slants of light in order to write.

Peter Straub
All there is is sitting down to work and trusting that the ignition key still turns everything on.

Evan Hunter
The time to go to the typewriter is when you're fresh and ready to do battle ... So sit down, make yourself comfortable, and begin. No outline at first, except the loose one in your head, draped casually around the idea.

Tom Robbins
All you do is, you write a sentence and see where it takes you. You take a trip on the page. You go where the sentences lead you. It's a journey.

Penelope Fitzgerald
I think secretly when we start writing we all feel that we can do it. Otherwise, why start?

· The writing process ·

'I keep to a pretty close schedule'

There are no rules — each writer does it differently:

Lawrence Durrell
The best regimen is to get up early, insult yourself a bit in the shaving mirror, and then pretend you're cutting wood.

Clarence Budington Kelland
I get up in the morning, torture a typewriter until it screams, then stop.

George Bernard Shaw
My method is to take the utmost trouble to find the right thing to say, and then to say it with the utmost levity.

Norman Cousins
William Faulkner would isolate himself in a small cell-like room and labour over his words like a jeweller arranging tiny jewels in a watch.

Evelyn Waugh
I put the words down and push them a bit.

E L Doctorow
I like the physical aspect of writing. I like to tear up a piece of paper and throw it down and put a new piece of paper in the typewriter. When I've decided to change something, I like to retype the whole page.

Arthur Kopit
I keep to a pretty close schedule. The best thing is to get a telephone that you can shut off ... I write standing up, or sitting in front of that drafting table ... And I do quite a lot of writing lying down, with a clipboard. The danger there, though, is that you often fall asleep.

Gore Vidal
Whenever I get up in the morning I write for about three hours. I write novels in longhand on yellow legal pads ... The first draft usually comes rather fast.

Nadine Gordimer
I work about four hours nonstop, and then I'll be very tired and nothing comes any more, and then I will do other things.

Truman Capote
I work four hours a day and then usually early in the evening I read over what I've written during the day and I do a lot of changing and shifting around. See, I write in longhand and I do two versions of whatever I'm doing.

Stephen King
I work four ... hours a day, seven days a week, around 2 000 words a day. The work that I do now I used to do more quickly ten years ago, and that's just a function of being ten years older. But it's also that I'm taking more time with it.

Barbara Cartland
I write every day, 750 words an hour ... I dictate everything to a secretary who is good at punctuation. Then a schoolmaster friend reads it all again, for grammar and punctuation.

John Updike
I write fairly rapidly if I get going, and don't change much, and have never been one for making outlines or taking out whole paragraphs or agonising much.

Doris Lessing
I write much better if I'm flowing. You start something off, and at first it's a bit jagged, awkward, but then there's a point where there's a click and you suddenly become quite fluent. That's when I think I'm writing well. I don't write well when I'm sitting there sweating about every single phrase.

Mary Stewart
I don't write easily. My work only flows after I've been hammering at it for ages and ages and ages. It's like pushing a rusty machine up a hill.

Pauline Smith
Every short story I wrote was written not in the joy of creation but in the pain of it, through a misery of diffidence and despair and in indifferent health which only his [Arnold Bennett's] dogged persistence and belief in me enabled me to find the courage to overcome.

James Michener
I slave over my books and work rather slowly. I work very painfully. I stop a lot of what I start and retype everything four, five, six times. The critical passages more, and everything at least three times. It takes me a while, a couple of years, to write a book.

Clive Cussler
On a good day of total effort, beginning at nine o'clock and ending at five ... I'm lucky if I turn out four finished pages or 1 000 words. And then I have to take a long walk, indulge in a martini and take a snooze prior to dinner, before I'm mentally rejuvenated enough to return to the land of the living.

Judith Krantz
Work has taken over my life to an extent I never thought possible. I have completed six books in twelve years, and in between there have been tours, promotion, research.

Clare Francis
Sometimes I have to look very hard for the story I want to write and other times it comes to me. I spend a long time planning and thinking about it, researching and so on, but once I'm away, I write every day from nine to five.

Nicholas Monsarratt
Once I was a sit-down-and-wait-for-inspiration writer. That was in the beginning. But you need a rich aunt for that sort of thing. Now it just comes. It has to. If it's going badly I still do it. This is a factory, it really is.

Kurt Vonnegut
It's like watching a teletype machine in a newspaper office to see what comes out. I work seven days a week. Some days I hit. Other days I only waste time. Most days are like that, just throwing stuff away. I am not at all prolific.

Of Kurt Vonnegut:
He sits on a padded Danish walnut easy chair. With his long legs drawn up and his back hunched, he leans forward to type on a machine set on a coffee table. Papers, folders and books are strewn about the table and on the floor ... His wife says she frequently hears him talking in his workroom.

Of John le Carré:
When writing dialogue, he speaks every line out loud before writing it down.

Tennessee Williams
I talk out the lines as I write.

James Thurber
I never quite know when I'm not writing. Sometimes my wife comes up to me at a party and says, 'Dammit, Thurber, stop writing.' She usually catches me in the middle of a paragraph. Or my daughter will look up from the dinner table and ask, 'Is he sick?' 'No,' my wife says. 'He's writing something.'

Frederick Forsyth
When I am writing I don't go out in the evening, but watch television which is like moving wallpaper and doesn't require a response. I think of the next day's writing. At the end of every day I make a list of things I have to do tomorrow.

Eudora Welty
Each story tells me how to write it, but not the one afterwards.

John Steinbeck
We work in our own darkness a great deal with little real knowledge of what we are doing.

Elizabeth Hardwick
I'm not sure I understand the process of writing.

The most unusual writing arrangements are those of ...

Maya Angelou
I have kept a hotel room in every town I've ever lived in. I rent a hotel room for a few months, leave my home at six, and try to be at work by 6.30. To write, I lie across the bed, so that this elbow is absolutely encrusted at the end, just so rough with calluses. I never allow the hotel people to change the bed, because I never sleep there. I stay until 12.30 or 1.30 in the afternoon, and then I go home and try to breathe; I look at the work around five; I have an orderly dinner: proper, quiet, lovely dinner; and then I go back to work the next morning ... I insist that all things are taken off the walls. I don't want anything in there. I go into the room, and I feel as if all my beliefs are suspended.

... and V S Naipaul
To keep in shape, he performs a daily exercise taught to him years ago by a family pundit in Trinidad. It is a difficult yoga bend that leaves the writer arched backward with his head on the floor.

· Order ·

'I write the big scenes first ...'

There are chronological writers – and there are those who approach their books quite differently:

Tom Robbins
I start with the first sentence – usually I start with the title; I write that on one page, then I turn the page and write the first sentence. Then I write the second sentence. It's very linear, very chronological, although the action and the plot might not be.

William Gass
The real writing process is simply sitting there and typing the same old lines over and over and over and over and sheet after sheet after sheet gets filled with the same shit.

Frank O'Connor
I write any sort of rubbish which will cover the main outlines of the story, then I can begin to see it.

Joyce Cary
I write the big scenes first, that is, the scenes that carry the meaning of the book, the emotional experience.

Vladimir Nabokov
The pattern of the things precedes the things. I fill in the gaps of the crossword at any spot I happen to choose. These bits I write on index cards until the novel is done.

John le Carré
A little controlled disorder helps.

· Working pace ·

'I write at high speed because boredom is bad for my health'

Some writers gallop along, some crawl and some just ooze:

Georges Simenon
I write fast because I have not the brains to write slow.

Doris Lessing
I have disciplined myself to write very fast in short periods of time. It was the only way when my children were small and I could write only when they were in school or playing.

Lawrence Durrell
It sounds stupid, but the fact is I write at a terrific speed, and ... you cross inner resistances like you cross a shoal of transmitters when you are fiddling with the dial on a radio.

William Saroyan
I believe in anything that works. With me it varies. When I'm seized by a chore, an assignment, a job, I need to do it quickly. This is not necessarily a virtue. It's just that I'm always afraid that if I don't do a thing right away I might never do it.

Isaac Asimov
I can write up to 18 hours a day. Typing 90 words a minute, I've done better than 50 pages a day ... If my doctor told me I had only six months to live, I wouldn't brood. I'd type a little faster.

Mary Stewart

Sometimes I get really excited writing. I write faster and faster until I find my hands shaking. When I'm nervous my fingers get pins and needles.

Noël Coward

I write at high speed because boredom is bad for my health. It upsets my stomach more than anything else. I also avoid green vegetables. They're grossly overrated.

Tom Wolfe

I try to be very methodical. I always have a clock in front of me. Sometimes, if things are going badly, I will force myself to write a page in half an hour.

Arthur Hailey

I'm a painfully slow writer. I bleed the words a few at a time and after that revise, revise, revise. I've tried to go faster but, for me, it doesn't work.

S J Perelman

I'm a bleeder. It's a good day when I get a page done.

· Amount ·

'I set myself a quota'

It's always difficult to measure creative output since it is dependent on mood and energy levels, and what is written or painted or composed today may be changed, rearranged or even scrapped tomorrow.

A writer's output is measured in words, and many of the older pen-pushers and typewriter-bashers are surprisingly rigid about their daily quota, counting the words as they go and stopping when it has been achieved. Writers of the keep-going-while-you're-hot school and those who have adapted to word processors tend to dash merrily along until they run out of steam, only then calculating how much they have written. (There are few satisfactions like that of hitting the relevant computer button after a creative spurt, and finding that you've managed a couple of thousand.)

The variation in output between one writer and the next is infinite:

Gabriel Garcia Marquez
On a good working day, working from nine o'clock in the morning to two or three in the afternoon, the most I can write is a short paragraph of four or five lines, which I usually tear up the next day.

V S Naipaul
I still write by hand ... 400 words in a good day and I have about three good days a week. I write very slowly and then transfer it to the screen. I transfer half a page to the screen and then I can print it out and play with it.

Norman Cousins *(on Thomas Mann)*:
[He] would consider himself lucky if, after a full day at his desk, he was able to put down on paper 500 words that he was willing to share with the world.

Graham Greene
Over twenty years I have probably averaged 500 words a day for five days a week ... Every now and then during the morning's work I count what I have done and mark off the hundreds on my manuscript.

Nicholas Monsarrat
Every day I write six hundred words. No more, no less.

Of *Arthur Hailey*:
His target is 600 [words] a day, and as each paragraph is completed he deducts the number of words it contains from that target. Occasionally, on a bad day when progress is slow, he will go back to his study after dinner to make up those 600 words.

Kingsley Amis
A page takes me quite a long time. Two pages a day is good. Three pages is splendid.

Tom Robbins
I work five days a week, ten to three, with a goal of two pages a day. Sometimes I don't get two pages, and sometimes I get a lot more. If I'm doing dialogue, which of course takes up more space anyway, I might get five or six pages.

Joseph Heller
I ordinarily write three or four handwritten pages and then rework them for two hours. I can work for four hours, or forty-five minutes. It's not a matter of time. I set a realistic objective: How can I inch along to the next paragraph?

Nadine Gordimer
A good day's work for me would be about 1 000 words, so roughly that is more or less my capacity at one sitting.

John Gordon Davis
I work a 12-hour day and manage on average 1 000 words – Frederick Forsyth turns out about 5 000.

Joseph Wambaugh
I write 1 000 words a day when I'm writing. Minimum. There's no deviation from that. I write 1 000 words a day, *every day*. And if an emergency would happen that I couldn't write 1 000 words on Monday, then I will write 2 000 words on Tuesday. Nothing will stop me, I mean *nothing*.

Edna O'Brien
There are writers who claim to write a minimum of 1 000 words a day and, if they are to be believed, there are more words than there are molecules in the universe.

Jon Cleary
I usually do between 1 500 and 2 000 words a day – five foolscap typed pages, triple-spaced. If there's a lot of dialogue ... that might be only 1 500 words that day. But when I finish those five pages, even if it's going well, I knock off.

Tom Wolfe
I set myself a quota – ten pages a day, triple-spaced, which means about 1 800 words. If I can finish that in three hours, then I'm through for the day. I just close up the lunch box and go home. If it takes me twelve hours, that's too bad, I've got to do it.

Erica Jong
I set myself to the task of writing ten pages a day in longhand, which comes out to about five typewritten pages.

Anthony Trollope
It had at this time become my custom – and it still is my custom, though of late I have become a little lenient to myself – to write with my watch before me, and to require from myself 250 words every quarter of an hour.

Of *Anthony Trollope*:
[He] trained himself to turn out 49 pages of manuscript a week, seven pages a day, and he was so rigorous about keeping to that exact number of pages that if he finished a novel halfway through the last day, he'd write the title of a new book ... and go right on until he'd done his proper quota of seven pages.

Evelyn Waugh
2 000 words a day is very good going.

Jilly Cooper
When things are going brilliantly, I can do 3 000 words a day. There are also days when I turn out nothing more than 100 words of complete rubbish.

Lawrence Durrell
What I do is try and write a slab of 10 000 words, and if it doesn't come off, I do it again.

Wilbur Smith
I can do 10 000 words a day when it's coming with a rush and a roar.

Yiddish Proverb:
Words should be weighed, not counted.

Dorothy Uhnak
No matter how remiss I am about regulating my work schedule, at least this much is structured: I work a scene through, beginning to end, whether it runs for four pages or 40, whether it takes 23 minutes or six hours. Maybe it's those six-hour binges that get the job done.

Graham Greene
I can produce a novel in a year, and that allows time for revision and the correction of the typescript.

William Styron
I can't turn out slews of stuff each day. I wish I could. I seem to have some neurotic need to perfect each paragraph – each sentence, even – as I go along.

Kurt Vonnegut
My published material is very small compared to what other people write.

· Number of books or projects ·
'I always work on two'

Most writers work on one book at a time:

John Barth
I work on one project at a time, until it's completed, whether it takes a month like some of my stories, or seven years like some of my novels. I've never been able to think about the next thing I'm going to write while I'm writing.

Irving Wallace
I only work on one book at a time.

Niki Daly
I always work on one book at a time – as I finish one another idea comes. One just trusts that something is there.

But there are many who prefer to have several projects on the go – the reasoning being that when you get stuck on one, you can move to the next. This seems a good idea, since a piece of writing can only benefit from being laid aside for a while and looked at critically again when the creative heat has cooled:

Stephen Birmingham
I always work on two things at a time. When one goes flat, I turn to the other.

Of John Gardner:
He works ... on three or four books at the same time, allowing the plots to cross-pollinate, shape and qualify each other.

· Stopping ·

'When my horse is running good, I don't stop to give him sugar'

Hemingway's famous advice to stop while you're going good (though Thomas Mann appears to have said it too) remains sound, but not all writers agree:

Ernest Hemingway
I learned never to empty the well of my writing, but always to stop when there was still something there in the deep part of the well, and let it refill at night from the springs that fed it.

Marguerite Young
I always leave off the day before. As Thomas Mann advised, when the going is good ... and you are in a moment of exuberance, you stop. When I hook on the next morning, if the going was good I just go. I feel it emotionally, almost in the blood, the pulse, the excitement.

Jon Cleary
It's better to go to bed knowing what I'm going to write tomorrow than to go to bed with an empty skull and lie awake all night wondering what I'm going to write.

William Faulkner
When my horse is running good, I don't stop to give him sugar.

John Updike
If a thing goes, it goes for me, and if it doesn't go, I eventually stop and get off.

Edward Albee
I find that in the course of the day when I'm writing, after three or four hours of intense work, I have a splitting headache, and I have to stop.

Graham Greene
I have always been very methodical, and when my quota of work is done I break off, even in the middle of a scene.

H G Wells
There comes a moment in the day, when you have written your pages in the morning, attended to your correspondence in the afternoon, and have nothing further to do. Then comes the hour when you are bored; that's the time for sex.

Tennessee Williams
When I stop [working], the rest of the day is posthumous. I'm only really alive when I'm working.

· Summing up ·

To sum up this chapter on how writers write, a quartet of voices:

George Henry Lewes
To write much, and to write rapidly, are empty boasts. The world desires to know *what* you have done, and not *how* you did it.

T S Eliot
There is no method except to be very intelligent.

Marcel Proust
Masterpieces are no more than the shipwrecked flotsam of great minds.

Saul Bellow
I don't know exactly how it's done. I let it alone a good deal.

Chapter Eight
General Advice about Writing

'Whether or not you write well, write bravely'

This chapter brings you a feast of general advice about writing. The would-be writer should study these quotes with particular care, since they contain the essence of what writing is about – or rather, what it would be in a perfect world.

First essentials

'Set a chime of words tinkling'

Harold Nicolson
The first essential is to know what one wishes to say; the second is to decide to whom one wishes to say it.

Logan Pearsall Smith
There is one thing that matters – to set a chime of words tinkling in the minds of a few fastidious people.

Voltaire
One should always aim at being interesting, rather than exact.

Robert Penn Warren
Your business as a writer is not to illustrate virtue but to show how a fellow may move toward it or away from it.

Kurt Vonnegut
One part of writing well is writing something that can be read well. Otherwise, the link between the writer and the reader is broken. Anytime the reader fails to get the message, it's the writer's fault.

Anthony Trollope
Of all the needs a book has, the chief need is that it be readable.

Carlos Fuentes
I'm very much in agreement with Virginia Woolf when she says that when you sit down to write, you must feel the whole of your tradition in your bones, all the way back to Homer.

Vladimir Nabokov
A creative writer must study carefully the works of his rivals, including the Almighty.

Bernard Malamud
The real mystery to crack is you.

'You're never going to be able to write if you don't read!'

John McGahern
I came to write through reading ... [and] I came to reading through pure luck. I had great good fortune when I was ten or eleven. I was given the run of a library. I believe it changed my life and without it I would never have become a writer.

Nadine Gordimer
You're never going to be able to write if you don't read!

Mary Wesley
Read, read and keep on reading. Books have been my education.

William Faulkner
Read, read, read. Read everything – trash, classics, good and bad, and see how they do it. Just like a carpenter who works as an apprentice and studies the master. Read! You'll absorb it. Then write. If it is good, you'll find out. If it's not, throw it out the window.

Henry Miller
It is in reading one's favourite authors that one becomes supremely aware of the value of practising the art of writing. One reads them with the right and the left eye. Without the least diminution of the sheer enjoyment of reading, one becomes aware of a marvellous heightening of consciousness.

Malcolm Bradbury
[A student of writing] ... has to be a good reader – to read creatively, not as a detached critic, but greedily, to feed his or her own writing, and have a love of language and of words, and be a good observer ... A writer is, after all, a reader, probably an indefatigable one.

Raymond Carver
Writers should read, yes, to see how it's done, for one thing, how the others are doing it; but there's also the sense of shared enterprise, the sense that we're all in this together.

James Michener
Read as many of the great books as you can before the age of 22.

Arthur Kopit
Read as much as possible, and while you're reading, try to see why the writing works.

Dorothea Brande
Consider a book in the light of what it can teach you about your own work ... Read with every faculty alert ... How does [the author] get the characters from one scene to another, or mark the passing of time? ... How does he get contrast?

André Maurois
Writing is a difficult trade which must be learned slowly by reading great authors, by trying at the outset to imitate them; by daring then to be original and by destroying one's first productions.

Arthur Brisbane
Read as much as you can of the best writers, and read Shakespeare all through life ... Read books that tell you what your predecessors on the earth have believed and

done, and how they escaped their superstitions. Read also some of the old classics ... In short, READ, always coming back to Shakespeare.

James Kisner
A good writer needs a sense of the history of literature to be successful ... and you need to read some Dickens, some Dostoyevsky, some Melville, and other great classics – because they are part of our world consciousness, and the good writers tap into the world consciousness when they create.

William Safire
Nobody who intends to be a writer can afford to be an unwary or passive reader ... Writers read ... with narrowed eyes, knowing that their emotions or thought processes are being manipulated and subtly directed by a fellow member of the scribe tribe. Writers read sceptically, often doubtfully, sometimes combatively ... Reading writers are never mere receptacles.

Malcolm Bradbury
In the end, every writer is a reader, and every reader is a critic. It is the task of all those who practise or study literature to have some strong sense of what all these functions are, and what they can become.

Of *Ernest Hemingway*:
A writer, Papa believed, had to read: for pleasure, for knowledge, for experience, but most importantly, to see what the competition is.

S I Hayakawa
It is not true that we have only one life to live; if we read, we can live as many lives and as many kinds as we wish.

· Advice to new writers ·

'Think straight and write simply'

Brander Matthews
To a beginner, the advice I would give would be to think straight and write simply. To be clear is the first duty of a writer; to charm and to please are graces to be acquired later.

Paddy Chayefsky

Artists don't talk about art. Artists talk about work. If I have anything to say to young writers, it's stop thinking of writing as art. Think of it as work ... It's hard physical work. You keep saying, 'No, that's wrong, I can do it better.'

Lorrie Moore

Perhaps one would be wise when young even to avoid thinking of oneself as a writer ... better to think of writing ... [as] an activity rather than an identity ... to keep working at the thing, at all hours, in all places, so that your life does not become a pose, a pornography of wishing.

Doris Lessing

You only learn to be a better writer by actually writing. I don't know much about creative writing programmes. But they're not telling the truth if they don't teach, one, that writing is hard work and, two, that you have to give up a great deal of life, your personal life, to be a writer.

Dorothy Uhnak

I'm not even sure anyone should presume to offer [young writers] any advice beyond that one tormenting, beautiful, obvious, obscure, demanding, torturous ecstasy: WRITE. Don't talk about it, whine about it, rap about it, agonise over it, dissect, analyse, study or anything else. Just do it. WRITE.

Ernest Hemingway

When you first start to write you get all the kick and the reader gets none, but after you learn to work it's your object to convey everything to the reader so that he remembers it not as a story he had read but something that happened to himself. That's the true test of writing. When you can do that, the reader gets the kick and you don't get any.

William Saroyan

I prefer a pattern of seeing a job through ... not having such a pattern is what holds many young writers back. Their high standards, the demands they make of themselves, are so great they get a novel about a third done and then give up because they think it's not good enough.

Doris Lessing

One bit of advice I might give a young writer is to get rid of the fear of being thought of as a perfectionist, or to be regarded as pompous. They should strike out for the best, to be the best.

May Sarton

My advice to young writers is that you must always keep trying. If you can't take the criticism, then you're not a writer. You've got to be able to take it. Hold on, trust your talent, and work hard ... Have the courage to write whatever your dream is for yourself.

John Jakes
Alas, the lesson of persistence is lost on many beginning writers – if indeed they ever hear it at all. If beginners did not give up so easily, the writing trade would be far more crowded and competitive than it is. That is a professional secret you should never forget.

James Baldwin
Don't describe it, show it. That's what I try to teach all young writers – take it out! Don't describe a purple sunset, make me see that it is purple.

William Faulkner
The young writer would be a fool to follow a theory. Teach yourself by your own mistakes; people learn only by error. The good artist believes that nobody is good enough to give him advice. He has supreme vanity. No matter how much he admires the old writer, he wants to beat him.

Ursula le Guin
The attempt to play complicated music on an instrument which one hasn't even learned the fingering of is probably the commonest weakness of beginning writers ... Beginners' failures are often the result of trying to work with strong feelings and ideas without having found the images to embody them

Gabriel Garcia Marquez
If I had to give a young writer some advice I would say to write about something that has happened to him; it's always easy to tell whether a writer is writing about something that has happened to him or something he has read or been told.

Athol Fugard
My first and last word of advice to any young writer remains: guard your secrets jealously.

James Michener
Young writers ought to find two or three authors in the last century who make them feel they knew what it was all about. And then try to figure out how they did it ... But I would certainly look at revolutionary and experimental forms in all fields: poetry, drama, painting, architecture.

E B White
Advice to young writers who want to get ahead without any annoying delays: don't write about Man, write about a man.

John Irving
[My teachers] told me things about my writing and about writing in general that I would probably have figured out for myself, but time is precious for a young writer ... This is what I can 'teach' a young writer: something he'll know for himself in a little while longer; but why wait?

Truman Capote
My point to young writers is to socialise. Don't just go up to a pine cabin all alone and brood. You reach that stage soon enough anyway.

James Jones
Boozing does not necessarily have to go hand in hand with being a writer ... I therefore solemnly declare to all young men trying to be writers that they do not actually have to become drunkards first.

William Saroyan (from his Letter to a Talented Young Unpublished Writer):
If you do not make the right beginning, you will never be able to write. They will put you down as one who has been influenced by another, and that will be the end. If they do that with your first stories, and your first book, there will never be any freedom from their judgement. The way not to write like anybody else in the world is to go to the world itself, to life itself, to the senses of the living body itself, and to translate in your own way what you see, and hear, and smell, and taste, and feel, and imagine, and dream and do ... Try to learn to breathe deeply, really to taste food when you eat, and when you sleep, really to sleep. Try as much as possible to be wholly alive, with all your might, and when you laugh, laugh like hell, and when you get angry, get good and angry. Try to be alive ... If you make the right beginning, nothing can stop you, and all you will have to do is survive.

Irwin Shaw
In my experience, I've found that if you're young enough, any kind of writing you do for a short period of time – up to two years, perhaps – is a marvellous apprenticeship.

William Styron
The purpose of a young writer is to write, and he shouldn't think too much. He shouldn't think that after he's written one book he's God Almighty and air all his immature opinions in pompous interviews.

Fyodor Dostoyevsky *(to a young writer)*:
Remember that you must never sell your soul ... Never accept payment in advance. All my life I have suffered from this ... Never give a work to the printer before it is finished. This is the worst thing you can do ... it constitutes the murder of your own ideas.

Kingsley Amis
I may not have many lessons to offer the ambitious young, but two are: take care what you publish early on, because someone might read it; and if you do succeed, don't pull earlier, failed stuff out of your bottom drawer, as at least three contemporaries of mine have done, to their cost.

Bernard Malamud
I urge young writers not to be too much concerned with the vagaries of the marketplace. Not everyone can make a first-rate living as a writer, but a writer who is serious and responsible about his work, and life, will probably find a way to earn a decent living, if he or she writes well.

Ray Bradbury
If I were to advise new writers ... I would advise like this: Tell me no pointless jokes ... Build in me no tention toward tears ... Do not clench my fists for me and hide the target. I might strike you, instead. Above all, sicken me not unless you show me the way to the ship's rail.

Irwin Shaw
Keep going. Writing is finally play, and there's no reason why you should get paid for playing. If you're a real writer, you write no matter what. No writer need feel sorry for himself if he writes and enjoys the writing, even if he doesn't get paid for it.

George Gissing
With a lifetime of dread experience behind me, I say that he who encourages any young man or woman to look for his living in 'literature', commits no less than a crime.

Fay Weldon
Consider, would-be writer, that if I, who have been writing for years, still have to carry on in this way, drafting and redrafting, refining and elaborating, searching for proper expression, whether this sort of thing is really how you wish to spend your life. The rewards are often negligible.

Lillian Hellman
If I had to give young writers advice, I would say don't listen to writers talking about writing or themselves.

Doris Lessing
I believe the worst enemy of any beginning writer is the group of loving friends. Most hope to be writers, and the story which the poor aspirant has entrusted to them is nothing like what they would attempt themselves.

· Practice makes perfect ·

'The way to learn to write is to write'

As successful writers are fond of pointing out, those who are serious about writing should (and will) keep going, no matter what:

Japanese Proverb:
Don't study an art, practise it.

Epictetus
If you wish to be a good writer, write.

Guy de Maupassant
Get black on white.

James Thurber
Don't get it right, just get it written.

Jean Auel
The way to learn to write is to write. Maybe by the time you've written a million words in your life – and that counts letters – you'll begin to discover what you need to know.

Bernard Malamud
You write by sitting down and writing. There's no particular time or place – you suit yourself, your nature.

J B Priestley
Write as often as possible, not with the idea at once of getting into print, but as if you were learning an instrument.

Ray Bradbury
The gift is part; it's there, but you have to rehearse it for many years ... Just write every day of your life. Read intensely. Then see what happens.

Catherine Cookson
I am of the firm belief that writers, especially beginners, should make a practice of writing some part of every day, if it's only one sentence.

Anton Chekhov
You must work without stopping all of your life ... What is needed is constant work, day and night; constant reading, study, will. Every hour is precious for it.

Anthony Trollope
All those who live as literary men – working daily as literary labourers – will agree with me that three hours a day will produce as much as a man ought to write. But then, he should so have trained himself that he shall be able to work continuously during those three hours – so have tutored his mind that it shall not be necessary for him to sit nibbling his pen, and gazing at the wall before him.

Lawrence Kasdan
You have to get lucky at some point, but you can only get lucky if you are still on the road, and for each of us that road, that journey, is of a different length. The thing is to keep doing it and doing it, any way you can.

John Jakes
Fundamental to success is practice. There is nothing mysterious about it ... Writing is a lot like playing golf, or the piano. To lift yourself out of the amateur class, you must do more than dabble; and once launched, you cannot, I believe, sustain a professional career without a continuing commitment to practice.

Stephen King
If you write for an hour and a half a day for ten years, you're gonna turn into a good writer.

Judith Krantz
Thousands of people plan to be writers, but they never get around to it. The only way to find out if you can write is to set aside a certain period every day *and try*. Save enough money to give yourself six months to be a full-time writer. Work every day and the pages will pile up.

Arnold Bennett
Only a small minority of authors over-write themselves. Most of the good and the tolerable ones do not write enough.

John Creasey
Nine out of ten writers, I am sure, could write more. I think they should and, if they did, they would find their work improving even beyond their own, their agent's, and their editor's highest hopes.

Aloysius Smith ('Trader Horn')
It's the busy fellers get the ideas. An idle man has too much time on his hands to get an idea. Sitting in an armchair never brought you nearer to good literary notions.

Raymond Carver
It really comes down to this: indifference to everything except that piece of paper in the typewriter.

· Be disciplined ·

'Life is tons of discipline'

Joseph Wambaugh
I feel that writing is a mix of talent and discipline.

Robert Frost
Discipline. Tightness. Firmness. Crispness. Sternness. And sternness in our lives. Life is tons of discipline. Your first discipline is your vocabulary; then your grammar and your punctuation ... Then, in your exuberance and bounding energy you say you're going to add to that.

Bernard Malamud
How one works, assuming he's disciplined, doesn't matter. If he or she is not disciplined, no sympathetic magic will help. The trick is to make time ... and produce the fiction. If the stories come, you get them written, you're on the right track. Eventually everyone learns his or her own best way.

Florence King
Discipline is never a restraint ... It's an aid. The first command of the romantic school is: 'Don't worry about grammar, spelling, punctuation, vocabulary, plot or structure – just let it come.' That's not writing; that's vomiting, and it leads to uncontrolled, unreadable prose.

Sidney Sheldon
I think it is important to set up a disciplined schedule. If you write only when the muse sits on your shoulder, it is unlikely that your project will ever get completed.

Arthur Kopit
Very important – don't wait to write when you 'feel like it'. Keep a schedule.

Evan Hunter
Set yourself a definite goal each day. Tack it on the wall ... Set the goal, make it realistic, and *meet it* ... At the end of each week, on your calendar, jot down the number of pages you've already written. Store your kernels. Watch the cache grow. Keep the thing moving.

Peter Elbow
Writing with power also means getting power over yourself and over the writing process; knowing what you are doing as you write; being in charge; having control; not feeling stuck or helpless or intimidated.

Paul Johnson
Six hours of uninterrupted writing produces several thousand words. And when a book takes something like five months solid merely to write, well, you have to be disciplined and adhere to a strict routine. You have to keep fit, you need a good diet and the right kind of exercise.

Rachel Carson
The discipline of the writer is to learn to be still and listen to what his subject has to tell him.

Though as usual, there is a dissenting voice:

John Fowles
All this advice from senior writers to establish a discipline – always to get down a thousand words a day whatever one's mood – I find an absurdly puritanical and impractical approach. Write, if you must, because you feel like writing, never because you feel you *ought* to write.

Strive to write well

'Always dream and shoot higher than you know you can do'

Aristotle
To write well, express yourself like the common people but think like a wise man.

Isaac Asimov
To write quickly and to write well are usually incompatible attributes, and if you must choose one or the other, you should choose quality over speed every time.

William Faulkner
He must never be satisfied with what he does. It is never as good as it can be done. Always dream and shoot higher than you know you can do. Don't bother just to be better than your contemporaries or predecessors. Try to be better than yourself.

Gay Talese
No good writer ever cares whether or not his book is a commercial success. What is important is always to do your best work.

Write from the heart

'Look into thy heart and write'

Philip Sidney
Look into thy heart and write.

Susan Howatch
Write straight from the heart, write a story you feel absolutely driven to commit to paper, and don't waste time worrying about how you can make it 'commercial'.

Thomas Carlyle
If a book comes from the heart, it will contrive to reach other hearts; all art and authorcraft are of small amount to that.

Ivan Turgenev
What you must study is mankind in general, and your own heart, and the truly great writers ... Would to God your horizon may broaden every day! The people who bind themselves to systems are those who are unable to encompass the whole truth.

Anthony Trollope
Let an author so tell his tale as to touch his reader's heart and draw his tears and he has ... done his work well.

William Faulkner
[The writer] must teach himself that the basest of all things is to be afraid; and, teaching himself that, forget it forever, leaving no room in his workshop for anything but the old verities and truths of the heart, the old universal truths lacking which any story is ephemeral and doomed – love and honour and pity and pride and compassion and sacrifice.

Leo Tolstoy
One ought only to write when one leaves a piece of one's flesh in the inkpot each time one dips one's pen.

D H Lawrence
Be still when you have nothing to say; when genuine passion moves you, say what you've got to say, and say it hot.

Lawrence Durrell
Stop writing and start feeling.

· Be yourself ·
'Follow your inner moonlight'

Christopher Isherwood
One should never write down or up to people, but out of yourself.

George Bernard Shaw
The man who writes about himself and his own time is the only man who writes about all people and about all time.

Allen Ginsberg
Follow your inner moonlight; don't hide the madness.

W B Yeats
To speak of one's emotions without fear or moral ambition, to come out from under the shadow of other men's minds, to forget their needs, to be utterly oneself, that is all the Muses care for.

F L Lucas
In literature, as in life, one of the fundamentals is to find, and be, one's true self ... In writing, in the long run, pretence does not work. As the police put it, anything you say may be used in evidence against you. If handwriting reveals character, writing reveals it still more.

Amelia E Barr
I put *myself*, my experiences, my observations, my heart and soul into my work. I press my soul upon the white paper. The writer who does this may have any style, he or she will find the hearts of their readers. You will see, then, that writing a book involves, not a waste, but a great expenditure of vital force.

John Mortimer
There's a lot of me in everybody I write about. It's the worst side of vanity, refusing to grow up. And there's the thing I learned from my father – saying things, not because I mean them, but just to start an argument ... I think people ought to be shocked regularly.

Terry Southern
Out of the old gut onto the goddamn page.

Lorrie Moore
One has to give to one's work like a lover. One must give of oneself, and try not to pick fights.

Joan Plowright
You have to reach into your own personality to illuminate things that, if possible, will surprise people, make them realise that you have understood things about life that they may not have. Your journey as a human being should make you more able to illuminate such things.

Virginia Woolf
The test of a book [to a writer] is if it makes a space in which, quite naturally, you can say what you want to say.

William Zinsser
Sell yourself, and your subject will exert its own appeal. Believe in your own identity and your own opinions. Proceed with confidence, generating it, if necessary, by pure willpower. Writing is an act of ego and you might as well admit it. Use its energy to keep yourself going.

Henry David Thoreau
Nothing goes by luck in composition. It allows of no tricks. The best you can write will be the best you are. Every sentence is the result of a long probation. The author's character is read from title-page to end. Of this he never corrects the proofs.

Samuel Taylor Coleridge
I could inform the dullest author how he might write an interesting book. Let him relate the events of his own life with honesty, not disguising the feelings that accompanied them.

John Burroughs
When [the writer] speaks from real insight and conviction of his own, men are always glad to hear him, whether they agree with him or not. Get down to your real self ... and let that speak. One's real self is always vital and gives the impression of vitality.

Truman Capote
At the end the personality of a writer has so much to do with the work. The personality has to be humanly there ... The writer's individual humanity, his word or gesture toward the world, has to appear almost like a character that makes contact with the reader.

James Dickey
You want to hold out for those things *only* you can say. You satisfy these two criteria: one, something that only you could say; and two, that you judge it good *even though* it's something only you could say. These are rare times when you get something like that, but you can tell.

Kurt Vonnegut
You should have something on your mind. You should have opinions on things. You should care about things.

Alison Lurie
You can't write well with only the nice parts of your character, and only about nice things. And I don't want even to try any more. I want to use everything, including hate and envy and lust and fear.

Hortense Calisher
To write in the first person seems the easiest ... Actually it may be the hardest – there are so many hazards. Garrulity. Lack of shape, or proportion. Or even of judgement. On the other hand, when you're really riding that horse well, it can feel as if you're on Bucephalus. And you really feel the wind on you.

Peter Elbow
Writing with power means getting power over words and readers; writing clearly and correctly; writing what is true or real or interesting; and writing persuasively or making some kind of contact with your readers so that they actually experience your meaning or vision.

Gustave Flaubert
This is one of my principles; you must not write of *yourself*. The artist must be within his work like God within the Creation; invisible and all-powerful; we feel him throughout, but we do not see him.

Stephen King
If the stuff you're writing is not for yourself, it won't work ... I think, 'Don't give them what they want – give them what you want.'

Katharine Hepburn
A book is only your point of view.

· Heed your subconscious ·

'You have to trust your intuition'

Dorothea Brande
Hitch your unconscious mind to your writing arm.

Mignon McLaughlin
If you jot down every silly thought that pops into your mind, you will soon find out everything you most seriously believe.

Tom Robbins
You have to trust your intuition. You can't be totally spontaneous – you've got to

shape your material – but at the same time, if you put too many restrictions on yourself, you're going to produce dull work. Constricted. Anal retentive.

Motto of **'Punchbowl'** *(the University of Pennsylvania magazine):*
Any damn fool can be spontaneous.

Doris Lessing
In the writing process, the more a thing cooks, the better. The brain works for you even when you are at rest. I find dreams particularly useful. I myself think a great deal before I go to sleep and the details sometimes unfold in the dream.

Rainer Maria Rilke
What is needed is, in the end, simply this: solitude, great inner solitude. Going into yourself and meeting no one for hours on end – that is what you must be able to attain.

· Use your imagination ·

'Imagination is more important than experience and inspiration'

B J Chute
The imagination, like the intellect, has to be used, and a creative writer ought to exercise it all the time. There is no idea, however insignificant or vague it may be, that the imagination cannot touch to new beginnings, turning it around and around in different lights, playing with it, *listening* to it.

David Madden
Imagination is more important than experience and inspiration. I don't want to give a faithful report on real-life incidents, I want to *transform* them in my imagination so that the story itself becomes the event.

Somerset Maugham
Imagination grows by exercise.

Iris Murdoch
One piece of imagination leads to another. You think about a certain situation and then some quite extraordinary aspect of it suddenly appears. The deep things that the

work is about declare themselves and connect ... Of course, actually writing it involves a different kind of imagination and work.

Hinda Teague Hill
Since imagination *cannot create material*, set about systematically to stock your mental storehouse. Cultivate the habit of curiosity ... Observe accurately. Increase the variety of your reading, your contacts with others, your emotional experiences, so that they may furnish richer material for the imagination to work with.

Henri de Montherlant
It is a feature of the artistic imagination that it should be able to reconstitute everything on the basis of very limited data. When Delacroix wanted to paint a tiger, he used his cat as a model.

Joseph Conrad
Let him mature the strength of his imagination amongst the things of this earth, which it is his business to cherish and know.

· Live life before trying to write about it ·

'Throw yourself into the hurly-burly of life'

Henry David Thoreau
How vain it is to sit down to write when you have not stood up to live!

Somerset Maugham
You cannot be a writer without experience ... You cannot describe life convincingly unless you have partaken of it ... Throw yourself into the hurly-burly of life. It doesn't matter how many mistakes you make, what unhappiness you have to undergo ... Experience is your material.

Neville Shute
An author must be prepared to put himself to hardship and inconvenience to extend his knowledge.

Etienne van Heerden
I often say [the time I spend writing a book] is as long as I've been living. A book is a concentration of skills and experiences and other texts that you've read over many years.

· *Give it all you've got* ·

'*Spend it all, shoot it, play it*'

Joyce Carol Oates
Be daring, take on anything. Don't labour over little cameo works in which every word is to be perfect.

Annie Dillard
One of the few things I know about writing is this: Spend it all, shoot it, play it, lose it, all, right away, every time. Do not hoard what seems good for a later place in the book, or for another book, give it, give it all, give it now.

Ray Bradbury
I have come up with a new simile to describe myself lately. It can be yours. Every morning I jump out of bed and step on a landmine. The landmine is me. After the explosion, I spend the rest of the day putting the pieces together.

Bill Stout
In your writing, be strong, defiant, forbearing. Have a point to make and write to it. Dare to say what you want most to say, and say it as plainly as you can. Whether or not you write well, write bravely.

Alfred, Lord Tennyson
> Authors – essayist, atheist, novelist,
>   realist, rhymster, play your part,
> Paint the mortal shame of nature
>   with living hues of Art.
> Rip your brothers' vices open, strip
>   your own foul passions bare;
> Down with Reticence, down with Reverence
>   – forward – naked – let them stare.

Lorrie Moore
Obviously one must keep a certain amount of literary faith, and not be afraid to travel with one's work into margins and jungles and danger zones.

Ellen Goodman
You have to care. That's the most important thing.

Doris Lessing
You have to learn how to use your energy and not squander it.

Ralph Waldo Emerson
Nothing great was ever achieved without enthusiasm.

· Be truthful ·

'Write truthfully but with cunning'

Ivan Turgenev
You need truth, remorseless truth, as regards your own sensations.

Peter Carey
The big question for a writer is: how can you know this? In what corner of yourself can you find what you need to write truthfully about things of which, objectively, you'd have no knowledge?

Wolfgang Amadeus Mozart
The golden mean, the truth, is no longer recognised or valued. To win applause one must write stuff so simple that a coachman might sing it, or so incomprehensible that it pleases simply because no sensible man can comprehend it.

Bernard Malamud
Watch out for self-deceit in fiction. Write truthfully but with cunning.

Emily Dickinson
> Tell the truth
> But tell it slant.

Be succinct

'Try to leave out all the parts readers skip'

Anatole France
The writer's first courtesy, is it not to be brief?

Samuel Butler
'Tis in books the chief
Of all perfections to be plain and brief.

Robert Southey
If you would be pungent, be brief; for it is with words as with sunbeams – the more they are condensed the deeper they burn.

Eudora Welty
You must know all, then not tell it all, or not tell too much at once; simply the right thing at the right moment.

John D Macdonald
When in doubt, opt for less rather than more.

Jules Renard
The less you write, the better it must be.

William Strunk, Jr
Be clear. Be concise. Be forceful. Know where you're going. Avoid windy locutions, repetitive mannerisms. Save your most important point for last.

Susan Howatch
For a start, don't ramble. Never write a scene unless it's absolutely necessary, and if it *is* necessary, then write it concisely.

John Simon
Concision is honest, honesty concision – that's one thing you need to know.

Morris West
You can't tell or show everything within the compass of a book ... Ask yourself what is the core of the matter you wish to communicate to your reader? Having decided ... all that you tell him must relate to it and illustrate it more and more vividly.

Somerset Maugham
The narrative passages should be vivid, to the point, and no longer than is necessary to make the motives of the persons concerned, and the situations in which they are placed, clear and convincing.

Stephen King
Leave in the details that impress you the most strongly; leave in the details you see the most clearly; leave everything else out.

Alan Paton
What is the gift [shared by Raymond Chandler and James Hadley Chase]? In the first place it is economy of writing. Every sentence says something. Every chapter advances the story. No padding. And the greatest gift of all I suppose is to arouse the interest at once, to make the reader want to know more.

Elizabeth Bowen
Relevance crystallises meaning. The novelist's – any writer's – object is, to whittle down his meaning to the exactest and finest possible.

David Westheimer
Try for the significant detail, the one that will engage the reader's interest, add to your story and give the impression you could say a great deal more on the subject if you wished.

Voltaire
The best way to be boring is to leave nothing out.

Elmore Leonard
My most important piece of advice to all you would-be writers: *when you write, try to leave out all the parts readers skip.*

Ernest Hemingway
I always try to write on the principle of the iceberg. There is seven-eighths of it under water for every part that shows. Anything you know, you can eliminate and it only strengthens your iceberg ... The reader, if the writer is writing truly enough, will have a feeling of those things as strongly as though the writer had stated them.

Spareness and bareness are all very well, but even the most pernickety writers stress the importance of well-chosen details:

Vladimir Nabokov
There is nothing wrong about the moonshine of generalisation when it comes after the sunny trifles of the book have been lovingly collected ... Caress the detail, the divine detail.

Georges Simenon
I consider myself an impressionist, because I work by little touches. I believe a ray of sun on a nose is as important as a deep thought.

Henri Troyat
No detail must be neglected in art, for a button half-undone may explain a whole side of a person's character. It is absolutely essential to mention that button. But it has to be described in terms of the person's inner life, and attention must not be diverted from important things to focus on accessories and trivia.

Judy Delton
To write with great restraint is to write dishonestly. To write effectively, a writer must be ready to spill a certain amount of blood on the sidewalk.

· Write clearly and simply ·

'You want to write a sentence as clean as a bone'

Leo Tolstoy
When a man has something to say he must try to say it as clearly as possible, and when he has nothing to say it is better for him to keep quiet.

Henry David Thoreau
If a man has anything to say, it drops from him simply and directly like a stone to the ground.

Truman Capote
I prefer to underwrite. Simple, clear as a country creek.

Anthony Trollope
The language should be so pellucid that the meaning should be rendered without an effort to the reader.

Stendhal
I see but one rule: to be clear. If I am not clear, all my world crumbles to nothing.

Walter Savage Landor
Clear writers, like clear fountains, do not seem so deep as they are; the turbid look the most profound.

Somerset Maugham
To write simply is as difficult as to be good.

James Baldwin
The hardest thing in the world is simplicity. And the most fearful thing, too. You have to strip yourself of all your disguises, some of which you didn't know you had. You want to write a sentence as clean as a bone. That's the goal.

Ernest Hemingway
It had gone so simply and easily that he thought it was probably worthless. Be careful, he said to himself, it is all very well for you to write simply ... But do not start to think so damned simply. Know how complicated it is and then state it simply.

William Shakespeare
An honest tale speeds best being plainly told.

H G Wells
I write as I walk because I want to get somewhere and I write as straight as I can, just as I walk as straight as I can, because that is the best way to get there.

Friedrich Nietzsche
It takes less time to learn to write nobly than to learn to write lightly and straightforwardly.

Rod McKuen
No matter how smart you think you are, how gifted or intellectual, never write over, under or around people. Write straight ahead. The only way to protect the language is to use it simply and straightforwardly.

Robert Graves
It is the greatest fun making things as easy as possible for the reader while keeping the sense and integrity of what you are writing.

Robert Louis Stevenson
In all narration there is only one way to be clever. And that is to be exact.

Anthony Hope Hawkins
Unless one is a genius, it is best to aim at being intelligible.

On the other hand:

Marshall McLuhan
Clear prose indicates the absence of thought.

Albert Camus
I ought not to have written; if the world were clear, art would not exist.

· Concentrate on communicating ·

'... the link between the writer and the reader ...'

Harlan Ellison
All you are, all I am, is what I write. Away from the typewriter I'm a man, but behind it I'm someone else entirely. I'm something more than a man. I can say what I believe, what I truly believe, and it will be read and understood by *someone, somewhere*, and I'll have communicated.

Kurt Vonnegut

One part of writing well is writing something that can be read well. Otherwise, the link between the writer and the reader is broken. Anytime the reader fails to get the message, it's the writer's fault. You say what you have to say. But you have to learn to say it in such a way that the reader can see what you mean.

Doris Lessing

I don't like to have to express myself in a complicated fashion. A book should be understandable for everyone.

Nadine Gordimer

In some people's writing you are very conscious of the writer – the writer is between you and the subject all the time. My own aim is to be invisible and to make the identification for the reader with what is being written about ... not to distance the reader.

Rod McKuen

Writers are only communicators. We are not some lofty breed meant to speak only to other writers. If we are given the gift to communicate, we should not abuse it.

· Be objective ·

'A writer ... must always be a stranger to the place he loves'

Anton Chekhov

To a chemist, nothing on earth is unclean. A writer must be as objective as a chemist; he must abandon the subjective line; he must know that dung heaps play a very respectable part in a landscape, and that evil passions are as inherent in life as good ones.

Willie Morris

When a writer knows home in his heart, his heart must remain subtly apart from it. He must always be a stranger to the place he loves, and its people.

Leo Tolstoy
I have found that a story leaves a deeper impression when it is impossible to tell which side the author is on.

Maxwell Perkins
You have to throw yourself away when you write.

· Be original ·

'The story … is yours alone'

François René Chateaubriand
The original writer is not he who refrains from imitating others, but he who can be imitated by none.

Ernest Hemingway
There is no use writing anything that has been written before unless you can beat it. What a writer in our time has to do is write what hasn't been written before or beat dead men at what they have done.

Yoshida Kenko
In everything, no matter what it may be, uniformity is undesirable. Leaving something incomplete makes it interesting, and gives one the feeling that there is room for growth.

Kaatje Hurlbut
Trust your genius: it is your creative function and its business is to create. Because it works at the level of origins, the story it creates is original; it is yours alone.

Bernard Malamud
Teach yourself to work in uncertainty. Many writers are anxious when they begin, or try something new.

Goethe
Dare to storm those gates which everyone gladly sneaks past.

Avoid platitudes & clichés

'Worn out and useless phrases'

William Zinsser
If a writer litters his prose with platitudes ... we can safely infer that the writer lacks an instinct for what gives language its freshness.

George Orwell
One can at least change one's own habits, and from time to time one can even, if one jeers loudly enough, send some worn out and useless phrase – some jackboot, Achilles' heel, hotbed, melting pot, acid test, veritable inferno or other lump of verbal refuse – into the dustbin where it belongs.

George Bernard Shaw
The writer who aims at producing the platitudes which are 'not for an age but for all time' has his reward in being unreadable in all ages.

Think before you write

'Think about the value of what you have to say'

Nicolas Boileau-Despréaux
Before writing, learn to think.

Susan Hill
There is nothing like having to write every word down for making you think about the value of what you have to say.

Miguel de Cervantes
Let every man take care how he talks, or how he writes of other men, and not set down at random, higgle-de-piggledy, whatever comes into his noddle.

On the other hand:

Harry Kemelman
Don't think and then write it down. Think on paper.

Pay attention to the sense

'The sound must seem an echo to the sense'

E B White
When you say something, make sure you have said it. The chances of your having said it are only fair.

Somerset Maugham
Have common sense and ... stick to the point.

Lewis Carroll
Take care of the sense and the sounds will take care of themselves.

Alexander Pope
> True ease in writing comes from art, not chance.
> As those move easiest who have learn'd to dance.
> 'Tis not enough no harshness gives offence,
> The sound must seem an echo to the sense.

Kathleen Krull
Take care to avoid getting asked the favourite question of Harold Ross, the *New Yorker*'s late editor: 'What the hell do you mean?'

More nuggets of practical advice

'Store your kernels. Watch the cache grow.'

Joanna Trollope
It's nice if you're a reader to do a little work yourself. The writer should leave paths for readers to follow, so that they have this sense of the moral pot pourri which exists in all of us.

Anne Bernays
Nice writing isn't enough. It isn't enough to have smooth and pretty language. You have to surprise the reader frequently ... Provoke the reader. Astonish the reader. Writing that has no surprises is as bland as oatmeal. Surprise the reader with the unexpected verb or adjective. Use one startling adjective per page.

William Goldman
Don't write stuff you can't handle. If you don't like romantic comedies, don't write *Annie Hall*. You have to always write your best, or you're dead.

Ignore the opinions of others

'If you write with someone looking over your shoulder, you'll never write'

Nadine Gordimer
The ideal way to write is as if you were dead and will be unaffected by any repercussions. You cannot protect yourself or worry about what you may uncover – even in yourself.

Nikki Giovanni
You must be unintimidated by your own thoughts because if you write with someone looking over your shoulder, you'll never write.

Norman Mailer
You have to assume that the act of writing is the most important of all. If you start worrying about people's feelings, then you get nowhere at all.

Catherine Cookson
You must first of all make up your mind to turn deaf ears to all those well-wishers who tell you that the markets are swamped already and that there isn't a hope in hell for newcomers; or that – take their word for it – there's no money in this game.

Dire warnings

'You cannot lie to your typewriter'

Leon Uris
You can lie to your wife or your boss, but you cannot lie to your typewriter. Sooner or later you must reveal your true self in your pages.

E L Doctorow
Planning to write is not writing. Outlining ... researching ... talking to people about what you're doing, none of that is writing. Writing is writing.

Matthew Arnold
Produce, produce, produce ... for I tell you the night is coming.

W H Auden
In relation to a writer, most readers believe in the Double Standard: they may be unfaithful to him as often as they like, but he must never, never be unfaithful to them.

E B White
No one can write decently who is distrustful of the reader's intelligence, or whose attitude is patronising.

Dorothy Parker
If you're going to write, don't pretend to write down.

Charles P Curtis
The author is like the host at a party. It is his party, but he must not enjoy himself so much that he neglects his guests. His enjoyment is not so much his own but theirs.

Anthony Trollope
Beware of creating tedium! I know no guard against this so likely to be effective as the feeling of the writer himself. When once the sense that the thing is becoming long has grown upon him, he may be sure that it will grow upon his readers.

Fay Weldon
It's a hideously personal kind of thing ... you're doing. You are working upon the inside of your head to make what's in there comprehensible to others. And ... what is worse, you must be prepared to do as adults what children so hate doing ... read your work *aloud* before you hand it in.

James Kisner
If you alter your writing to pander to a market trend then you're compromising your craft, number one, and number two, you're no longer a writer, you're a hack. The only concession a writer should make to the market is to maintain a contemporary style and viewpoint.

Irwin Shaw
You must avoid giving hostages to fortune, like getting an expensive wife, an expensive house, and a style of living that never lets you afford the time to take the chance to write what you wish.

· Rules of writing ·

'It's not wise to violate the rules until you know how to observe them'

Writers love talking about the rules of writing – often to the point of making lists of rules. Here, for what they're worth, is a selection:

Truman Capote
Writing has laws of perspective, of light and shade, just as painting does, or music. If you are born knowing them, fine. If not, learn them. Then arrange the rules to suit yourself.

T S Eliot
It's not wise to violate the rules until you know how to observe them.

Stendhal
I see but one rule: *to be clear*. If I am not clear, all my world crumbles to nothing.

James Michener
The rules seem to be these: if you have written a successful novel, everyone invites you to write short stories. If you have written some good short stories, everyone wants you to write a novel. But nobody wants anything until you have already proved yourself by being published somewhere else.

Somerset Maugham
A good rule for writers; do not explain overmuch.

Anthony Trollope
I deemed it expedient to bind myself to certain self-imposed laws. It was also my practice to allow myself no mercy.

Walter Savage Landor
Elegance in prose composition is mainly this: A just admission of topics and of words; neither too many nor too few of either; enough of sweetness in the sound to induce us to enter and sit still; enough of illustration and reflection to change the posture of our minds when they would tire; and enough of sound matter in the complex to repay us for our attendance.

Irving Stone *(on how to write)*:
1. Dramatise
2. Plenty of dialogue
3. Bring the characters to life
4. Use anecdotes and humour

E B White
Place yourself in the background; write in a way that comes naturally; work from a suitable design; write with nouns and verbs; do not overwrite; do not overstate; avoid the use of qualifiers; do not affect a breezy style; use orthodox spelling; do not explain too much; avoid fancy words; do not take shortcuts at the cost of clarity; prefer the standard to the offbeat; make sure the reader knows who is speaking; do not use dialect; revise and rewrite.

Stephen King

Use vivid verbs. Avoid the passive voice. Avoid the cliché. Be specific. Be precise. Be elegant. Omit needless words. Most of these rules ... will take care of themselves almost automatically if you will ... take two pledges: First, not to insult your reader's interior vision; and second, to see everything before you write it.

Sheridan Baker

- Economise. Think of explaining what you have to say clearly, simply and pleasantly to a small mixed group of intelligent people.
- Never use a long word when you can find a short one, or a Latin word when you can find a good Old English one.
- Suspect yourself of wordiness whenever you see an *of*, a *which* or a *that*. Inspect all areas surrounding any form of *to be*. Never use *exist*.
- Make sure that each word really makes sense. No one who had inspected the meaning of his words could have written: 'Every seat in the auditorium was filled to capacity.'
- The important thing is, I think, to pick up each sentence in turn, asking ourselves if we can possibly make it shorter.

George Orwell

- Never use a metaphor, simile or other figure of speech which you are used to seeing in print.
- Never use a long word where a short one will do.
- If it is possible to cut a word out, always cut it out.
- Never use the passive where you can use the active.
- Never use a foreign phrase, a scientific word or a jargon word if you can think of an everyday British equivalent.
- Break any of these rules sooner than say anything outright barbaric.

Judith Krantz's 12 Rules

1. Don't be intimidated by the work of other writers
2. Read copiously in the area you want to write in
3. Don't try to imitate; find your own voice
4. Start with an outline, though it may change as you go
5. Visualise your characters clearly
6. Have your own special place to work in, and insist on not being disturbed
7. Work regular hours; don't let yourself get distracted
8. Keep pads of paper and pencils all over the house to record odd bits of inspiration

9. Don't talk about your work, except perhaps with one other whom you rely on for criticism and comment
10. Learn to write directly on to a typewriter
11. Don't let yourself get discouraged
12. Rewrite

F L Lucas
1. Make your own characters seem good.
2. Make clear connections between sentences.
3. Don't say too many things at once.
4. Don't get lured off the line of argument.
5. Use short paragraphs rather than long.
6. Avoid monotony.
7. Be simple.
8. Omit needless words.
9. Write less; rewrite more.
10. Variety is courtesy to the reader.

William Strunk, Jr
1. Choose a suitable design and hold to it
2. Make the paragraph the unit of composition
3. Use the active voice
4. Put statements in positive form
5. Use definite, specific, concrete language
6. Omit needless words
7. Avoid a succession of loose sentences
8. Express co-ordinate ideas in similar form
9. Keep related words together
10. In summaries, keep to one tense
11. Place the emphatic words of a sentence at the end

William Safire *(on how to write good)*:
- Avoid run-on sentences that are hard to read.
- No sentence fragments.
- It behooves us to avoid archaisms.
- Also, avoid awkward or affected alliteration.
- Don't use no double negatives.
- If I've told you once, I've told you a thousand times, 'Resist hyperbole.'
- Avoid commas, that are not necessary.
- Verbs has to agree with their subjects.
- Avoid trendy locutions that sound flaky.
- Writing carefully, dangling participles should not be used.

- Kill all exclamation points!!!
- Never use a long word when a diminutive one will do.
- Proofread carefully to see if you any words out.
- Take the bull by the hand, and don't mix metaphors.
- Don't verb nouns.
- Never, ever use repetitive redundancies.
- Last but not least, avoid clichés like the plague.

Ray Bradbury

To sum it all up, if you want to write, if you want to create, you must be the most sublime fool that God ever turned out and sent rambling.
- You must write every single day of your life
- You must read dreadful dumb books and glorious books, and let them wrestle in beautiful fights inside your head, vulgar one moment, brilliant the next
- You must lurk in libraries and climb the stacks like ladders to sniff books like perfumes and wear books like hats upon your crazy heads
- I wish for you a wrestling match with your Creative Muse that will last a lifetime
- I wish craziness and foolishness and madness upon you
- May you live with hysteria, and out of it make fine stories – science fiction or otherwise
- Which finally means, may you be in love every day for the next 20 000 days. And out of that love, remake a world.

William Carlos Williams

I have never been one to write by rule, not even by my own rules.

Edward Coplestone

Write what will sell! To this Golden Rule every minor canon must be subordinate.

Henry David Thoreau

When I read some of the rules for speaking and writing the English language correctly ... I think – *Any fool can make a rule, and every fool will mind it.*

Wesley Price

Three rules of professional comportment for writers: Never make excuses, never let them see you bleed, and never get separated from your baggage.

Somerset Maugham

There are three rules for writing the novel. Unfortunately, no one knows what they are.

Some final words of advice

William Faulkner
The writer's only responsibility is to his art.

J M Coetzee
Whatever the process is that goes on when one writes, one has to have some respect for it. It is in one's own interest, one's own very best interest, even one's material interest, to maintain that respect.

John Steinbeck
In utter loneliness a writer tries to explain the inexplicable …The writer must believe that what he is doing is the most important thing in the world. And he must hold to this illusion even when he knows it is not true.

William Makepeace Thackeray
Ah, ye knights of the pen! May honour be your shield, and truth tip your lances! Be gentle to all gentle people. Be modest to women. Be tender to children. And as for the Ogre Humbug, out sword and have at him!

Benjamin Franklin
If you would not be forgotten, as soon as you are dead and rotten, either write things worth reading, or do things worth the writing.

Ken Follett
Why are good books so boring? We wondered about this as students, plodding through Henry James or Virginia Woolf while we longed to get back to *My Gun Is Quick*. Perhaps we were afraid to ask, for fear of seeming naive. As writers I think we should be asking the question still. It could turn out to be the most important question around.

Ernest Hemingway
The great thing is to last and get your work done and see and hear and learn and understand and write when there is something that you know; and not before; and not damned much after.

Colette
The writer who loses his self-doubt, who gives way as he grows old to a sudden euphoria, to prolixity, should stop writing immediately: the time has come for him to lay aside his pen.

Phyllis Whitney
You must want to *enough*. Enough to take all the rejections, enough to pay the price in disappointment and discouragement while you are learning.

Frank Conroy
For God's sake, don't do it unless you have to ... It's not easy. It shouldn't be easy, but it shouldn't be impossible, and it's damn near impossible.

William Faulkner
Do not look toward writing as a profession. Work at something else. Dig ditches if you have to, but keep writing in the status of a hobby that you can work at in your spare time. Writing, to me, is a hobby – by trade I'm a farmer.

James Michener
Many writers can get jobs in public relations or elsewhere to supplement their incomes, and with the understanding of your spouse, you can organise your life so there is time to plug away at what you want to do.

John Gardner
Write in any way that works for you. Write in a tuxedo or in the shower with a raincoat or in a cave deep in the woods.

Jack Kerouac
>Be in love with yr life
>Be crazy dumbsaint of the mind
>Blow as deep as you want to blow
>Write what you want bottomless from the
>   bottom of the mind
>Remove literary, grammatical and syntactical
>   inhibition
>Write in recollection and amazement for
>   yourself.

More Quotes

Chapter Nine
Choosing a Genre

One of the most pleasurable activities for would-be writers is the contemplation of what genre they will choose to write in – when, of course, they choose to write.

The choice is important since a correct decision can beget agreeable perks. In non-fiction these include the subsidised travel and exotic locations enjoyed by travel writers, and the biographer's licence to poke around in someone else's affairs.

J A Cuddon
Genre: A French term for a kind, a literary type or class. The major classic genres were: epic, tragedy, lyric, comedy and satire, to which would now be added novel and short story.

Herbert E Meyer & Jill M Meyer
The absolute first thing to do when you launch a writing project is to resist the impulse to start writing. You need to relax, to settle down and above all YOU NEED TO THINK ...The first real step in the writing process [is choosing] the correct category of writing product.

Autobiography

'The pearl is the oyster's autobiography'

> **Autobiography is ...**
>
> ... an unrivalled vehicle for telling the truth about other people. **Philip Guedalla**
>
> ... an obituary in serial form with the last instalment missing. **Quentin Crisp**
>
> ... a kind of writing in which you tell the story of yourself as truthfully as you can, or as truthfully as you can bear to. **J M Coetzee**

Creative people often maintain that their autobiography is apparent in their body of work:

Jean Cocteau
The work of every creator is autobiography, even if he does not know it or wish it, even if his work is 'abstract'. It is why you cannot re-do your work.

Anthony Trollope
The man of letters is, in truth, ever writing his own biography.

Theodore Lessing
All good books are autobiographies; but bad autobiographies are the worst of all books.

Federico Fellini
All art is autobiographical; the pearl is the oyster's autobiography.

There are varying opinions as to the best age to write an autobiography:

Beverley Nichols
Twenty-five seems to me the latest age at which anybody should write an autobiog-

raphy. It has an air of finality about it, as though one had clambered to the summit of a great hill, and were waving goodbye to some distant country which can never be revisited.

Bertrand Russell
I have a certain hesitation in starting my biography too soon for fear of something important having not yet happened. Suppose I should end my days as President of Mexico; the biography would seem incomplete if it did not mention this fact.

Evelyn Waugh
Only when one has lost all curiosity about the future has one reached the stage to write an autobiography.

And there is no lack of advice on how to go about it:

Samuel Taylor Coleridge
I could inform the dullest author how he might write an interesting book. Let him relate the events of his own life with honesty, not disguising the feelings that accompanied them.

Laurie Lee
In writing autobiography, especially one that looks back at childhood, the only truth is what you remember. No one else who was there can agree with you because he has his own version of what he saw.

J M Coetzee
Autobiography is usually thought of not as a kind of fiction-writing but as a kind of history-writing, with the same allegiance to the truth as history has.

Ellery Sedgwick
Autobiographies ought to begin with Chapter Two.

Ned Rorem
To start writing about your life is, from one standpoint, to stop living it. You must avoid adventures today so as to make time for registering those of yesterday.

Abraham Cowley
It is a hard and nice thing for a man to write of himself. It grates his own heart to say anything of disparagement, and the reader's ears to hear anything of praise from him.

Laurie Lee
Perhaps the widest pitfall in autobiography is the writer's censorship of self. Unconscious or deliberate, it often releases an image of one who could never have lived. Flat, shadowy, prim and bloodless, it is a leaf pressed dry on the page, the surrogate chosen for public office so that the author might survive in secret.

With **Georges Bernanos** *making the most telling point:*
When writing of oneself one should show no mercy. Yet why – at the first attempt to discover one's own truth – does all inner strength seem to melt away in floods of self-pity and tenderness and rising tears?

Writers of autobiographies generally have a good motivation tucked away in case it should seem an exercise in vanity:

Anthony Burgess
The professional novelist will sometimes have a sly and perhaps unworthy reason for writing about himself. In a fallow time, when he does not have the energy to invent, he will be glad to fall back on reminiscence ... An autobiography may be a substitute for the novel that cannot be written.

Michel de Montaigne
And because I found I had nothing else to write about, I presented myself as a subject.

Doris Lessing
Why an autobiography at all? Self-defence: biographies are being written. It is a jumpy business, as if you were walking along a flat and often tedious road in an agreeable half-dark but you know a searchlight may be switched on at any minute.

Last words on autobiography to:

Gore Vidal
I find ruminating on the past interesting when I focus on someone else; less so when confronted with my youthful self, an elusive – even blank – figure whom I don't remember much about.

Donal Henahan
Next to the writer of real estate advertisements, the autobiographer is the most suspect of prose artists.

Henri-Philippe Pétain
To write one's memoirs is to speak ill of everybody except oneself.

A C Benson
If the dullest person in the world would only put down sincerely what he or she thought about his or her life, about work and love, religion and emotion, it would be a fascinating document.

Hilaire Belloc
Just as there is nothing between the admirable omelette and the intolerable, so with autobiography.

· Biography ·

'Biography is about chaps'

Biography is …

… one of the new terrors of death. **Dr John Arbuthnot**

… ancient. Christianity itself is based on four biographies. **Ben Pimlott**

… a form of textual interpretation – the life as key to the work. **James Allan**

… by nature the most universally profitable, universally pleasant of all things; especially the biography of distinguished individuals. **Thomas Carlyle**

… of the various kinds of narrative writing, that which is most eagerly read and most easily applied to the purposes of life. **Samuel Johnson**

Aneurin Bevan
All biography is lies.

> ## Biographies are ...
>
> ... like detective stories: you start off with a series of lies and deceptions, then hopefully get somewhere near the truth. **Peter Alexander**
>
> ... but the clothes and buttons of the man – the biography of the man himself cannot be written. **Mark Twain**

Edmund Clerihew Bentley
The art of Biography.
Is different from Geography.
Geography is about maps,
But Biography is about chaps.

Philip Guedalla
Biography, like big game hunting, is one of the recognised forms of sport, and it is unfair as only sport can be.

Ben Pimlott
A serviceable answer to the question 'What is the purpose of biography?' is 'understanding' – of a person, a period, a setting, perhaps even the human condition.

Most people consider biography to be a facet of history, which accounts for its popularity:

Thomas Carlyle
No great man lives in vain. The history of the world is but the biography of great men.

Benjamin Disraeli
Read no history; nothing but biography, for that is life without theory.

Philip Guedalla
Biography is a region bounded on the north by history, on the south by fiction, on the east by obituary, and on the west by tedium.

Opinions as to the duties of a biographer vary:

Philip Toynbee
The primary duty of a serious biographer is to illuminate his subject's life work, not to play the spy in his bedroom.

Lytton Strachey
To preserve ... a becoming brevity – a brevity which excludes everything that is redundant and nothing that is significant – that surely is the first duty of a biographer. The second, no less surely, is to maintain his own freedom of spirit. It is not his business to be complimentary; it is his business to lay bare the facts of the case, as he understands them ... dispassionately, impartially, and without ulterior intentions.

James Allan
In the new biography, life illuminates art. The biographer's task is to reveal the work's emotional genesis, to anatomise the private and public events that brought it into being.

B L Reid
A biographer's first duty is to recover the actual; and what is more powerful in a man's life than the detail of his days? ... I confess to feeling an odd little private thrill when I found a ragged notebook that included Roger Casement's laundry list for 12th May 1899 in Loanda on the west coast of Africa. I felt my nostrils flaring.

Ben Pimlott
To achieve [understanding], biographers have to think of themselves as more than evidence-accumulators. They need to see their subjects not as deities to be revered ... They should, above all, stop regarding themselves as the valets of the great and treating their work as a minor branch of the public service.

And the choice of subject is crucial:

Evelyn Waugh
The best sort of book to start with is biography. If you want to make a success of it, choose as a subject someone very famous who has had plenty of books written about him quite recently. Many young writers make the mistake of choosing some forgotten ... eighteenth-century traveller.

Advice on the writing of biographies is freely available from practitioners of the art:

Paul Murray Kendall
[The biographer] must be as ruthless as a board meeting smelling out embezzlement, as suspicious as a secret agent riding the Simplon–Orient Express, as cold-eyed as a pawnbroker viewing a leaky concertina.

Tim Couzens
Given the same material there are many ways to write a biography. It is a craft, not a production belt. The flip side of this, though, is that truth has a fascination, a quirkiness, that fiction doesn't.

Caroline Drinker Bowen
In writing biography, fact and fiction shouldn't be mixed. And if they are, the fiction parts should be printed in red ink, the fact parts in black ink.

Alan Paton
Then you take it all – the chronology, the letters, the interviews, your worn knowledge, the newspaper cuttings, the history books, the diary, the thousand hours of contemplation, and you try to make a whole of it, not a chronicle but a drama, with a beginning and an end.

Harold Nicolson
Biography, if it is to enhance understanding, add to history or interpret character, must be constructive and not destructive.

Julian Barnes
The trawling net fills, then the biographer hauls it in, sorts, throws back, stores, fillets and sells. Yet consider what he doesn't catch; there is always far more of that ... Think of everything that got away, that fled with the last deathbed exhalation of the biographee.

Rebecca West
Just how difficult it is to write biography can be reckoned by anybody who sits down and considers just how many people know the real truth about his or her love affairs.

Noël Coward
With my usual watchful eye on posterity, I can only suggest to any wretched future biographer that he gets my daily engagement book and from that fills in anything he can find and good luck to him, poor bugger.

Impartiality in a biographer is a moot point:

A J Balfour
Biography should be written by an acute enemy.

And not everyone admires biographers and their works:

Sigmund Freud
Whoever turns biographer commits himself to lies, to concealment, to hypocrisy, to embellishments, and even to dissembling his own lack of understanding, for biographical truth is not to be had, and even if one had it, one could not use it.

Thomas Macaulay
Many of the greatest men that ever lived have written biography. Boswell was one of the smallest men that ever lived, and he has beaten them all ... He had, indeed, a quick observation and a retentive memory. These qualities, if he had been a man of sense and virtue, would scarcely of themselves have sufficed to make him conspicuous; but because he was a dunce, a parasite, and a coxcomb, they have made him immortal.

Thomas Carlyle
A well-written Life is almost as rare as a well-spent one.

Ben Pimlott
Modern biographies come in two bits: the text and then the notes. The latter ... are meant to make you believe the former ... Before the invention of the reference note, the biographer tried to tell a story that would make the reader happier, sadder, even a bit wiser.

Hannah More
This new-fashioned biography seems to value itself upon perpetuating every thing that is injurious and detracting.

However, the writing of biography does have its excitements ...

Tim Couzens
What are the rewards of writing biography? Firstly, it fulfills all those failed ambitions one had as a child to join the Brixton Murder and Robbery Squad, or to emulate Hercule Poirot. Biography is intellectual detective work, with all the excitement of

the hunt or car chase, sometimes culminating in a shoot-out, sometimes in a libel case. Secondly, biography is disguised tourism on a grand scale. You never know where you're going to be, or who you're going to meet. But you have an excuse to be there … Thirdly, biography, being at the intersection of history and literature, satisfies the would-be novelist in every historian.

… and admirers:

Elbert Hubbard
Biography broadens the vision and allows us to live a thousand lives in one.

Doris Lessing
What is better than a really good biography? Not many novels.

Though **Thomas Carlyle** *did not hold the same high opinion of his compatriots as biographers:*
How delicate, decent, is English biography, bless its mealy mouth!

Biographies of writers fall into a category of their own:

Godfrey Smith
I find biographies of writers riveting, though they do tend to end sadly.

Vladimir Nabokov
The best part of a writer's biography is not the record of his adventures but the story of his style.

George Painter
The biographer must discover, beneath the mask of the artist's everyday, objective life, the secret life from which he extracted his work.

Joyce Cary
It is very pleasant to be written up, even by a writer.

Last words on biography to:

Arthur Wilson
A biographer is like a contractor who builds roads: It's terribly messy, mud everywhere, and when you get done, people travel over the road at a fast clip.

Julian Barnes
The biography stands, fat and worthyburgerish on the shelf, boastful and sedate; a shilling life will give you all the facts, a 10-pound one all the hypotheses as well.

Marie Dressler
I enjoy reading biographies because I want to know about the people who messed up the world.

Tony Tanner
After you have traced a man down to the last munched bath bun you are still left with the whole mystery of 'the madness of art'.

Ben Pimlott
Is biography ceasing to be an art, and becoming a form of monumental masonry?

· Travel writing ·

'Literature and travel are anciently, inevitably tangled'

Why do people choose to write about travel in the first place? Some celebrated travel writers give us their reasons:

Paul Theroux
Anyone can sit in a room and write, but doing something extremely physical and then writing about it, that's very satisfying.

Jonathan Raban
Simple wanderlust is relatively easy to fend off, but when it starts to get tangled up with a literary motive it becomes irresistible; and literature and travel are anciently, inevitably tangled.

Miles Kington
Topographical writers are those who are interested in other places; travel writers are those who are only interested in themselves.

Travel writing has a distinct set of problems:

Jonathan Raban
The writer's working conditions tend to drive him to travel, just as they often drive him to drink.

Paul Theroux
What is required is the lucidity of loneliness to capture that vision which, however banal, seems in my private mood to be special and worthy of interest. There is something in feeling abject that quickens my mind and makes it intensely receptive to fugitive impressions.

Norah Lofts
The armchair traveller is a far more cerebral creature than the man on the spot whose mind is subject to physical concerns: will his money last out, has the last train gone, what was in that queer-looking fish that now lies so uneasily in his stomach, could that really be a bedbug? It is all too possible to look upon the Bridge of Sighs or the Leaning Tower and to be preoccupied with the site of the nearest lavatory.

> *The vicarious thrills enjoyed by armchair travellers are spiced by the question: How much of this stuff is true?*

Luke Alfred
Much travel writing hovers uncomfortably between fact and fiction. Travel books are never entirely factual, because they contain the subjective narration of dramatic incidents, but neither are they fictional, because the travel writer must nevertheless describe actual experience in real places.

· Summing up ·

To sum up the matter of non-fiction genres, who better than:

Lawrence Durrell
I've had to do a lot of potboiling in my career. Let me say this: if one stays absolutely sincere and honest towards a form ... every form thoroughly exploited and honestly dealt with is not shameful.

Chapter Ten
Publishers, Publishing and Publicity

· Publishers ·

'Part chameleon, part humming-bird ... part warrior ant'

The relationship between writers and publishers is mainly that of sparring partners:

Jacques Barzun
In spite of good will, and frequently of true friendship, Author and Publisher are natural antagonists. Authors, as everybody knows, are difficult – they are unreliable, arrogant, and grasping. But publishers are impossible – grasping, arrogant, and unreliable. Many publishing tangles come from the fact that authors and publishers are far too much alike.

Michael Legat
The list of authors who have written nastily about their publishers is lengthy and distinguished. Why there should be so much acrimony is hard to explain ... but I think it stems partly from the fact that very few authors understand much about

publishing and even more from the other fact that, as a group, authors are trusting, not to say gullible.

Jack Morpurgo
Publishers are convinced that most authors are ignorant of the techniques of the publishing craft and suspect, often with justification, that many sustain this ignorance by a lofty conviction that comprehending the technical and commercial practicalities of publishing is somehow beneath their dignity and an unnecessary distraction from their prime duty.

Mario Puzo
For hundreds of years, writers have been giving it away like warm-hearted country girls in the big city, and it is not astonishing that their lovers (that is, the publishers) balk at giving a mink coat when a pair of nylons will do the job.

Hilaire Belloc
The more enormous one's output the more the publishers get to regard you as a reliable milch cow.

A common complaint is that the old-style publisher is vanishing, to be replaced by crass commercialism ...

Irving Wallace
Most publishers are basically commercial-minded. They have no time for literary idealism.

John Hersey
Publishing has changed in my years ... [Alfred Knopf Sr] was dazzled by authorhood; he cared more about his relationship with authors than he did about his relationship with books. His concern was ... always for the growth of the person as a craftsman. Now ... the heads of firms are more apt to be businessmen.

Kurt Vonnegut
I would say that younger writers are being discriminated against because publishers are putting less money into them than they used to, and publishers aren't as patient to let writers develop now.

P D James
Publishers don't nurse you; they buy and sell you.

... though the average comment is far more vitriolic:

Mark Twain
Take an idiot man from a lunatic asylum and marry him to an idiot woman, and the fourth generation of this connection should be a good publisher from the American point of view.

Anne Bernays
Publishers never tell writers anything. They're all crazy and they drive me crazy.

Cyril Connolly
As repressed sadists are supposed to become policemen or butchers, so those with irrational fear of life become publishers.

Thomas Campbell
Now Barabbas was a publisher.

William James
Publishers are demons, there's no doubt about it.

Voltaire
I could show you all society poisoned by this class of person – a class unknown to the ancients – who, not being able to find any honest occupation, be it manual labour or service, and unluckily knowing how to read and write, become the brokers of literature, live on our works, steal our manuscripts, falsify them, and sell them.

George Bernard Shaw
I object to publishers: the one service they have done me is to teach me to do without them. They combine commercial rascality with artistic touchiness and pettiness, without being either good business men or fine judges of literature. All that is necessary in the production of a book is an author and a bookseller, without any intermediate parasite.

Brenda Maddox
The worst sin of publishers, to my mind ... is their suicidal wish not to sell the books they publish.

Jack Higgins
The last person I'd ever listen to would be a publisher. I've always found them to be wrong.

Saul Bellow
You write a book, you invest your imagination in it, and then you hand it over to a bunch of people who have no imagination and no understanding of their own enterprise.

Le Roi Jones
Publishers are usually not very intelligent, or they might be intelligent, but it's usually hard to tell. Publishers don't publish a lot of fine books they should publish.

John Irving
So much bitterness exists between writers and their publishers, you have to eliminate the distractions. You've got to keep focused.

Amanda Ros
I don't believe in publishers who wish to butter their bannocks on both sides while they'll hardly allow an author to smell treacle. I consider they are too grabby altogether and like Methodists they love to keep the Sabbath and everything else they can lay their hands on.

Miguel de Cervantes
There are men that will make you books and turn 'em loose into the world with as much dispatch as they would do a dish of fritters.

Fay Weldon
Initially I had a horrendous time. Publishers would tell you their contracts were standard and you believed them because they were nicely printed. If you were a new writer, they would take away your foreign and TV rights without telling you they existed. Once you get well known though, they tend to improve.

Richard le Gallienne
The publisher is a being slow to move, slow to take in changed conditions, always two generations, at least, behind his authors.

Roy Blount, Jr
Every author pisses and moans about his publisher.

J M Barrie
Times have changed since a certain author was executed for murdering his publisher.

Publishers' faults include myopia ...

Patrick Dennis
[*Auntie Mame*] circulated for five years, through the halls of fifteen publishers, and finally ended up with Vanguard Press, which, as you can see, is rather deep into the alphabet.

... and a tendency to entertain at the drop of a first edition:

Kazuo Ishiguro
You could almost make a career out of just going to publishers' parties [in London].

Publishers reject the vituperation, inky hands on hearts, and point out that they have their own problems ...

Stanley Unwin
Publishers are neither rogues nor philanthropists ... Publishers are much abused people. It is doubtful whether, in proportion to their numbers, any class in the community comes in for quite so much criticism, or has so much publicity given to its every shortcoming.

Jason Epstein
If publishers knew what would turn up, publishing would be a lot easier.

Kurt Vonnegut
Publishers are wary of young writers, too, because they haven't been that faithful to the publishers who have invested money in them.

... stressing the necessity for trust ...

Alfred A Knopf
Trust your publisher and he can't fail to treat you generously.

A N Wilson
It's rather important to an author to know who will be publishing their books abroad. You need to trust your publisher to make foreign deals which are appropriate.

... and the qualities that make for good editing and publishing:

Cass Canfield
The good editor or publisher is ... part chameleon, part humming-bird, tasting every literary flower, and part warrior ant.

Last words on the subject of publishers to:

Oscar Wilde
A publisher is simply a useful middle-man.

Anthony Blond
Editors have to be able to spell: publishers can be illiterate.

Gore Vidal
It is not wise to solicit the opinions of publishers – they become proud if you do.

Heinrich Heine
No author is a man of genius to his publisher.

Norman Douglas
It is with publishers as with wives: one always wants somebody else's.

Ursula le Guin
Of course most publishers are men, but most publishers now aren't even human: they're corporations.

Christopher Sinclair-Stevenson
The thing that has struck me more and more over the past five years ... is that authors want to be involved ... This can sometimes be extremely tiresome. But generally speaking, I think the author's involvement is not only a good thing, it's actually essential. It's their book. We're just tradesmen.

· Publishing ·
'Publishing is a horse race'

There are good things to say about publishing ...

John Buchan
The book-trade is a spiritual barometer of a nation's well-being.

Robert J Burdette
Books have been published for the consolation of the distressed; for the guidance of the wandering; for the relief of the destitute; for the hope of the penitent; for uplifting the burdened soul above its sorrows and fears; for the general amelioration of the condition of all mankind; for the right against wrong; for the good against bad; for the truth.

George Rainbird
Publishing can take you round the world and I made it pay for my travels. It's given me all I ever wanted from life.

Ursula le Guin
There is less sexism in book and magazine publishing than in any field I know about ... Many editors and other human beings in publishing are women or unmacho men. And thirty to fifty per cent of living authors are women. With talent and obstinacy, a woman can and will get her writing published.

Jay McInerney
[Publishing paperback originals] is applying some good marketing sense to an industry that hasn't changed in a hundred years. We're in a very vital period of fiction, and it's important to reach general readers – not just the 5 000 who are always going to pick up a book that's reviewed by the *New York Times*.

J M Barrie
The printing press is either the greatest blessing or the greatest curse of modern times, one sometimes forgets which.

... and there are bad things:

Peter Owen
Publishing is a literary mafia.

Thomas Browne
Things evidently false are not only printed, but many things of truth most falsely set forth.

John D MacDonald
If you would be thrilled by watching the galloping advance of a major glacier, you'd be ecstatic watching changes in publishing.

Richard Brautigan
I wonder whether what we are publishing now is worth cutting down trees to make paper for the stuff.

Though there is no argument over the bald fact that books, far from being literary ventures, are seen as commodities today and expected to make money:

Kingsley Amis
Since my first book was published it has got harder for a first book to be published unless it seems surer of making money than mine did. The author's importance is receding to that of supplying raw material for expert moulding and marketing.

The Economist *(on the trend towards the 'global' book):*
One early example was Alex Haley's *Roots*. Umberto Eco's *The Name of the Rose* is another. Now books by authors as diverse as Gore Vidal, John le Carré and Gabriel Garcia Marquez sell worldwide, just as records by Michael Jackson or Pavarotti do. This changing environment makes publishing look deceptively like just another entertainment business ... It relies heavily on a few hits to pay for all the misses.

Graham Watson
Publishers expect to pay for the losses of their unsuccessful books by the substantial profits on their successful ones. This also applies to the agent, but to a lesser degree. Both make most of their money from a small proportion of their authors.

Elizabeth Hardwick
I don't think it's a good idea for writers to think too much about the publishing world. I sense in a good many books, even by the best writers, an anxiety about how it will do in the market-place. You can feel it on the page, a sort of sweat of calculation.

Judith Krantz
Publishing is a horse race. And you can't not worry whether your horse will win, place or show.

George Rainbird
Those who start with a lot of money and think they're God's gift to publishing are the ones who go broke.

Publishers have to make difficult decisions:

Michael Pountney
The key decision a publisher makes is whether or not to publish. If they offload that decision on to booksellers ... their *raison d'être* disappears. Authors and agents might just as well send their manuscripts direct to the bookselling cabal, and they would then farm out the chosen twenty per cent to selected manufacturers.

Thomas Wolfe
Publishing is a very mysterious business. It is hard to predict what kind of sale or reception a book will have, and advertising seems to do very little good.

Though the system of 'previews' obviates some of the guess-work for American publishers:

J A Sutherland
There is something characteristically premature about the way in which Americans put their books out. Books are often paid for before they are written; editors interfere with them before they are complete; the Kirkus Book Service ... offers a 'tip-sheet' assessment of books months before their publication ... 'Previews' are thus much more important than reviews.

But however daunted by the economics of publishing, writers should never forget that the industry depends on us, and talent will out in the end:

Doris Lessing
It does no harm to repeat, as often as you can, 'Without me the literary industry would not exist.'

Alan Garner
When you start, the world of publishing seems like a great cathedral citadel of talent, resisting attempts to let you inside. It isn't like that at all. It may be more difficult now, and take longer than when I started to write, but there's a great, empty warehouse out there looking for simple talent.

Kurt Vonnegut
I am persuaded that anybody who writes awfully well is going to be published because readers are going to like these books. The thing is to write compellingly and you're going to do very well.

Publication

'Publication is the male equivalent of childbirth'

There are few highs for a writer equal to the thrill of being published ...

Hortense Calisher
First publication is a pure, carnal leap into that dark which one dreams is life.

Publication is ...

... the auction of the Mind of Man. **Emily Dickinson**

... a self-invasion of privacy. **Marshall McLuhan**

... the male equivalent of childbirth. **Richard Acland**

J M Barrie
For several days after my first book was published I carried it about in my pocket, and took surreptitious peeps at it to make sure the ink had not faded.

Andy Rooney
Having a book published is one of the all-time most satisfying experiences. It can't be matched by 10 000 hours of appearing on television. There it is, that tidy little package that represents so much of yourself.

Hortense Calisher
Not yet published a writer lies in the womb ... waiting for the privilege to breathe. Outside is the great, exhaling company of those who have expressed.

... not to mention being able to admire your own books on the shelves of book shops, and to dispense them to friends:

Catullus
> Here's my small book out, nice and new,
> Fresh-bound – who shall I give it to?

Charles Lamb
A presentation copy ... is a copy of a book which does not sell, sent you by the author, with his foolish autograph at the beginning of it; for which, if a stranger, he only demands your friendship; if a brother author, he expects from you a book of yours, which does not sell in return.

Though there is a down side to publication:

Calvin Trillin
As part of my research for *An Anthology of Authors' Atrocity Stories About Publishers*, I conducted a study ... that showed the average shelf-life of a trade book to be somewhere between milk and yogurt. It is true that some books by Harold Robbins ... last longer on the shelves, but they contain preservatives.

Sherwood Anderson
When a man publishes a book, there are so many stupid things said that he declares he'll never do it again. The praise is almost always worse than the criticism.

Jane Gardam
Once it is published a novel is no longer your own. Like your child (and sometimes you don't like your child) it leaves you to reveal new things about itself to new people.

Konrad Lorenz
During the final stages of publishing a paper or book, I always feel strongly repelled by my own writing ... it appears increasingly hackneyed and banal and less worth publishing.

Edna St Vincent Millay
A person who publishes a book wilfully appears before the populace with his pants down ... If it is a good book nothing can hurt him. If it is a bad book, nothing can help him.

Kingsley Amis
We authors like having a say in our jackets; but while the thing can still be changed, not after ... We like blurbs to get our characters' names right and also not to give away any little surprises our plot may have up its sleeve ... And we know all about the boldly illiterate copy-editing, the printer's 'corrections' let in after that, the garbled, unproofed biographical note, the boobs and bad choice in the publicity quotes, above all constantly finding us too far away at the end of a telephone.

Last words on publication to:

Doris Lessing
The act of getting a story or a novel published is an act of communication, an attempt to impose one's personality and beliefs on other people.

William Gass
I publish a piece in order to kill it, so that I won't have to fool around with it any longer.

Katherine Anne Porter
I think it is a curious lack of judgment to publish before you are ready. If there are echoes of other people in your work, you're not ready. If anybody has to help you rewrite your story, you're not ready. A story should be a finished work before it is shown.

Fran Lebowitz
Having been unpopular in high school is not just cause for book publication.

P D James
Don't you know that when a writer can no longer be published she may as well be dead?

Duke of Wellington *(in 1825, when an ex-mistress threatened to tell of their affair in her memoirs):*
Publish and be damned!

Richard Ingrams
My own motto is publish and be sued.

John Creasey
Never buy an editor or publisher a lunch or a drink until he has bought an article, story or book from you. This rule is absolute and may be broken only at your peril.

Publicity and promotion

'I've had enough publicity to last an army of super rats'

Some writers accept (and even enjoy) the necessity of promoting their books and the attendant publicity:

Truman Capote
A boy's gotta hustle his book.

Kingsley Amis
No writer, especially a young and unknown writer, resents publicity of any kind – whatever he may say.

Robertson Davies
Publishers make [publicity] tours flattering to writers whose home life may not be luxurious. The successful author is carried from place to place on a silver tray; air tickets and private cars are provided; he stays at good hotels and may eat and drink himself into a stupor if he is silly enough to do it.

Joseph Heller
I make no secret of it. I love to have my novels acknowledged; I love getting good reviews, and the whole publicity process.

Joyce Cary
It is very pleasant to be written up, even by a writer.

Some have mixed feelings:

Ray Bradbury
The publicity is pleasant, but it never belongs to you. You're never quite convinced the name on that printed page is you.

Mary Stewart
Sometimes I am recognised and I love it and hate it. I hate publicity, but love it when people know my name and say, 'Aren't you the author?' ... This feeds my vanity and is a very necessary food. It restores my self-confidence which, as you know, we writers haven't got much of.

Harold Brodkey
Without publicity you lose the sense of an audience that has learned how to read you, or not. Everyone waits not so much for the book as for the essays and talk about the book.

Some can't see the necessity of publicity at all, disliking the invasion of privacy:

Rosellen Brown
I get very tired of reading about writers, I don't even understand why people want to read novels about them. There's apparently some glamour, but I'll be damned if I can see it.

E M Forster
I am more interested in works than in authors.

Michael Ondaatje *(after co-winning the Booker Prize)*:
I think it's easier to write out of anonymity.

Malcolm Bradbury
Success is at the other side of that vast fissure that for me has always opened up between the lonely self that actually does the writing and the second self that has to represent and personalise its outcome.

Roy Blount Jnr
To promote a book you are expected to get it up eight or ten times a day, sometimes in Philadelphia.

John Updike
I'm interviewed too much. I fight them off, but even one is too many. In any interview, you do say more or less than you mean. You leave the proper ground of your strength and become one more gassy monologist.

Mary Stewart
What I hate about modern publicity is the notion that if you are good at your particular trade – and my trade is writing – then you must be Sir Oracle on everything else; and you find yourself on television being asked your opinion on things you know nothing whatever about.

John le Carré

The press cast me increasingly as the master spy, and there wasn't much I could do to stop them. So I learned to keep my distance from them, and get on with my fictions in my own way. It was no loss. If you have ever been a diplomat, you have learned to loathe the press for life anyway, and the compliment is cordially returned.

Julian Barnes

It's like that nowadays. People assume they own part of you, on no matter how small an acquaintance; while if you are reckless enough to write a book, this puts your bank account, your medical records, and the state of your marriage irrevocably into the public domain.

Candia McWilliam

Confronted with the problem of whether to be or not to be hyped, most authors who want to earn a living and are feeling reasonably tough decide to grin and bare it ... There is no point in being snooty about publicity, if it works, but a writer who believes in his own publicity is probably sunk. It is easy in the artificial world of hype to forget its purpose: to nudge readers who would not, without it, be readers.

And many are cynical about the process:

Truman Capote

I've had enough publicity to last an army of super rats. I don't know anybody who gets as much publicity as I do for doing nothing.

H L Mencken

A writer is always admired most, not by those who have read him, but by those who have merely heard about him.

Martin Amis

The truth is that we are more interested in writers than we are in writing. A writer is much easier to understand than a body of work.

Doris Lessing

Writers these days see themselves as showbiz entertainers and this makes them very competitive. All that literary malice is very new. When I was young we didn't crave instant success and recognition; we certainly didn't write with the idea of getting the Booker Prize.

David Lodge
There is a risk that the aesthetic status of the novel is diminished by all the gossip surrounding it.

Bill Adler
If your publisher promises you a full-page ad in the *New York Times*, get it in writing ...When you are interviewed by a talk-show host, don't expect the host to have read your book.

Joyce Grenfell
Have you read my book, Mr Wimble? No, I know it is so difficult to find time to read what one really wants to. No, it was only since you have so kindly invited me to come on to your television programme in order to discuss my book I thought – you know – that you might just possibly have read it.

Philip Roth
All this talk about ourselves, all these symposiums and pronouncements – sometimes I have the feeling that everybody is out reading the interviews and nobody's at home with the novels.

New writers have an extra problem: it is difficult to get written about nowadays, since both book editors and reviewers are only too aware of their precarious situation between the twin rocks of commercial expectations and dwindling numbers of readers:

Jonathan Raban
Many first novels, carrying all their authors' hopes with them, fail to get a single review. Many more get only a mention at the end of the weekly round-up ...Too few people, with too little space at their disposal, are responsible for recognising new writing, and, by recognising it, enabling the second, third, fourth novel to be written.

The general attitude, however, is that authors should grit their teeth and submit with good grace to the publicity attendant on publication and fame. In other words – flash the necessary smiles, give the interviews and sign the books with good grace, then shut up and go back to your writing.

Last words on publicity to:

E M Forster
Some reviews give pain. That is regrettable, but no author has any right to whine. He was not obliged to be an author. He invited publicity, and he must take the publicity that comes along.

Charles Newman
If a writer proclaims himself as isolated, uninfluenced and responsible to no one, he should not be surprised if he is ignored, uninfluential, and perceived as irresponsible.

Jay McInerney
As far as I can tell, the only healthy attitude for a writer is to consider praise, blame, book chat, and table position at Elaine's irrelevant to the writing, and to get on with it.

Gabriel Garcia Marquez
It is much more important to write than to be written about.

More Quotes

Chapter Eleven

Critics & Criticism

· Critics ·

*'Like eunuchs in a harem ... Haunters of unquiet graves ...
Tickbirds of the literary rhinoceros ... Race of cockchafers'*

A critic is ...

... a man who knows the way but can't drive the car. **Kenneth Tynan**

... a legless man who teaches running. **Channing Pollock**

... a man who expects miracles. **James Gibbons Huneker**

... a man who writes about things he doesn't like. **H L Mencken**

... a man created to praise greater men than himself, but he is never able to find them. **Richard le Gallienne**

... a necessary evil, and criticism is an evil necessity. **Carolyn Wells**

... a gong at a railroad crossing clanging loudly and vainly as the train goes by. **Christopher Morley**

... a haunter of unquiet graves. He tries to evoke the presence of a living art, but usually succeeds only in disturbing the peace of the dead. **M J C Hodgart**

Critics are ...

... like pigs at the pastry cart. **John Updike**

... like fleas: they love clean linen and adore any form of lace. **Gustave Flaubert**

... like brushers of noblemen's clothes. **Francis Bacon**

... like eunuchs in a harem: they know how it's done, they've seen it done every day, but they're unable to do it themselves. **Brendan Behan**

As can be seen by the above, critics are not favourite people. Reactions to them range from vigorous vilification ...

Gustave Flaubert
Critics! Eternal mediocrity living off genius by denigrating and exploiting it! Race of cockchafers slashing the finest pages of art to shreds!

Edward Young *(of literary critics):*
> Hot, envious, noisy, proud, the scribbling fry
> Burn, hiss and bounce, waste paper, stink, and die.

François Rabelais
As for you, little envious Prigs, snarling, bastard, puny Criticks, you'll soon have railed your last: Go hang yourselves.

Ben Jonson
There be some men born only to suck out the poison of books.

C N Bovee
There is probably no hell for authors in the next world – they suffer so much from critics and publishers in this one.

... to scorn ...

Cyril Garbett
Any fool can criticise, and many of them do.

Irwin Shaw
There's an almost unavoidable feeling of smugness, of self-satisfaction, of teacher's pettishness, that sinks into a critic's bones.

Samuel Johnson
There is a certain race of men that either imagine it their duty, or make it their amusement, to hinder the reception of every work of learning or genius, who stand as sentinels in the avenues of fame, and value themselves upon giving Ignorance and Envy the first notice of a prey.

Doris Lessing
There is always, in any culture where there are praised writers and artists, a sump or a well of hatred for them, and always people are ready to do them down.

George Jean Nathan
Show me a critic without prejudices, and I'll show you an arrested cretin.

Eugene O'Neill *(of critics)*:
I love every bone in their heads.

... to comparison with animals and insects ...

Jonathan Miller
If you were ever to say as much about critics as they have said about me, there would be a porcine squeal as they slither with their dirty little trotters in their zinc troughs.

John Irving
I have a friend who says that reviewers are the tickbirds of the literary rhinoceros – but he is being kind. Tickbirds perform a valuable service to the rhino and the rhino hardly notices the birds. Reviewers perform no service to the writer and are noticed too much.

J B Priestley
They will review a book by a writer much older than themselves as if it were an over-ambitious essay by a second-year student ... It is the little dons I complain about, like so many corgis trotting up, hoping to nip your ankles.

Christopher Hampton
Asking a working writer what he thinks about critics is like asking a lamp-post how it feels about dogs.

John Steinbeck
These curious sucker fish who live with joyous vicariousness on other men's work and discipline with dreary words the thing which feeds them.

Mark Twain
The critic's symbol should be the tumble-bug; he deposits his egg in somebody else's dung, otherwise he could not hatch it.

Friedrich Nietzsche
Insects sting, not from malice, but because they want to live. It is the same with critics – they desire our blood, not our pain.

Anton Pavlovitch
Critics are like horse-flies which prevent the horse from ploughing.

J B Priestley
The greater part of critics are parasites, who, if nothing had been written, would find nothing to write.

... to heartfelt moans:

Nelson Algren
To literary critics a book is assumed to be guilty until it proves itself innocent.

Frank Moore Colby
Many a critic seems more like a committee framing resolutions than a man writing down what he likes.

Ernest Hemingway
One battle doesn't make a campaign, but critics treat one book, good or bad, like a whole war.

Mickey Spillane
Why did all these giants descend on me and my little stories? I wasn't doing anything of national import. All I was trying to do was entertain the public and make a buck.

Few (and mostly French) are the voices raised in their defence:

Molière
There is no reward so delightful, no pleasure so exquisite, as having one's work known and acclaimed by those whose applause confers honour.

François Mauriac
A good critic is the sorcerer that makes some hidden spring gush forth unexpectedly under our feet.

Anatole France
A good critic is one who narrates the adventures of his mind among masterpieces.

John Crosby
[The critic] is forced to be literate about the illiterate, witty about the witless and coherent about the incoherent.

Jean Rostand
Sometimes an admirer spends more talent extolling a work than the author did in creating it.

Most writers, indeed, believe themselves superior beings to critics ...

William Faulkner
The artist is a cut above the critic, for the artist is writing something which will move the critic. The critic is writing something which will move everybody but the artist.

Gustave Flaubert
A man is a critic when he cannot be an artist, in the same way that a man becomes an informer when he cannot be a soldier.

Samuel Johnson
A fly, Sir, may sting a stately horse and make him wince; but one is but an insect, and the other is a horse still.

... and vice versa:

Octavio Paz
After 1950, there had been a fresh cultural development – not just in France, in fact, but throughout the world. This was the seizure of power by the professors, the new pre-eminence of critics over creators. The theoreticians had managed to drive out the poets and the novelists.

Some say that writers don't make good critics and shouldn't involve themselves in the nitpicking details of Lit Crit ...

Jim Bishop
A good writer is not, *per se*, a good book critic. No more than a good drunk is automatically a good bartender.

Lillian Hellman
I am not an intelligent critic of those I like. It is not that I am overgenerous or over-loyal, it's that their work ... is too close to what I know about them ... and thus I am

so occupied by the revelations of the author ... that I cannot be cool about the work itself.

Max Beerbohm
[George Bernard] Shaw's judgments are often scatter-brained, but at least he has brains to scatter.

Malcolm Bradbury
Writers normally do well not to become enmeshed in totalistic explanations of language, text, and history, the business of critical commissariats; these rarely link in with the intimate experiences of writing.

... and the view is widely held that critics are mostly failed writers:

Benjamin Disraeli
You know who critics are – the men who have failed in literature and art.

Samuel Taylor Coleridge
Reviewers are usually people who would have been poets, historians, biographers ... if they could; they have tried their talents at one or at the other, and have failed; therefore they turn critics.

Though **T S Eliot** *disagrees:*
The only critics worth reading are the critics who practise, and practise well, the art of which they write.

Sarcasm rules when it comes to defining characteristics:

Hortense Calisher
An artist is born kneeling; he fights to stand. A critic, by nature of the judgment seat, is born sitting.

A E Housman
It has become apparent what the modern conservative critic really is: a creature moving about in worlds not realised. His trade is one which requires, that it may be practised in perfection, two qualifications only: ignorance of language and abstinence from thought.

Danny Abse
Passionately held political convictions are likely to unhinge one who sets himself up as a literary critic, especially if he lacks a sense of humour.

Richard Eder
The critic's job is ... confining, frequently enervating, often beguiling, and generally exposed. There is some resemblance to working in a coal mine. The work is done in the dark, it is done alone, and the roof keeps falling in.

David Lister
All critics live in a world of virtual reality, seldom sharing an equal experience with the rest of the audience. The literary variety speed-read where the rest of us take an almost sensual pleasure in poring over a novel.

John Steinbeck
Time is the only critic without ambition.

Christopher Hope
There is no more discerning critic than one who knows your material better than you do, no harsher judge of the missed accent, the needless modulation, the imperfect rhyme, the parading of sentiment in place of real emotion, of the spuriously poetical, the pretentious, and the silly.

Gabriel Garcia Marquez
Critics are for me the biggest example of what intellectualism is. First of all, they have a theory of what a writer should be. They try to get the writer to fit their model, and if he doesn't fit, they still try to get him in by force.

Bernard Malamud
I dislike particularly those critics who preach their aesthetic or ideological doctrines at you. What's important to them is not what the writer has done but how it fits, or doesn't fit, the thesis they want to develop. Nobody can tell a writer what can or ought to be done ... in his fiction.

Penelope Gilliatt
Critics are probably more prone to clichés than fiction writers who pluck things out of the air.

And there are variations of opinion as to a critic's duties, methods, modus and function:

Michael Roberts
The critic's first duty is neither to condemn nor to praise, but to elucidate technique and meaning.

James Russell Lowell
A wise scepticism is the first attribute of a good critic.

Eugène Ionesco
The critic should describe, and not prescribe.

V S Pritchett
I think the critic must first of all clear his own mind. Someone who has worked on a book, perhaps for years, and succeeded in getting it published, must have some quality. What is it? The critic has to sort him out and look for his merits.

H L Mencken
The critic, to interpret his artist, even to understand his artist, must be able to get into the mind of his artist; he must feel and comprehend the vast pressure of the creative passion.

John Gardner
If a critic is concerned with only how well the sentences go, or how neat the symbolic structure is, or how new the devices are, he's going to exaggerate the importance of mediocre books.

Joseph Addison
A true critic ought to dwell rather upon excellencies than imperfections, to discover the concealed beauties of a writer, and communicate to the world such things as are worth their observation.

Allen Ginsberg
A lot of critics ... seem to take pride in showing how smart they are through put-downs. It's not helpful. You should be pointing arrows toward the road you want to be on.

Mark Schorer
Critics of literature have the same essential function as teachers of literature; this is not to direct the judgement of the audience, but to assist the audience in those disciplines of reading on which any meaningful judgement must rest.

T S Eliot
It is part of the business of the critic to preserve tradition – where a good tradition exists. It is part of his business to see literature steadily and to see it whole; and this is eminently to see it not as consecrated by time, but to see it beyond time; to see the best work of our time and the best work of twenty-five hundred years ago with the same eyes.

Fintan O'Toole
Critics should be honest enough to accept that they represent nobody but themselves – not the art form, not even in any real sense the newspapers that employ them. Their job is not to report on how a work was received by an audience. It is not to sell books or tickets. It is not to reform or mould the practise of theatre or music or poetry. And it is not to maintain, as arbiters of taste and value, the authority of the institutions who print their opinions. The job of the critic is to try to ignore the magnifying effect of print and hyperbole, to preserve a sense of proportion, and to give a genuinely individual opinion. It is a modest but by no means contemptible task. And it is one that is inextricable from the artistic process itself.

There is sound advice on how to handle critics:

Jean Sibelius
Pay no attention to what the critics say; no statue has ever been put up to a critic.

Rainer Maria Rilke
I never read anything concerning my work. I feel that criticism is a letter to the public which the author, since it is not directed to him, does not have to open and read.

John Berryman
I would recommend the cultivation of extreme indifference to both praise and blame because praise will lead you to vanity, and blame will lead you to self-pity, and both are bad for writers.

Somerset Maugham
It is salutary to train oneself to be no more affected by censure than by praise.

Dick Francis
I pay no attention to critics. I don't pretend to write great literature.

Truman Capote
I've developed a very thick skin about criticism. I've had to. I can read the most devastating things about myself now, and it doesn't make my pulse skip a beat.

Evelyn Waugh
Most writers in the course of their careers become thick-skinned and learn to accept vituperation, which in any other profession would be unimaginably offensive, as a healthy counterpoise to unintelligent praise.

Thornton Wilder
The important thing is that you make sure that neither the favourable nor the unfavourable critics move into your head and take part in the composition of your next work.

Andrew Greeley
Don't give up, because those who don't like your work may very well be wrong. And after you're published, don't pay any attention to the critics.

Shirley Hazzard
There will always be those who seize on an open expression of thought or feeling as if it were self-exposure ... But one can't concern oneself with that sort of thing – one would end up peering over one's defences, as if knowledge and opinion were an armed camp.

Truman Capote
Never demean yourself by talking back to a critic, never. Write those letters to the editor in your head, but don't put them on paper.

Bernard Baruch
Never answer a critic, unless he's right.

Tennessee Williams
The best thing you can do about critics is never say a word. In the end you have the last say, and they know it.

Jean Cocteau
Listen carefully to first criticisms made of your work. Note just what it is about your work that the critics don't like and cultivate it. That's the only part of your work that's individual and worth keeping.

James Dickey
I've known writers who are absolutely destroyed by adverse opinion, and I think this is a lot of shit. You shouldn't allow this to happen to yourself, and if you do, then it's your fault.

But however well you may deal with it, criticism still hurts ...

Arthur Miller
Criticism hurt me when I had failures. I thought: I'll never write another play. But I'm an alligator. Only the alligators remain. The others get out of the water.

John Steinbeck
I don't think I am ill tempered about adverse criticism. It does seem kind of meaningless. But, do you know, you never get over the ability to have your feelings hurt by deliberately cruel and destructive attacks. Even if you know why the attack was made, it still hurts.

Peter Carey
I worry about everything. That's why bad reviews are so devastating: there isn't a single thing a bad review will say that I won't have thought.

John Updike *(on reading an unfavourable review of one of his novels)*:
My ears close up, my eyes go warm, my chest feels thin as an eggshell, my voice churns silently in my stomach.

John Mortimer
You put so much of yourself into writing, any criticism makes you feel totally exposed. It goes back to being an only child, you think you have to make an impression. I lurch from insecurity to insecurity. Anybody's more secure than writers.

Virginia Woolf
Literature is strewn with the wreckage of men who have minded beyond reason the opinion of others.

Bernard Malamud
Some of it [affects me]. Not the crap, the self-serving pieces, but an occasional insightful criticism, favourable or unfavourable, that confirms my judgement of my work.

Phyllis Reynolds Naylor
All right, so it hurts. But it is not a death sentence. It does not say that you will never write a good novel as long as you live. As novelists – observers or listeners – we of all people should trust our ability to grow and change.

... as does being ignored by the critics:

May Sarton
I hope I'm a good writer, but the critics have no handle on what I am because not many distinguished writers work in as many forms as I do. That's why I feel I'm brushed aside by the most important reviewers, not taken as seriously as I'd like.

The ability to criticise your own work is a necessity for all creative people, not only writers:

P G Wodehouse
I do think one can learn from criticism. In fact, I'm a pretty good critic of my own work. I know when it isn't as good as it ought to be.

Anthony Burgess
When critics express a like, or even greater, dissatisfaction, I can only nod glumly in agreement. The horrid truth, though, is that one cannot really make oneself any better. The results in one's work are less faults of artistic application than inbuilt and inextricable flaws in one's personal make-up.

William Styron
There's only one person a writer should listen to, pay any attention to. It's not any damn critic. It's the reader. And that doesn't mean any compromise or sell-out. The writer must criticise his own work as a reader.

And so we come to the hundred dollar question: do critics help writers – or not?

Stephen King
I think that you really ought to listen to the critics, because sometimes they're telling you something is broken that you can fix ... None of us like 'em, but if they're all saying something's a piece of junk, they're right.

Joyce Carol Oates
Critics sometimes appear to be addressing themselves to works other than those I remember writing.

Françoise Sagan
When the articles were agreeable, I read them through. I never learned anything at all from them but I was astonished by their imagination and fecundity. They saw intentions I never had.

Robert Morley
If the critics were always right we should be in deep trouble.

Tom Stoppard
I remember my play *M Is For Moon* mainly because it received a passing favourable mention in a newspaper on a day when, riding on the top deck of a bus ... my con-

fidence had dropped to zero. I got on the bus a writer without hope and got off the bus feeling I could write anything.

What about the readers, then?

Gabriel Garcia Marquez
[Critics] have claimed for themselves the task of being intermediaries between the author and the reader. I've always tried to be a very clear and precise writer, trying to reach the reader directly without having to go through the critic.

Doris Lessing
My attitude towards criticism is it is of no use to writers and of not much use to readers. It may be of use to other critics ... To the people who actually read books and enjoy them, finding use for them, it is quite irrelevant.

Last words on critics to:

Gustave Flaubert
How rare it is to see a critic who knows what he's talking about!

Mario Puzo
Never show your work to a friend; only to a teacher. A friend may tell you what you want to hear. Only a teacher can tell you what you need to hear.

Kenneth Tynan
Western man, especially the Western critic, still finds it very hard to go into print and say: 'I recommend you to go and see this because it gave me an erection.'

Vladimir Nabokov
It's a short walk from the hallelujah to the hoot.

Robert Hughes
In England you can dump on God, Churchill or Prince Charles, but touch Jane Austen and you're toast.

Criticism

'I love criticism just so long as it's unqualified praise'

The act (art?) of criticism is variously defined and practised:

Elia Kazan
Criticism – a big bite out of someone's back.

Frank Moore Colby
The main use in criticism is in showing what manner of man the critic is.

Criticism is …

… the art of praise. **Richard le Gallienne**

… easy, art is difficult. **Philippe Destouches**

… prejudice made plausible. **H L Mencken**

… a study by which men grow important and formidable at very small expense. **Samuel Johnson**

… the art wherewith a critic tries to guess himself into a share of the artist's fame. **George Jean Nathan**

Arthur Symons
The aim of criticism is to distinguish what is essential in the work of a writer. It is the delight of a critic to praise; but praise is scarcely part of his duty … What we ask of him is that he should find out for us more than we can find out for ourselves.

Randall Jarrell
An age of criticism is not an age of writing, nor an age of reading … People still read, still write – and well; but for many of them it is the act of criticism which has become the representative or archetypal act of the intellectual.

H L Mencken
Anyone can be accurate and even profound, but it is damned hard work to make criticism charming.

And literary criticism is in a class of its own:

Jonathan Raban
It is in the reviews, more than in seminar-rooms ... that the main dialogue about modern literature is sustained, that new writers are discovered, old ones revalued, that standards of comparison are established and the essential small-talk of literary culture goes on.

Tim Couzens
I could be cynical and say I am glad that so many critics are currently obsessed with pure theory since it gives the few of us who plough our own furrows an emptier field. But it does sadden me, too ... There is not enough fun in our literary criticism.

John Davidson
Literary criticism is constantly attempting a very absurd thing – the explanation of passionate utterance by utterance that is unimpassioned: it is like trying to paint a sunset in lamp-black.

John Updike
Writing criticism is to writing fiction and poetry as hugging the shore is to sailing the open sea.

Doris Lessing
Most literary criticism is just sheer bloody-minded malice.

Criticism can, however, be uplifting and instructive ...

Charles Caleb Colton
Criticism is like champagne: nothing more execrable if bad, nothing more excellent if good; if meagre, muddy, vapid, and sour, both are fit only to engender colic and wind; but if rich, generous and sparkling, they communicate together in a glow of the spirits, improve the taste, expand the heart, and are worthy of being introduced at the symposium of the gods.

George Jean Nathan
Criticism is the windows and chandeliers of art: it illuminates the enveloping darkness in which art might otherwise rest only vaguely discernible, and perhaps altogether unseen.

Vladimir Nabokov
Criticism can be instructive in the sense that it gives readers, including the author of the book, some information about the critic's intelligence, or honesty, or both ... I find criticism most instructive when an expert proves to me that my facts or my grammar are wrong.

Truman Capote
Before publication, and if provided by persons whose judgement you trust, yes, of course criticism helps.

Robert Martin Adams
It is through the vigilant, the militant use of our critical faculties that we can confer any real benefit on the authors whom we love.

... though there are many who curse and damn it ...

Hilaire Belloc
Of all the fatiguing, futile, empty trades, the worst, I suppose, is writing about writing.

Gustave Flaubert
Criticism occupies the lowest place in the literary hierarchy: as regards form, almost always; and as regards moral value, incontestably. It comes after rhyming-games and acrostics, which at least require a certain inventiveness.

Molière
There is no fate more distressing for an artist than to have to show himself off before fools, to see his work exposed to the criticism of the vulgar and ignorant.

... or bemoan the state of modern criticism:

G K Chesterton
A great deal of contemporary criticism reads to me like a man saying: 'Of course I do not like green cheese; I am very fond of brown sherry.'

C Day-Lewis
I cannot feel happy about that school of modern criticism which treats literature as a mine-field, to be approached in a suspicious attitude, with infinite caution ... nor do I believe the chief task of the critic to be the exploding of reputations, however scientific the instruments employed.

And writers have valid objections ...

George Orwell
Prolonged, indiscriminate reviewing of books involves constantly *inventing* reactions towards books about which one has no spontaneous feelings whatever.

George Santayana
To substitute judgments of fact for judgments of value, is a sign of pedantic and borrowed criticism.

John Cheever
The whole business [academic criticism] is a subsidiary undertaking, like extracting useful chemicals from smoke.

Jonathan Raban
As with cartoons, there's a congenital streak of cruelty in the form of the review ... The reviewer, especially if he's new to the job and trying to make his name, finds a style of pert mockery ready and waiting for him like an off-the-peg suit. The style is boisterously smartyboots in tone and fake-Augustan in its grammar.

... often tinged with understandable sarcasm:

Blaise Pascal
We find fault with perfection itself.

Ralph Waldo Emerson
Taking to pieces is the trade of those who cannot construct.

George Santayana
Tomes of aesthetic criticism hang on a few moments of real delight and intuition.

Lorrie Moore
Later on in life you will learn that writers are merely open, helpless texts with no real understanding of what they have written and therefore must half-believe anything and everything that is said of them.

Most writers have firm ideas on what criticism should – and should not – be:

Ralph Waldo Emerson
Criticism should not be querulous and wasting, all knife and root-puller, but guiding, instructive, inspiring, a south wind, not an east wind.

George Jean Nathan
Impersonal criticism is like an impersonal fist fight or an impersonal marriage, and as successful.

Henry Miller
Honest criticism means nothing; what one wants is unrestrained passion, fire for fire.

Arthur Symons
While there is a great mass of valuable criticism done by critics, the most valuable criticism of all, the only quite essential criticism, has been done by creative writers, for the most part poets.

Leo Tolstoy *(to a friend)*:
Don't praise my book! ... I ask you, be a friend; either do not write to me about the book at all, or else write and tell me everything that is wrong with it. If it is true, as I feel, that my powers are weakening, then, I beg of you, tell me. Our profession is dreadful, writing corrupts the soul. Every author is surrounded by an aura of adulation which he nurses so assiduously that he cannot begin to judge his own worth or see when it starts to decline.

And then there are the pragmatists who say that they don't mind criticism at all, as long as it is favourable:

Noël Coward
I love criticism just so long as it's unqualified praise.

Mark Twain
I like criticism, but it must be my way.

Somerset Maugham

People ask you for criticism, but they only want praise.

Truman Capote
After something is published all I want to read or hear is praise. Anything less is a bore, and I'll give you fifty dollars if you produce a writer who can honestly say he was ever helped by the prissy carpings and condescensions of reviewers.

Jeanette Winterson
Praise and blame are much the same for the writer. One is better for your vanity, but neither gets you much further with your work.

Last words on criticism to:

Terry McMillan
The bottom line is I told the story I wanted to tell. And so my attitude is this – I'm willing to take whatever criticism happens as a result. I put myself out there. I will take, handle and deal with any kind of criticism I get, if I choose to.

Ogden Nash
I don't care how unkind the things people say about me are so long as they don't say them to my face.

Marvin Harris
I don't see how you can write anything of value if you don't offend someone.

William Phillips
Boredom, after all, is a form of criticism.

George Eliot
It seems to me much better to read a man's own writing than to read what others say about him, especially when the man is first-rate and the 'others' are third-rate.

Doris Lessing
Why don't you read what I have written and make up your own mind about what you think, testing it against your own life, your own experience?

More Quotes

Chapter Twelve

Epilogue

· Some closing quotes ·

We – the compiler, editor and publisher – hope that you have not only been amused and diverted, but positively inspired by our collection. If just one would-be writer leaps up shouting 'Eureka!' and dashes off a manuscript that gets published, we will be delighted. If a whole bevy of writers is stimulated to embark on the mysterious process that leads to successful authorship, we will be overjoyed, for there will never be enough readable books.

At all costs, we must avoid the situation prognosticated tongue-in-cheek by:

Alan Bennett
Books are on their way out nowadays ... Words are on their last legs ... The sentence, that dignified entity with subject and predicate, is shortly to be made illegal. Wherever two or three words are gathered together, you see, there is a grave danger that thought might be present. All assemblies of words will be forbidden, in favour of patterns of light, videotape, every man his own telecine.

Though there are, serendipitously, those who disagree:

D T Max
The book has great advantages over the computer: it is light and it's cheap. That it has changed little in over 400 years suggests an uncommonly apt design ... You can drop

a book in the bathtub, dry it out on the radiator, and still read it. You can put it in the attic, pull it out 200 years later, and probably decipher the words. You can curl up in bed with it or get suntan lotion on it. These are definitely not possibilities suggested by the computer. However much dictionaries and encyclopaedias might be superseded, a well-thumbed paperback blowing in a beach breeze represents a technological stronghold the computer may never invade.

John Irving
It seems to me the book has not just aesthetic values – the charming little clothy box of the thing, the smell of the glue, even the print, which has its own beauty. But there's something about the sensation of ink on paper that is in some sense a ... phenomenon.

The road ahead for would-be writers will not be easy:

Mary Wesley
Writing is much harder than it may seem. I've been lucky. I wouldn't recommend it for anyone.

Ernest Hemingway
The better you write the harder it is because every story has to be better than the last one. It's the hardest work there is.

Lillian Hellman
Nothing you write, if you hope to be any good, will ever come out as you first hoped.

But there is no lack of sage advice from those who have gone before:

Gustave Flaubert
The author in his book must be like God in his universe, everywhere present and nowhere visible.

John Gardner
Mastery is not something that strikes in an instant, like a thunderbolt, but a gathering power that moves through time, like weather.

Kurt Vonnegut
You say what you have to say. But you have to learn to say it in such a way that the reader can see what you mean.

Epilogue

Edward de Bono *(on how to write a book):*
The first stage is to sit down and write random notes as rapidly as possible. Use a fresh sheet of paper for each new train of thought. The next stage is to go back, read the notes and pick out chapters. Number the chapters and at the top of each sheet of notes put the number of the chapter it will go in ... Pick a chapter, revise your notes, sit down and write. The main thing is to keep the style simple ... [and] also avoid adjectives as much as possible. The aim is not to have everything so detailed that it becomes very boring to write it all down. You want to surprise yourself as well as the reader. That is the fun of writing. When you start a sentence, you may not know how it's going to end. You're after a dynamic flow rather than a series of static points ... The key thing is the discipline not to try to make it perfect. Never reread anything. Once you start reading it over, you modify one thing and then the next thing doesn't balance and you have to adjust that, rather like trimming sideburns.

Very last words to ...

Doris Lessing
In an age of committee art, public art, people may begin to feel again a need for the small personal voice; and this will feed confidence into writers and, with confidence because of the knowledge of being needed, the warmth and humanity and love of people which is essential for a great age of literature.

Athol Fugard
There is no life to beat a writer's, if you've had success.

The idea is simply to keep going:

Clare Francis
I'll stay with writing. It's been my full-time occupation for fourteen years and, like with most writers, it's a love–hate relationship but I can't let it go. Writers never retire, they go on and on.

Marguerite Duras
Yes, she writes, does Marguerite Duras. She has her pens and pencils, and she writes. That's it ... Nothing more.

Rainer Maria Rilke
This before all: ask yourself in the quietest hour of your night: must I write? Dig down into yourself for a deep answer. And if this should be in the affirmative, if you

may meet this solemn question with a strong and simple, I must, then build your life according to this necessity.

You'll never know what you can do unless you try:

Lewis Carroll
'I can't believe that,' Alice said.

'Can't you?' the Queen said in a pitying tone. 'Try again: draw a long breath, and shut your eyes.'

Alice laughed. 'There's no use trying,' she said: 'one can't believe impossible things.'

'I daresay you haven't had much practice,' said the Queen. 'When I was your age, I always did it for half-an-hour a day. Why, sometimes I've believed as many as six impossible things before breakfast.'

Frank Kermode
Good books can happen to good writers anywhere.

· Postscript ·

J M Barrie
It is all very well to be able to write books, but can you waggle your ears?

Bibliography

The Agony and the Ego, edited by Clare Boylan (Penguin, 1993).

An Author's Guide to Publishing by Michael Legat (Robert Hale, 1982).

Bloomsbury Guide to English Literature, edited by Marion Wynne-Davies (Bloomsbury, 1989).

Bloomsbury Treasury of Quotations, edited by John Daintith & Anne Stibbs (Bloomsbury, 1994).

The Book of Quotes compiled by Barbara Rowes (Dutton, 1979).

Collins Dictionary of Literary Quotations, compiled by Meic Stephens (HarperCollins, 1991).

The Concise Oxford Dictionary of Literary Terms by Chris Baldick (Oxford University Press, 1990).

Conversations : Interviews with Australian Writers, edited by Paul Kavanagh & Peter Kuch (Imprint, 1991).

Dancing at the Edge of the World by Ursula le Guin (Paladin, 1992).

A Dictionary of Literary Terms by J A Cuddon (Penguin, 1982).

Flaubert's Parrot by Julian Barnes (Picador, 1985).

For Love & Money by Jonathan Raban (Picador, 1988).

Good Advice on Writing, edited by William Safire and Leonard Safir (Simon & Schuster, 1992).

International Thesaurus of Quotations, compiled by Rhoda Thomas Tripp (Penguin, 1976).

The New Penguin Dictionary of Quotations, compiled by J M & M J Cohen (Penguin, 1992).

The Novel Today, edited by Malcolm Bradbury (Fontana, 1990).

Novels & Novelists, edited by Martin Seymour-Smith (Windward).

On Being a Writer, intro by Will Blythe (Writer's Digest Books, 1989).

The Oxford Dictionary of Quotations, second edition, third impression (Oxford University Press, 1956).

Personal Best 2: Stories and Statements by Australian Writers, edited by Garry Disher (Imprint, 1991).

The Pleasure of Reading, edited by Antonia Fraser (Bloomsbury, 1992).

Scribblers for Bread by George Greenfield (Hodder & Stoughton, 1989).

A Small Personal Voice by Doris Lessing, edited by Paul Schlueter (Flamingo, 1994).

Under My Skin & Walking in the Shade by Doris Lessing (HarperCollins, 1994 & 1997).

The Way To Write by John Fairfax & John Moat (Elm Tree Books, 1981).

The Writer's Chapbook, edited from the Paris Review interviews (Penguin, Revised edition, 1992).

The Writer's Handbook, edited by Sylvia K Burack (The Writer Inc, 1983).

Writers At Work series (Penguin).

Writers On Writing by Jon Winokur (Headline, 1986).

Writing the Blockbuster Novel by Albert Zuckerman (Little, Brown, 1994).

Writing With Power by Peter Elbow (Oxford University Press).

Also ...

Newspaper and magazine interviews between 1965 and 1998.

Author Index

A

Abse, Danny (1923–), Welsh/Jewish doctor & poet 310
Acland, Richard (1906–1990), English politician & writer 296
Adams, Franklin P(ierce) (1881–1960), American columnist & humorist 39
Adams, John (1704–1740), American clergyman 51
Adams, Robert Martin (1915–), American critic & academic 320
Addison, Joseph (1672–1719), English poet & essayist 12, 312
Adler, Bill 34, 118, 302
Adler, Renata (1938–), American essayist & critic 82
Aeschylus (525–456 BC), Greek dramatist 77
Aiken, Conrad (1889–1993), American novelist, poet & critic 88
Alain (E A Chartier) (1868–1951), French philosopher & essayist 190
Albee, Edward (1928–), American playwright 14, 49, 124, 218, 233
Aldiss, Brian (1925–), English novelist & science fiction writer 59
Aldrich, Thomas Bailey (1836–1907), American poet & novelist 112
Alexander, Peter 280
Alfred, Luke 286
Algren, Nelson (1909–1981), American novelist & short story writer 23, 89, 308
Allan, James (1949–), American writer, illustrator & sculptor 279, 281
Allende, Isabel (1942–), Chilean/Peruvian novelist 69, 121, 147, 198
Allingham, William (1824–1889), Irish poet 212
Amis, Kingsley (1922–1997), English novelist & poet 21, 51, 87, 130, 229, 242, 294, 297, 299
Amis, Martin (his son) (1949–), English novelist & journalist 186, 187, 301
Anderson, Jessica, Australian novelist, short story writer & playwright 38
Anderson, Sherwood (1876–1941), American novelist & short story writer 127, 297
Angelou, Maya (Marguerite Johnson) (1928–), American poet, novelist & playwright 65, 150, 219, 226
Anouilh, Jean (1910–1987), French playwright 33
Arbuthnot, Dr John (1667–1735), Scottish physician & satirist 279
Archer, Jeffrey (1940–), English novelist 201, 211
Aristotle (384–322 BC), Greek philosopher 191, 247
Armstrong, Campbell, Scottish novelist 66
Arnold, Matthew (1822–1888), English poet & critic 185, 191, 266
Ashbery, John (1927–), American poet & writer 51
Asch, Sholem (1880–1957), Polish/American novelist, poet & playwright 125
Asimov, Isaac (1920–1992), American novelist (mainly science fiction), short story & non-fiction writer 9, 77, 86, 102, 135, 216, 227, 247
Atchity, Kenneth 53, 161
Atkinson, Brooks (1894–1984), American critic 25, 99
Auden, W H (Wystan Hugh) (1907–1973), English poet, critic & playwright 83, 87, 88, 209, 266
Auel, Jean M (1936–), American novelist 6, 129, 180, 215, 243

B

Bach, Richard (1936–), American novelist 58
Bacon, Francis (1561–1628), English philosopher, politician & essayist 122, 306
Bagehot, Walter (1826–1877), English economist & journalist 6
Bainbridge, Beryl (1934–), English novelist 109, 128, 171, 204, 206, 215
Baker, Sheridan (1918–), American academic & author 178, 269
Baldwin, James (1924–1987), American novelist, playwright & non-fiction writer 34, 50, 59, 81, 147, 204, 240, 259
Balfour, Arthur J (1848–1930), British statesman & essayist 283
Ballard, J G (James Graham) (1930–), English novelist & science fiction writer 87
Balzac, Honoré de (1799–1850), French novelist 12, 129
Banville, John (1945–), Irish journalist & novelist 211
Baring, Maurice (1874–1945), English poet & novelist 81
Barnes, Clive (1927–), English dance & drama critic 115
Barnes, Julian (1946–), English novelist 37, 186, 192, 282, 285, 301
Barr, Amelia E(dith) (1831–1919), American novelist 249
Barrie, J M (Sir James Matthew) (1860–1937), Scottish novelist & playwright 290, 293, 296, 328
Barth, John (1930–), American novelist 38, 42, 76, 80, 142, 209, 231
Barthelme, Donald (1933–1989), American short story writer 143
Barthes, Roland (1915–1980), French literary critic 118, 162
Baruch, Bernard (1870–1965), American financier 314
Barzun, Jacques (1907–), French-born American academic 153, 166, 181, 200, 287
Bawden, Nina (1925–), English novelist 4
Beckett, Samuel (1906–1989), Irish novelist & playwright (Nobel Prize for Literature, 1969) 108, 150, 154
Beecher, Henry Ward (1813–1887), American clergyman 150, 211
Beerbohm, Sir Max (1872–1956), English writer 310
Behan, Brendan (1923–1964), Irish writer 15, 69, 306
Belcher, Susan 30, 73
Belloc, Hilaire (1870–1953), French-born English poet, essayist & historian 10, 67, 136, 140, 279, 288, 320
Bellow, Saul (1915–), American novelist & playwright (Nobel Prize for Literature, 1976) 5, 24, 234, 290
Benchley, Robert (1889–1945), American humorist 43, 104, 213
Bennett, Alan (1934–), English playwright 325
Bennett, Arnold (1867–1931), English novelist & non-fiction writer 37, 245
Benson, A C (Arthur Christopher) (1862–1925), English novelist & essayist 279
Bentley, Edmund Clerihew (1875–1956), English journalist 280
Bernanos, George 278
Bernays, Anne (1930–), American academic, novelist & non-fiction writer 265, 289
Bernstein, Leonard (1918–1990), American conductor & composer 46
Berryman, John (1914–1972), American poet & critic 313
Betti, Ugo (1892–1953), Italian playwright 155
Bevan, Aneurin (1897–1960), Welsh politician 279
Bierce, Ambrose (1842–1914), American journalist & satirical writer 153
Billington, Rachel (1942–), English short story writer, novelist & playwright 19
Binchy, Maeve (1940–), Irish novelist 16, 50
Birmingham, Stephen (1931–), English novelist 232
Bishop, Jim (1907–) 309

Author index

Bishop, John Peale (1892–1944), American poet 132
Blake, William (1757–1827), English poet, painter & mystic 106
Block, Lawrence (1938–), American novelist & non-fiction writer 35, 180, 217
Blond, Anthony, English publisher 292
Blount Jr, Roy (1941–) 290, 300
Blythe, Will (1957–), American editor & writer 120, 199
Bogomoletz, Alexander A 30
Bohialian, Christopher A 45
Boileau-Despréaux, Nicolas (1636–1711), French poet 263
Bolitho, Hector (1898–), New Zealand biographer 140
Böll, Heinrich (1917–1985), German novelist & non-fiction writer (Nobel Prize for Literature, 1972) 90
Boothroyd, Basil, English humorist 10, 62
Borges, Jorge Luis (1899–1987), Argentinian short story writer & poet 57, 67, 113, 114, 157
Bovee, C N (1820–1904) 306
Bowen, Catherine Drinker 156, 282
Bowen, Elizabeth (Dorothea Cole) (1899–1973), Irish novelist & short story writer 257
Bowles, Paul (1910–), American composer, novelist, short story writer & poet 208
Boylan, Clare (1948–), Irish journalist, novelist & short story writer 99, 146, 211
Bradbury, Malcolm (1932–), English novelist, academic & screenwriter 142, 146, 237, 238, 244, 300, 310
Bradbury, Ray (1920–), American novelist & short story writer, best known for his science fiction 30, 36, 42, 61, 78, 125, 135, 213, 242, 254, 271, 299
Bradley, David 64
Brande, Dorothea (1893–1948), American novelist & non-fiction writer 237, 251
Brautigan, Richard (1935–1984), American novelist & poet 294
Brenan, Gerald (Edward Fitzgerald Brenan) (1894–1987), English writer 24, 200
Brennan, Maeve 79
Breslin, Jimmy (1930–), American humorist 54
Breton, André (1896–1966), French poet, essayist & critic 152
Brewster, Kingman 31
Breytenbach, Breyten (1939–), South African writer 119
Brink, André P(hillipus) (1935–), South African novelist, playwright & academic 126
Brisbane, Arthur (1864–1936), American columnist 237
Brittain, Vera (1893–1970), English novelist 145
Brodkey, Harold (1930–), American novelist 300
Brodsky, Joseph (1940–), Russian-born American poet (Nobel Prize for Literature, 1987) 70
Brontë, Charlotte (1816–1855), English novelist 17
Brontë, Emily (1818–1848), English novelist 92
Brookner, Anita (1928–), English novelist 61, 102
Brophy, Brigid (1929–1995), English novelist & critic 177
Brown, Rita Mae (1944–), American novelist & poet 177
Brown, Rosellen (1939–), American novelist & poet 300
Browne, Sir Thomas (1605–1682), English doctor & author 293
Browning, Elizabeth Barrett (1806–1861), English poet 14
Browning, Robert (her husband) (1812–1889), English poet 44
Bruner, Jerome (1915–), American psychologist & author 125
Bruyère, Jean de la (1645–1696), French writer 134, 136, 139
Buchan, John, Lord Tweedsmuir (1875–1940), Scottish novelist & statesman 292
Buechner, Frederick (1926–), American priest & novelist 196

Buffon, Comte George-Louis (1707–1788), French naturalist 134
Bukowski, Charles (1920–1994), American poet & novelist 206
Burdette, Robert J (1844–1914), American editor & humorist 293
Burgess, Anthony (1917–1994), English novelist, critic & non-fiction writer 11, 46, 47, 54, 86, 87, 108, 137, 214, 278, 316
Burroughs, John (1837–1921), American essayist 44, 250
Burroughs, William (1914–1997), American novelist 59, 88, 154
Burton, Isobel (1831–1896), English writer 194
Burton, Robert (1577–1640), English clergyman & scholar 105
Bussy, George 138
Butler, Guy (1918–), South African academic & writer 164
Butler, Samuel (1612–1680), English satirist 67, 195, 256
Byatt, A S (Antonia Susan) (1936–), English novelist 165
Byron, George Gordon, Lord (1788–1824), English poet 47, 104

C

Caldwell, Erskine (1903–1987), American novelist 2, 25, 91
Calisher, Hortense (1911–), American novelist 251, 296, 310
Callaghan, Morley (1903–), Canadian novelist 39
Campbell, Roy (1901–1957), South African poet 18, 168
Campbell, Thomas (1777–1844), English poet 289
Camus, Albert (1913–1960), French novelist & non-fiction writer (Nobel Prize for Literature, 1957) 14, 64, 68, 76, 114, 131, 148, 189, 260
Canfield, Cass, American publisher 292
Capote, Truman (1924–1984), American novelist 10, 25, 35, 57, 87, 113, 142, 162, 187, 192, 196, 210, 213, 223, 241, 250, 259, 267, 299, 301, 313, 314, 320, 323
Carey, Peter (1943–), Australian novelist 89, 255, 315
Carleton, Will (1845–1912), American poet 63
Carlyle, Thomas (1795–1881), Scottish historian & essayist 179, 247, 279, 280, 283, 284
Carroll, Lewis (Charles Lutwidge Dodgson) (1832–1898), English writer & mathematician 264, 328
Carson, Rachel (1907–1964), American science writer 246
Carter, Angela (1940–1992), English novelist & scriptwriter 130
Cartland, Dame Barbara (1901–), English romantic novelist 224
Carver, Raymond (1938–1988), American poet & short story writer 102, 109, 141, 143, 202, 214, 237, 245
Cary, Joyce (Arthur Joyce Lunel) (1888–1957), English novelist 227, 284, 299
Case, Diane (1955–), South African children's writer 127
Cassavetes, John (1929–1989), American actor, director, screenwriter & playwright 32
Cassill, R V (Ronald Verlin) (1919–), American novelist 122
Catullus, Gaius Valerius (?84–54 BC), Roman lyric poet 296
Céline, Louis-Ferdinand (Louis-Ferdinand Destouches) (1894–1961), French novelist & physician 55
Celyn-Jones, Russell 141
Cendrars, Blaise (Frédéric Sauser) (1887–1961), French-Swiss writer 11, 207
Cerf, Bennett, American humorist 115
Cervantes, Miguel de (1547–1616), Spanish playwright & poet 211, 264, 290
Chandler, Raymond (1888–1959), American crime novelist 10, 172, 183
Chateaubriand, François-August-René, Vicomte de (1768–1848), French diplomat & writer 262
Chatwin, Bruce (1940–1989), English novelist & travel writer 105, 216, 220
Chaucer, Geoffrey (?1340–1400), English poet 137
Chayevsky, Paddy (1923–), American playwright 239

Cheetham, Anthony (1943–), English publisher 53
Cheever, John (1912–1982), American novelist & short story writer 26, 97, 160, 195, 321
Chekhov, Anton (1860–1904), Russian short story writer & playwright 85, 244, 261
Chesterfield, Philip Dormer Stanhope, Earl of (1694–1773), British statesman & letter-writer 133, 185
Chesterton, G K (Gilbert Keith) (1874–1936), English writer 21, 41, 159, 320
Christie, Dame Agatha (1890–1976), English crime novelist 7, 139, 213
Churchill, Sir Winston Spencer (1874–1965), English statesman & writer (Nobel Prize for Literature, 1953) 123, 147, 157, 160, 163
Chute, B J 90, 186, 252
Cioran, E M (1911–) 89, 145
Cixous, Hélène (1937–), Algerian-born French writer 7
Claudel, Paul (1868–1955), French playwright & poet 138
Cleary, Jon (1917–), Australian novelist 204, 230, 233
Cleaver, Eldridge (1935–), American writer 57
Cobb, Irvin S (1876–1944), American humorist 4
Cobbold, Marika, Swedish–born English novelist 130
Cocteau, Jean (1889–1963), French poet & artist 6, 29, 46, 121, 191, 276, 314
Coetzee, J M (John Maxwell) (1940–), South African novelist & academic 10, 80, 130, 132, 202, 272, 276, 277
Colby, Frank Moore (1865–1925), American academic & essayist 81, 308, 318
Coleridge, Samuel Taylor (1772–1834), English poet, philosopher & critic 105, 114, 123, 250, 277, 310
Colette, Sidonie Gabrielle (1873–1954), French novelist 148, 272
Colton, Charles Caleb (?1780–1832) 319
Condon, Richard (1915–), American novelist 100
Connolly, Cyril (1903–1974), English essayist & critic 12, 20, 23, 70, 97, 189, 289
Conrad, Joseph (Teodor Josef Konrad Korzeniowski) (1857–1924), Polish-born English novelist 64, 69, 85, 110, 150, 203, 253
Conroy, Frank (1936–) 273
Conroy, Pat (1945–), American novelist 44
Cookson, Catherine (1906–1998), English novelist 48, 145, 204, 215, 244, 266
Cooper, Jilly (1937–), English novelist & humorist 97, 231
Coplestone, Edward 271
Costain, Thomas B(ertram) (1885–1965), Canadian writer 38
Cotterell, Geoffrey (1919–), English novelist 15
Cousins, Norman (1912–1990), American editor & writer 152, 223, 229
Couzens, Tim (1944–), South African writer & academic 282, 283, 319
Coward, Sir Noël (1899–1973), English playwright & composer 22, 66, 159, 228, 282, 322
Cowley, Abraham (1618–1667), English poet & essayist 277
Cowley, Malcolm (1898–1989), American poet & critic 3, 14, 35, 82, 87
Creasey, John (1908–1973), English thriller writer 245, 298
Crisp, Quentin (1930–), English writer 24, 52, 53, 276
Crosby, John 309
Cuddon, J A (1928–), English playwright, novelist & travel writer 181, 275
Curtis, Charles P 267
Cussler, Clive (1931–), American advertising executive & novelist 62, 224

Dahl, Roald (1916–1990), English short story & children's writer 4, 42, 62, 95, 139, 203
Daly, Niki (1946–), South African children's writer and illustrator 31, 84, 232

Darien, George 37
Davidson, John (1857–1909), English poet 319
Davies, Robertson (1913–1995), Canadian novelist & playwright 36, 72, 80, 100, 299
Davis, John Gordon (1936–), South African novelist 230
Davis, Richard Harding (1864–1916), American journalist, short story writer & novelist 135
Day-Lewis, Cecil (1904–1972), Irish-born English novelist, non-fiction writer & poet 49, 320
De Beauvoir, Simone (1908–1986), French novelist & non-fiction writer 17, 72, 139
De Bono, Edward (1933–), Maltese writer & lecturer, renowned for his theories on lateral thinking 30, 327
Deighton, Len (1929–), English thriller writer 93
Delacroix, Eugène (1798–1863), French painter 12
De la Mare, Walter (1873–1956), English poet & novelist 99, 157
Delton, Judy 176, 258
De Maupassant, Guy (1850–1893), French novelist & short story writer 243
Dennis, Patrick (Edward Everett Tanner III) (1921–1976), American humorist & novelist 218, 291
Destouches, Philippe (1680–1754), French playwright 318
De Vries, Peter (1910–), American novelist & journalist 10, 45
Dickens, Charles (1812–1870), English novelist 21, 218
Dickinson, Emily (1830–1886), American poet 255, 296
Dickey, James (1923–1997), American poet & novelist 7, 25, 41, 64, 93, 126, 151, 167, 250, 314
Didion, Joan (1934–), American novelist & non-fiction writer 3, 26, 51, 91, 124, 162, 170
Dillard, Annie (1945–), American journalist 7, 111, 204, 254
Disraeli, Benjamin, Earl of Beaconsfield (1804–1881), English/Jewish statesman & novelist 76, 148, 170, 280, 310
D'Israeli, Isaac (his father) (1766–1848), English/Jewish novelist & man of letters 75, 187
Dobereiner, Peter, English journalist 129
Doctorow, E L (Edgar Lawrence) (1931–), American novelist, academic & editor 36, 68, 71, 85, 118, 132, 223, 266
Donleavy, J P (James Patrick) (1926–), American-born Irish novelist & playwright 25
Dos Passos, John (1896–1970), American novelist 60, 202, 205
Dostoyevsky, Fyodor (1821–1881), Russian novelist 55, 175, 242
Douglas, Norman (1868–1952), Scottish scientist, non-fiction writer & novelist 292
Drabble, Margaret (1939–), English novelist & non-fiction writer 31, 88
Dressler, Marie (1869–1934), Canadian actress 285
Du Maurier, Dame Daphne (1907–1989), English novelist 76
Durante, Jimmy (1893–1980), American comedian 172
Duras, Marguerite (1914–), French novelist, born in Indochina 115, 327
Durrell, Lawrence (1912–1990), English novelist, poet & non-fiction writer 43, 82, 83, 104, 108, 187, 222, 227, 231, 248, 286

E

Eco, Umberto (1929–), Italian novelist 53
Edel, Leon (1907–), American academic & biographer 188
Eder, Richard (1932–), American journalist & critic 311
Edwards, Oliver 114
Einstein, Albert (1879–1955), German-born American physicist & mathematician 38
Elbow, Peter, English writer 40, 77, 198, 246, 251
Eliot, George (Mary Ann Evans) (1819–1880), English novelist 92, 136, 168, 323
Eliot, T S (Thomas Stearns) (1888–1965), American-born English poet & playwright (Nobel Prize for Literature, 1948) 48, 57, 60, 75, 106, 132, 154, 156, 163, 233, 268, 310, 312

Elkin, Stanley (1930–1995), American novelist 46, 145
Ellin, Stanley (1916–1986), American writer 11
Ellis, Henry Havelock (1859–1939), English essayist & psychologist 188, 190
Ellison, Harlan (1934–), American novelist & short story writer 1, 6, 40, 46, 48, 126, 144, 260
Emerson, Ralph Waldo (1803–1882), American poet & essayist 35, 48, 96, 106, 132, 136, 160, 164, 255, 321, 322
Epictetus (c.55–c.135 AD), Greek philosopher 243
Epstein, Jason (1928–), American publisher 291
Erdrich, Louise (1954–), American novelist 211
Essex, Peter (Dr Peter Essex-Clark) (1937–) South African doctor & novelist 45, 107

Fadiman, Clifton (1904–), American writer 173
Falck, Colin 158
Farrell, James T (1904–1979), American novelist & academic 48
Faulkner, William (1897–1962) American novelist & short story writer (Nobel Prize for Literature, 1949) 20, 36, 40, 44, 47, 48, 56, 61, 64, 66, 67, 82, 108, 135, 138, 183, 195, 207, 216, 233, 237, 240, 247, 248, 272, 273, 309
Feiffer, Jules (1929–), American humorist 104
Fellini, Federico (1920–1993), Italian film director 276
Fénelon, François (1651–1715), French theologian & writer 187
Ferber, Edna (1887–1968), American novelist 9, 76, 112, 134, 207, 212
Finch, Anne, Countess of Winchilsea (1661–1720), English poet 19
Fischer, Martin H 155
Fitzgerald, F(rancis) Scott (1896–1940), American novelist & short story writer 34, 35, 51, 67, 78, 86, 132, 154, 175
Fitzgerald, Penelope (1916–), English novelist 222
Fitz-Gibbon, Bernice (1895–1982), American advertising executive 31
Flaubert, Gustave (1821–1880), French novelist 6, 55, 90, 109, 118, 156, 165, 185, 196, 251, 306, 309, 317, 320, 326
Follett, Ken (1949–), English novelist 156, 164, 272
Ford, Ford Madox (Ford Madox Hueffer) (1873–1939), English poet, novelist & critic 183
Forster, E M (Edward Morgan) (1879–1970), English novelist 49, 53, 75, 114, 300, 303
Forsyth, Frederick (1938–), English blockbuster novelist 54, 80, 138, 201, 214, 225
Fowler, Gene (1890–1960), American writer 119
Fowler, H W (Henry Watson) (1858–1933), English philologist & lexicographer 157, 171, 172
Fowles, John (1926–), English novelist 43, 100, 246
Fox, Henry Edward 81
France, Anatole (Anatole Thibault) (1844–1924) French writer (Nobel Prize for Literature, 1921) 47, 104, 138, 256, 308
Francis, Clare (1946–), English sailor & novelist 224, 327
Francis, Dick (1920–), English crime novelist 99, 209, 313
Franco, Marjorie, American writer 71
Frankau, Pamela (1908–1967), English novelist & short story writer 79
Frankel, Charles (1917–1979), American educator & writer 31
Franklin, Benjamin 1706–1790), American statesman, scientist & author 272
Freely, Maureen, English novelist 103
Freud, Anna (1895–1982), Austrian psychiatrist 32
Freud, Sigmund (her father) (1856–1939), Austrian psychiatrist 283
Frost, Robert (1875–1963), American poet 8, 37, 160, 171, 185, 245

Fry, Christopher (1907–), English playwright 64
Fuentes, Carlos (1928–), Mexican novelist 5, 16, 26, 52, 101, 111, 124, 131, 203, 213, 236
Fugard, Athol (1933–), South African playwright & actor 8, 36, 70, 240, 327
Fuller, Thomas (1608–1661), English biographer 208

G

Galsworthy, John (1867–1933), English novelist & playwright (Nobel Prize for Literature, 1932) 167
Garbett, Cyril, Archbishop of York (1875–1955), English clergyman & writer 306
Gardam, Jane (1928–), English novelist & short story writer 96, 121, 144, 297
Gardner, John (1933–1982), American novelist & academic 11, 86, 104, 126, 141, 143, 193, 232, 273, 312, 326
Garner, Alan (1934–), English children's writer 295
Garner, Helen (1942–), Australian novelist 7, 173
Gass, William (1924–), American novelist 61, 161, 178, 226, 298
Gasset, José Ortega y (1883–1955), Spanish philosopher & writer 178
Gide, André (1861–1951), French novelist, poet & non-fiction writer (Nobel Prize for Literature, 1947) 12, 47, 57, 101
Gilliatt, Penelope (1924–), English novelist 311
Ginsberg, Allen (1926–1997), American Beat poet 118, 249, 312
Ginzburg, Natalia 17
Giovanni, Nikki (1942–), American poet 166, 176, 266
Gissing, George (1857–1903), English novelist 56, 242
Godden, Rumer (1907–), English novelist 99, 141, 207, 209, 212
Godwin, Gail (1937–), American novelist & short story writer 120
Goethe, Johann Wolfgang von (1749–1832), German novelist, poet, playwright & non-fiction writer 72, 191, 263
Golding, Sir William (1911–1993), English novelist (Nobel Prize for Literature, 1983) 15, 51
Goldman, William (1931–), American novelist & screenwriter 265
Goncourt, Rémy de 98
Goodman, Ellen (1941–), American columnist 97, 255
Gordimer, Nadine (1923–) South African novelist, short story writer (Nobel Prize for Literature, 1991) 3, 17, 33, 61, 97, 100, 111, 122, 149, 186, 200, 213, 217, 223, 230, 236, 261, 265
Gordin, Jeremy (1952–), South African poet & journalist 136
Gosse, Sir Edmund (1849–1928), English poet & critic 190
Gould, Jay R, American journalist 117
Gould, Lois 176
Gowers, Sir Ernest (1880–1966), English lawyer, civil servant & author of books on the use of plain English 137, 160, 175
Goyen, William (1915–1983), American novelist 31, 90, 126
Gracian y Morales, Baltasar (1601–1658), Spanish novelist 115
Graves, Robert (1895–1985), English novelist, poet & critic 180, 260
Gray, Francine du Plessix (1930–), French-American journalist, novelist, academic & critic 93, 147
Greeley, Andrew (1928–), American crime writer 314
Green, Henry (Henry Vincent Yorke) (1905–1973), English novelist 123, 187
Green, Julien (1900–1998), French/American novelist & playwright 84
Greenberg, Clement (1909–) 16
Greene, Graham (1904–1991), English novelist & critic 39, 40, 43, 44, 69, 82, 98, 115, 182, 205, 209, 229, 231, 233
Greenfield, George, English publisher & literary agent 209
Grenfell, Joyce (1910–1979), English actress & humorist 302

Grenier, Jean (1898–1971) 126
Grigson, Geoffrey (1905–1985), English poet, critic & editor 174, 196
Gross, Miriam (1939–), English editor 104
Guedalla, Philip (1889–1944), English barrister & historian 276, 280

H

Haecker, Theodore 160
Hailey, Arthur (1920–), English/Canadian blockbuster novelist 228, 229
Halligan, Marion (1940–), Australian novelist & short story writer 61, 154, 175
Hampton, Christopher (1946–), English playwright 307
Hardwick, Elizabeth (1916–) American novelist & critic 58, 120, 181, 225, 294
Hardy, Thomas (1840–1928), English novelist & poet 190, 194
Hare, David (1947–), English playwright & director 126
Harris, Marvin (1927–), American cultural anthropologist 323
Harrison, Jim (1937–), American writer 91
Hart, Josephine, English publisher, producer & novelist 65, 129, 212
Hawkins, Sir Anthony Hope (1863–1933), English novelist 260
Hawthorne, Nathaniel (1804–1864), American novelist & short story writer 26, 48, 54, 165, 188, 191
Hayakawa, S I 238
Hazlitt, William (1778–1830), English essayist & critic 124, 150, 165, 189
Hazzard, Shirley (1931–), Australian-born American novelist 30, 40, 77, 212, 314
Heald, Tim, English crime novelist 146
Heine, Heinrich (1797–1856), German poet & essayist 36, 292
Heller, Joseph (1923–), American novelist 23, 60, 84, 99, 100, 110, 126, 129, 166, 213, 229, 299
Hellman, Lillian (1905–1984), American playwright 3, 66, 76, 97, 112, 242, 309, 326
Helps, Sir Arthur (1813–1875), English essayist 191
Hemingway, Ernest (1898–1961), American novelist & short story writer (Nobel Prize for Literature, 1954) 9, 23, 27, 33, 38, 41, 43, 63, 66, 69, 74, 75, 78, 79, 84, 98, 132, 133, 138, 139, 148, 167, 173, 179, 188, 199, 201, 210, 232, 238, 239, 257, 259, 262, 272, 308, 326
Henahan, Donal 278
Henry, O (William Sydney Porter) (1862–1910), American short story writer 69
Hepburn, Katharine (1909–), American actress 251
Hersey, John (1914–1993), American novelist 121, 288
Higgins, Jack (1929–), English thriller writer 289
Hill, Hinda Teague 253
Hill, Reginald (1936–), English novelist 133
Hill, Susan (1942–), English novelist, journalist, editor & biographer 126, 151, 263
Hodge, Alan 180
Hodgart, M J C (1916–) 30
Høeg, Peter, Danish novelist 32, 101, 118, 129
Holmes, Marjorie (1932–), American short story writer 33
Holmes, Oliver Wendell (1809–1894), American medical professor & novelist 22, 81, 153
Homer (?800 BC), Greek epic poet 158
Hood, Thomas (1799–1845), English editor & satirist 155
Hope, Christopher (1944–), South African novelist, poet & non-fiction writer 144, 311
Horace (Quintus Horatius Flaccus) (65–8 BC), Roman poet 84, 134
Housman, A E (Alfred Edward) (1859–1936), English poet 310
Hove, Chenjerai (1954–), Zimbabwean novelist 125
Howard, Phillip (1933–), English editor & author 175
Howatch, Susan (1940–), English novelist 70, 247, 256

Howell, James (1594–1666), Welsh diplomat & historian 168
Hubbard, Elbert (1856–1915), American novelist 170, 284
Hughes, Robert (1938–), Australian-born American art critic & writer 196, 317
Hugo, Victor (1802–1885), French poet, novelist & playwright 167
Hulme, T E (Thomas Ernest) (1883–1917), English poet & essayist 164
Huneker, James Gibbons (1857–1921), American critic & novelist 305
Hunter, Evan (1926–), American novelist 126, 222, 246
Hurlbut, Kaatje, American writer 138, 262
Hurst, Fannie (1887–1968), American novelist, short story writer & scriptwriter 89
Hutchens, John K 99
Huxley, Aldous Leonard (1894–1963), English novelist, poet & non-fiction writer 34, 58, 69, 79, 94, 136, 152, 155

I

Ibsen, Henrik (1828–1906), Norwegian playwright 123
Ingrams, Richard (1937–), English editor & satirist 298
Ionesco, Eugène (1912–1994), Rumanian-born French playwright 79, 312
Irving, John (1942–), American novelist 5, 126, 241, 290, 307, 326
Isherwood, Christopher (1904–1986), English/American novelist & screenwriter 123, 248
Ishiguro, Kazuo (1954–), Japanese/English novelist 291

J

Jackson, Charles (1903–1968), American novelist 114
Jakes, John (1932–), American academic & author 76, 141, 240, 244
James, Clive (1939–), Australian writer, critic & TV personality 9, 43, 122, 125
James, Henry (1843–1916), American/English novelist & short story writer 32, 92
James, P D (Dame Phyllis Dorothy) (1920–), English crime novelist 206, 288, 298
James, William (1842–1910), American psychologist & writer 289
Jarrell, Randall (1914–1965), American novelist & poet 318
Jefferson, Thomas (1743–1826), author & President of America 171
Jenkins, Geoffrey (1920–), South African novelist 49, 93, 101, 202
Jensen, Eileen 131
Johnson, Paul (1928–), English writer, mainly of history & political commentary 31, 73, 89, 90, 94, 153, 219, 246
Johnson, Dr Samuel (1709–1784), English essayist & lexicographer 42, 55, 65, 106, 115, 170, 205, 279, 307, 309, 318
Jolley, Elizabeth (1923–), English-born Australian novelist & short story writer 120, 143, 147, 168, 173
Jones, Bobi 11
Jones, James (1921–1977), American novelist 60, 88, 221, 241
Jones, James Earl (1931–), American actor 152
Jones, Le Roi (Imamu Amiri Baraka) (1934–), American academic & novelist 290
Jones, Nicolette, English journalist 142
Jong, Erica (1942–), American novelist & poet 34, 117, 140, 206, 230
Jonson, Ben (1573–1637), English poet & playwright 192, 306
Joseph, Michael (1897–1958), English publisher 3
Josipovici, Gabriel (1940–), English academic, playwright & novelist 134, 173
Joubert, Joseph (1754–1824), French writer & critic 154

Author index

Joubert, Elsa (1922–), South African novelist 215
Jung, Carl Gustav (1875–1961), Swiss psychologist 9

Kafka, Franz (1883–1924), Czech novelist & short story writer 10
Kane, Thomas S 163
Kanga, Firdaus (1961–), Indian novelist 126
Kanin, Michael 9
Kasdan, Lawrence (1949–), American film director & screenwriter 244
Katz, Gloria 109
Kazan, Elia (1909–), Turkish-born American actor, screenwriter & film director 318
Kazin, Alfred (1915–), American literary critic 50, 58, 124
Keane, Molly (1904–1996), Irish novelist & playwright 212
Keats, John (1795–1821), English poet 218
Kelland, Clarence Budington (1881–1964), American novelist 223
Kelman, James (1946–), Scottish novelist 71, 110
Kemelman, Harry (1908–), American rabbi & novelist 264
Kendall, Paul Murray, English biographer 282
Kenko, Yoshida, Japanese writer 262
Kennedy, William (1928–), American writer 33, 74
Kermode, Sir Frank (1919–), English academic, author & literary critic 66, 80, 143, 328
Kernahan, Coulson 83
Kerouac, Jack (1922–1969), American Beat poet & novelist 52, 92, 273
Kesey, Ken (1935–), American novelist 219
Kilpatrick, James J (1920–), American columnist 161, 177
Kincaid, Jamaica (1949–), West Indian-born American poet 72
King, Florence, American novelist & critic 135, 246
King, Stephen (1947–), American suspense novelist 147, 177, 199, 202, 223, 244, 251, 257, 269, 316
Kingsolver, Barbara (1955–), American poet & novelist 63
Kington, Miles (1941–), English journalist & humorist 175, 285
Kipling, Rudyard (1865–1936), English novelist, short story writer & poet (Nobel Prize for Literature, 1907) 150
Kisner, James 238, 267
Knopf, Alfred A (1894–1984), American publisher 291
Koenig, Rhoda 103
Koestler, Arthur (1905–1983), Hungarian-born English novelist 67, 95, 179
Kopit, Arthur (1937–), American playwright 140, 220, 223, 237, 246
Kosinski, Jerzy (1933–1991), Polish/American novelist & non-fiction writer 75
Krantz, Judith (1928–), American romantic novelist 7, 8, 62, 65, 129, 203, 224, 244, 269, 294
Kraus, Karl (1874–1936), American writer 2, 5, 65, 190, 193
Kruger, Charles Rayne (1922–), South African novelist 73
Krull, Kathleen (1952–), American writer of non-fiction & children's books 264

Lamb, Charles (1775–1834), English poet & essayist 297
Landor, Walter Savage (1775–1864), English poet & writer 3, 12, 24, 82, 259, 268
Langland, William (1332–1400), English cleric & poet 170
Lanham, Richard A 161, 166
Lardner, Ring (Ringgold Wilmer) (1885–1933) American humorist & short story writer 37

Larkin, Philip (1922–1986), English poet & essayist 48, 76, 168
Lawrence, D H (David Herbert) (1885–1930), English novelist, short story writer, poet & playwright 61, 248
Leavis, F R (Frank Raymond) (1895–1978), English literary critic & academic 11
Lebowitz, Fran (1951–), American humorist 9, 95, 145, 298
Le Carré, John (David Cornwell) (1931–), English spy novelist 3, 26, 201, 225, 227, 301
Lee, Laurie (1914–1997), English poet & autobiographer 1, 157, 207, 277, 278
Lee, Patrick (1952–), South African journalist & screenwriter 135
Le Gallienne, Richard (1866–1947), English journalist, poet, essayist & novelist 290, 305, 318
Legat, Michael, English editor, publisher, author & academic 1, 18, 287
Le Guin, Ursula (1929–), American novelist, children's & non-fiction writer, best known for her fantasy novels 3, 19, 77, 123, 125, 156, 164, 171, 176, 210, 240, 292, 293
L'Engle, Madeleine (1918–), American poet & children's writer 46
Leonard, Elmore (1925–), American crime novelist 158, 174, 257
Lessing, Doris (1919–), English novelist, short story & non-fiction writer, born in Iran & brought up in Zimbabwe 3, 13, 19, 38, 44, 46, 49, 54, 58, 61, 64, 70, 89, 107, 121, 125, 126, 144, 154, 158, 186, 202, 214, 217, 224, 227, 239, 243, 252, 255, 261, 278, 284, 295, 298, 301, 307, 317, 319, 323, 327
Lessing, Theodore 276
Levin, Bernard (1928–), English journalist, critic & author 221
Lewes, George Henry (1817–1878), English journalist 233
Lewis, C S (Clive Staples) (1898–1963), English novelist, critic, poet & writer on religion 133, 153
Lewis, Sinclair (1885–1951), American novelist & playwright (Nobel Prize for Literature, 1930) 15, 76
Lindbergh, Anne Morrow (1906–), American novelist, poet, memoirist & aviator 117
Linklater, Eric (1899–1974), Scottish novelist 4
Lister, David 311
Llosa, Mario Vargas (1936–), Peruvian novelist & politician 131
Lodge, David (1935–), English novelist 83, 302
Lofts, Norah (1904–1986), English historical novelist 286
London, Jack (1879–1916), American novelist, short story & non-fiction writer 55
Lorenz, Konrad (1903–1989), Austrian zoologist, writer & Nobel prizewinner 297
Lowell, James Russell (1819–1891), American poet, critic & academic 205, 214, 312
Lowell, Robert (1917–1977), American writer 139
Lowenkopf, Shelly, American writer 180
Lowry, Malcolm (1909–1957), English novelist 94
Lucas, F L (Frank Lawrence) (1894–1967), English writer & critic 249, 270
Lukas, J Anthony (1933–) 173
Lurie, Alison (1926–), American novelist 29, 250
Luther, Martin (1483–1546), German Protestant theologian 83

M

Macaulay, Thomas Babington, Lord (1800–1859), English historian & essayist 23, 283
MacDiarmid, Hugh (Christopher Murray Grieve) (1892–1978) Scottish poet 145
MacDonald, John D (1916–1986), American crime novelist 3, 57, 152, 256, 293
Mackay, Shena (1945–), Scottish novelist & short story writer 8, 151, 154, 163
MacLeish, Archibald (1892–1982), American playwright 52, 58, 137
Madden, David (1933–), American academic & novelist 252
Maddocks, Melvin 71

Maddox, Brenda 289

Maeterlinck, Comte Maurice (1862–1949), Belgian poet & playwright (Nobel Prize for Literature, 1911) 155

Mailer, Norman (1923–), American novelist & non-fiction writer 10, 55, 66, 70, 78, 83, 85, 112, 150, 185, 190, 192, 207, 220, 266

Malamud, Bernard (1914–1986), American novelist 70, 80, 95, 120, 165, 178, 186, 220, 236, 242, 243, 245, 255, 262, 311, 315

Malaquais, Jean 119

Malouf, David (1934–), Australian novelist & poet 29, 93, 114, 121, 151

Manley, Seon 30, 73

Mann, Jessica 8

Mann, Thomas (1875–1955), German novelist & non-fiction writer (Nobel Prize for Literature, 1929) 68

Mansfield, Katherine (Kathleen Mansfield Beauchamp) (1888–1923), New Zealand novelist & short story writer 8, 61, 85, 93

Mantel, Hilary (1952–), English novelist 10, 20, 38, 39, 42, 130

Marquand, John P(hillips) (1893–1960), American novelist 107

Marquez, Gabriel Garcia (1928–), Colombian novelist & short story writer (Nobel Prize for Literature, 1982) 39, 69, 84, 96, 119, 128, 134, 138, 169, 182, 201, 206, 215, 216, 229, 240, 303

Marquis, Don (1878–1937), American humorist, novelist & playwright 105, 126

Marx, Karl (1818–1883), German/Jewish founder of Communism 56

Masters, John (1914–), English soldier turned novelist 4

Matshikiza, John (1954–), South African actor, writer, playwright & director 146, 147

Matthews, Brander (1852–1929), American literary historian & critic 238

Matthiessen, Peter (1927–), American novelist 7

Maugham, W S (William Somerset) (1874–1965), English novelist, short story writer & playwright 1, 20, 21, 52, 69, 75, 132, 134, 144, 147, 158, 170, 178, 188, 205, 252, 253, 257, 259, 264, 268, 271, 313, 322

Mauriac, François (1885–1970), French novelist (Nobel Prize for Literature, 1952) 37, 99, 115, 205, 308

Maurois, André (Emile Herzog) (1885–1967), French biographer 185, 237

Max, D T 325

Maxwell, William (1908–), American novelist & short story writer 2, 78, 202, 206

May, Rollo (1909–1994), American psychoanalyst & writer 30

McCarthy, Mary (1912–1989), American novelist & non-fiction writer 206

McGahern, John (1934–), Irish novelist 120, 152, 182, 236

McGinley, Phyllis (1905–1978), American writer of light verse & children's books 210

McInerney, Jay (1956–), American novelist 21, 44, 126, 142, 293, 303

McKuen, Rod (1933–), American poet 1, 33, 118, 146, 200, 206, 210, 260, 261

McLaughlin, Mignon 251

McLuhan, Marshall (1911–1980), Canadian author of works analysing the mass media 105, 260, 296

McMillan, Terry (1951–), American academic & author 18, 323

McPhee, John (1931–), American writer 118

McWilliam, Candia, English journalist 301

Melville, Herman (1819–1891), American novelist 7, 114

Mencken, H L (Henry Louis) (1880–1956) American journalist, critic and essayist 49, 54, 60, 61, 83, 99, 301, 305, 312, 318

Meredith, George (1828–1909), English novelist & poet 192

Merrill, James (1926–1995), American poet & novelist 88

Metalious, Grace (1924–1964), American novelist 14

Meyer, Herbert E & Jill M 275

Michener, James (1907–1997), American novelist 25, 108, 115, 189, 202, 224, 237, 240, 268, 273
Millay, Edna St Vincent (1892–1950), American poet 92, 297
Miller, Arthur (1915–), American playwright 314
Miller, Henry (1891–1980), American novelist & non-fiction writer 4, 38, 72, 85, 111, 113, 183, 203, 217, 237, 322
Miller, Dr Jonathan (1934–), English medical doctor, actor & theatre director 307
Miller, Olin 118
Milne, A A (Alan Alexander) (1882–1956), English journalist, novelist & playwright 54, 174
Mizner, Wilson (1876–1933) 60
Moggach, Deborah (1948–), English journalist, novelist, short story & scriptwriter 17
Mokae, Dr Gomolemo, South African medical doctor, novelist & playwright 16
Molière (Jean-Baptiste Poquelin) (1622–1673), French playwright 14, 53, 165, 170, 308, 320
Monsarratt, Nicholas (1910–1979), English novelist 225, 229
Montagu, Lady Mary Wortley (1689–1762), English letter-writer 55
Montaigne, Michel de (1533–1592), French essayist 107, 278
Montesquieu, Baron de (1688–1755), French writer 108
Montherlant, Henri Millon de (1896–1972), French novelist & playwright 253
Moore, Brian (1921–), Irish novelist 36
Moore, George Augustus (1852–1933), English novelist & playwright 47
Moore, Lorrie (1957–), American novelist, short story writer & academic 20, 103, 110, 120, 131, 165, 239, 249, 255, 321
Moore, Marianne (1887–1972), American poet 98
Moravia, Alberto (1907–1990), Italian novelist & short story writer 13, 46, 69
More, Hannah (1745–1833), English playwright & religious writer 283
Morley, Christopher (1890–1957), American novelist, poet & essayist 305
Morley, John, Viscount (1838–1923), English statesman & man of letters 117
Morley, Robert (1908–1992), English actor 316
Morpurgo, Jack (1918–), English academic & author 288
Morris, Willie (1934–), American editor, novelist & author, mainly of children's books 261
Morrison, Blake (1950–), English poet & critic 103
Morrison, Toni (1931–), American novelist (Nobel Prize for Literature, 1993) 51, 59, 166, 206, 222
Mortimer, John (1923–), English barrister, playwright & novelist 3, 32, 96, 102, 125, 199, 249, 315
Moyana, T T, South African academic 16
Mozart, Wolfgang Amadeus (1756–1791), Austrian composer 47, 255
Mphahlele, Es'kia (Ezekiel) (1919–), South African critic, novelist, short story & non-fiction writer 49, 204, 217
Muir, Frank (1920–1997), English humorous writer & broadcaster 4, 76, 122
Munger, Theodore F 193
Munro, Alice (1931–), Canadian short story writer 64
Murdoch, Iris (1919–), Irish-born English novelist & philosopher 131, 252
Murray, Donald M 222
Murry, J(ohn) Middleton (1889–1957), English critic 12, 166, 189

Nabokov, Vladimir (1899–1977), Russian/American novelist & short story writer 13, 24, 188, 195, 207, 210, 227, 236, 258, 284, 317, 320
Naipaul, V S (Vidiadhar Surajprasad) (1932–), West Indian novelist 6, 163, 187, 198, 217, 226, 229
Nash, Ogden (1902–1971), American humorist 179, 323
Nathan, George Jean (1882–1958) American drama critic, editor & non-fiction writer 140, 307, 318, 319, 322

Naylor, Phyllis Reynolds (1933–), American writer, mainly of children's books 315
Neto, Agostinho, poet & President of Angola 123
Newman, Charles (1938–) 303
Nichols, Beverley (1898–1983), English writer & columnist 276
Nicolson, Sir Harold (1886–1968), English novelist, critic & diarist 235, 282
Nietzsche, Friedrich (1844–1900), German philosopher, poet & critic 42, 64, 79, 169, 259, 308
Nin, Anaïs (1903–1977), French diarist & writer 70
Nixon, Richard Milhous (1913–1994), American President 129
Noonan, Peggy, American writer & speechwriter 151

O

Oates, Joyce Carol (1938–), American novelist 182, 206, 254, 316
O'Brien, Edna (1932–), Irish novelist & short story writer 56, 101, 130, 207, 212, 230
O'Connor, Flannery (1925–1964), American novelist 148
O'Connor, Frank (1903–1966), Irish short story writer 50, 56, 62, 226
Okri, Ben (1959–), Nigerian novelist 44
Olivier, Sir Laurence (1907–1989), English actor & theatre director 129, 218, 221
Omotoso, Kole (Bankole) (1943–), Nigerian writer & academic 168
Ondaatje, Michael (1943–), Sri Lankan-born Canadian novelist & academic 300
O'Neill, Eugene (1888–1953), American playwright (Nobel Prize for Literature, 1936) 307
Orwell, George (Eric Blair) (1903–1950), English novelist & essayist 60, 108, 130, 135, 189, 263, 269, 321
Osborn, Alex F 30
Osborne, John (1929–1994), English playwright 25
Ostriker, Alicia (1937–), American poet & critic 19
O'Toole, Fintan, Irish critic 313
Owen, Peter, English publisher 293
Ozick, Cynthia (1928–), American novelist 169

P

Painter, George (1914–), English biographer 284
Palmer, Eve (1916–), South African writer 201
Paretsky, Sara (1947–), American crime novelist 95, 124
Parker, Dorothy (1893–1967), American short story & satirical writer 8, 16, 34, 54, 56, 213, 217, 266
Pascal, Blaise (1623–1662), French philosopher & mathematician 196, 321
Pasternak, Boris (1890–1960), Russian novelist & poet 2, 12
Patchen, Kenneth (1911–), American poet & novelist 4
Patmore, Coventry (1823–1896), English poet 55
Paton, Alan (1903–1988), South African novelist & biographer 53, 257, 282
Pavlovitch, Anton (1860–1904), Russian playwright & short story writer 308
Paz, Octavio (1914–), Mexican poet & essayist (Nobel Prize for Literature, 1990) 128, 309
Péguy, Charles (1873–1914), French poet & essayist 151
Percy, Walker (1916–1990), American novelist 96
Perelman, S J (Sidney Joseph) (1904–1979), American humorist 61, 111, 169, 228
Perkins, Maxwell (1884–1947), American editor 262
Perrick, Penny, English journalist 103
Pétain, Henri-Philippe (1856–1951), French marshal & pro-Nazi statesman 279
Petrarch (Francesco Petrarca) (1304–1374), Italian poet & scholar 211
Phillips, Caryl (1958–), English writer & academic 142

Phillips, William (1878–1968), American diplomat 323
Pimlott, Ben (1945–), English academic & biographer 279, 280, 281, 283, 285
Pinter, Harold (1930–), English playwright 133
Plath, Sylvia (1932–1963), American poet & novelist 111
Plomer, William (1903–1973), South African-born English novelist, poet & man of letters 29, 211
Plowright, Joan (Lady Olivier) (1929–), English actress 249
Poe, Edgar Allan (1809–1849), American short story writer 170
Pollock, Channing (1880–1946), American playwright, journalist & critic 305
Polya, George (1887–1985), Hungarian-born American mathematician 193
Pope, Alexander (1688–1744), English poet & satirist 264
Poppy, John 31
Porter, Katherine Anne (1890–1980), American novelist & short story writer 46, 59, 85, 137, 180, 187, 201, 298
Porter, Peter (1929–), Australian poet 52
Potter, Dennis (1935–1994), English writer & playwright 128
Pound, Ezra (1885–1972), American poet, critic & translator 26, 71, 165, 168, 176, 198
Pountney, Michael, English journalist 295
Powell, Anthony Dymoke (1905–), English novelist 74
Powell, Lawrence Clark (1906–), American writer, critic & librarian 98
Pratchett, Terry (1948–), English fantasy novelist 126
Prentice, George Dennison (1802–1870), American editor & poet 176, 211
Price, Wesley 271
Priestley, J B (John Boynton) (1894–1984), English novelist & playwright 70, 221, 243, 307, 308
Pritchett, V S (Sir Victor Sawdon) (1900–1997), English short story writer, novelist & essayist 13, 213, 312
Profumo, David 150
Proust, Marcel (1871–1922), French novelist 68, 131, 234
Ptahotep 8
Puzo, Mario (1920–), novelist & screenwriter 288, 317

Queen, Ellery (Frederick Dannay) (1905–1971), American crime novelist 140

Raban, Jonathan (1942–), English travel writer, critic & playwright 14, 53, 136, 139, 179, 197, 285, 302, 319, 321
Rabelais, François (1490–1553), French satirist 306
Rainbird, George, English publisher 293, 294
Rama Rau, Santha (1923–), Indian academic & author 42
Raphael, Frederic (1931–), American/English novelist & screenwriter 26, 70
Rascoe, Burton (1892–1957), American critic, editor & columnist 102
Ray, John (1627–1705), English naturalist 154
Reid, B L, English biographer 281
Renard, Jules (1894–1910), French writer 33, 117, 150, 256
Renault, Mary (Eileen Mary Challans) (1905–1983), English-born South African historical novelist 68
Rendell, Ruth (1930–), English crime novelist; also writes as Barbara Vine 219
Rhys, Jean (1894–1979), English novelist 51, 81, 100
Richler, Mordecai (1931–), Canadian novelist 75, 200
Rilke, Rainer Maria (1875–1926), Austro-German poet 62, 252, 313, 327

Author index

Roberts, Michael (1902–1948), English writer 311
Robbins, Tom (1936–), American novelist 165, 177, 195, 208, 214, 226, 229, 251
Robinson, Edwin Arlington (1869–1935), American poet 123
Robinson, James Harvey (1863–1936), American historian 30
Ronge, Barry (1947–), South African journalist, critic & TV personality 150
Rooney, Andy (1919–), American journalist & columnist 296
Rorem, Ned (1923–), American writer & composer 33, 46, 168, 277
Ros, Amanda (Anna Margaret Ross) (1860–1939), Irish novelist & poet 290
Rose, Phyllis (1942–), American biographer & critic 17
Rosenberg, Harold (1906–), American poet, critic & philosopher 22
Rossner, Judith (1935–), American novelist 2
Rostand, Jean (1894–), French biologist & essayist 309
Rosten, Leo (1908–), Polish-born American teacher & humorist 48
Roth, Philip (1933–), American novelist 65, 198, 199, 302
Roy, Arundhati, Indian novelist & screenwriter 169
Runyon, Damon (1884–1946), American journalist, columnist & short story writer 67
Russell, Lord Bertrand (1872–1970), English philosopher (Nobel Prize for Literature, 1950) 277

S

Saccai 216
Safire, William (1929–), American columnist 30, 118, 168, 189, 238, 270
Sagan, Françoise (1935–), French novelist 52, 117, 316
Saint-Exupéry, Antoine de (1900–1944), French novelist 169
Sanchez, Thomas (1944–) 100
Sand, George (Amandine Dupin) (1804–1876), French novelist 5
Sandburg, Carl (1878–1967), American poet 158, 167
Sansom, William (1912–), American novelist & short story writer 59
Santayana, George (1863–1952), Spanish-born American philosopher, poet & critic 150, 321
Saro-Wiwa, Ken (–1995), Nigerian novelist & political activist 2
Saroyan, William (1908–1981), American novelist 27, 41, 74, 100, 112, 121, 136, 227, 239, 241
Sarton, May (1912–1995), Belgian-born American poet & novelist 17, 23, 152, 201, 219, 239, 315
Sartre, Jean-Paul (1905–1980), French novelist, poet & philosopher 111, 114, 150
Sayer, Paul 10, 94
Scargill, Arthur (1938–), English trade unionist 153
Schopenhauer, Arthur (1788–1860), German philosopher 185, 192, 193
Schorer, Mark (1908–), American novelist & critic 312
Schrader, Paul (1946–), American film director & scriptwriter 180
Schwanitz, Dietrich, German academic & critic 148
Schwartz, Delmore (1913–1966), American poet & critic 82
Scott, Bill 161
Sedgwick, Ellery 277
Seferis, George (Giorgios Seferiadis) (1900–1971), Greek poet & diplomat (Nobel Prize for Literature, 1963) 57
Seneca (Lucius Annaeus the Younger) (?4 BC–65 AD), Roman philosopher, statesman & playwright 194
Serling, Rod (1925–1975), American playwright 4
Settle, Mary Lee 56
Shakespeare, William (1564–1616), English playwright & poet 33, 152, 178, 259
Shange, Ntozake (Paulette Williams) (1948–), American poet, playwright, novelist & academic 18
Sharpe, Tom (1928–), English satirical novelist 215

Shaw, George Bernard (1856–1950), Irish-born English playwright (Nobel Prize for Literature, 1925) 12, 24, 51, 72, 81, 139, 167, 185, 190, 207, 223, 248, 263, 289
Shaw, Irwin (1913–1984), American novelist & playwright 42, 87, 94, 117, 241, 242, 267, 306
Sheed, Wilfred (1930–), American novelist 4
Sheldon, Sidney (1917–), American novelist 5, 58, 67, 112, 203, 246
Shelley, Mary Wollstonecraft (1797–1851), English writer 42
Shenker, Israel 118
Shute, Nevil (1899–1960), Australian novelist 253
Sibelius, Jean (1865–1957), Finnish composer 313
Sidney, Sir Philip (1554–1586), English poet 247
Simenon, Georges (1903–1989), Belgian crime novelist 21, 27, 89, 118, 227, 258
Simon, John (1925–), American theatre & film critic 256
Sinclair-Stevenson, Christopher (1939–), English publisher & literary agent 292
Singer, Isaac Bashevis (1904–1991), Polish/American novelist & short story writer (Nobel Prize for Literature, 1978) 13, 24, 31, 41, 84, 169, 199, 216
Sitwell, Sir Osbert (1892–1969), English writer 155
Slovo, Gillian (1952–), South African novelist & thriller writer 49
Small, Adam (1936–), South African poet, playwright, non-fiction writer & academic 131
Smith, Alexander (1830–1867), Scottish poet 151
Smith, Aloysius ('Trader Horn') (1861–1931), traveller & writer of bestsellers about his African adventures 245
Smith, Carol, English literary agent & novelist 200
Smith, Godfrey (1926–), English editor & novelist 151, 284
Smith, H Allen 159
Smith, Logan Pearsall (1865–1946), American essayist 13, 83, 186, 235
Smith, Pauline (1882–1959), South African novelist & short story writer 224
Smith, Red (1905–1982), American sports writer 119, 171
Smith, Sydney (1771–1845), English clergyman & writer 74, 193
Smith, Wilbur (1933–), South African blockbuster novelist born in Zambia (then Northern Rhodesia) 78, 231
Solzhenitzyn, Alexander Isayevich (1918–), Russian novelist (Nobel Prize for Literature, 1970) 12
Sontag, Susan (1933–), American writer 89, 108
Southern, Terry (1924–), American novelist & short story writer 249
Southey, Robert (1774–1843), English poet & biographer 256
Spark, Muriel (1918–), Scottish poet & novelist 107, 126, 132, 159, 211
Spencer, Scott (1945–) 204
Spender, Sir Stephen (1909–1995), English poet & critic 122
Spillane, Mickey (1918–), American crime novelist 2, 13, 22, 50, 55, 75, 213, 308
Steel, Danielle (1947–), American romantic novelist 65
Steinbeck, John (1902–1968), American novelist (Nobel Prize for Literature, 1962) 36, 58, 65, 79, 91, 94, 113, 119, 148, 158, 210, 225, 272, 307, 311, 315
Stendhal (Henri Beyle) (1783–1842), French novelist 193, 259, 268
Stephen, J F 72
Sterne, Laurence (1713–1768), Irish-born English novelist 122
Stevenson, Adlai (1900–1968), American statesman 159
Stevenson, Robert Louis (1850–1894), Scottish novelist & essayist 6, 260
Stewart, Mary (1916–), Scottish novelist 19, 50, 57, 77, 93, 97, 98, 113, 128, 135, 197, 204, 218, 224, 228, 299, 300
Stone, Irving (1903–1989), American novelist 203, 221, 268

Stone, Robert (1937–), American novelist, short story writer & academic 65, 127, 128, 142, 195
Stoppard, Tom (1937–), English playwright 164, 316
Stout, Bill 162, 254
Strachey, Lytton (1880–1932), English biographer & critic 281
Stravinsky, Igor (1882–1971), Russian-born American composer 92
Strunk Jnr, William (1869–1946) 161, 256, 270
Styron, William (1925–), American novelist 50, 68, 87, 95, 99, 101, 130, 134, 188, 196, 231, 241, 316
Sutherland, J A (John Andrew) (1938–), English academic & author of books on language & literature 295
Suzman, Janet (1937–), South African-born English actress 162
Swift, Graham (1949–), English novelist 7, 38
Swift, Dean Jonathan (1667–1745), Irish-born English satirist 186
Symons, Arthur (1865–1945), Welsh poet & critic 318, 322

T

Tabori, Paul 109
Tacitus (Publius Cornelius) (?55–120 AD), Roman historian & orator 188
Talese, Gay (1932–), American novelist 247
Tanner, Tony 285
Tennyson, Alfred, Lord (1809–1892), English poet 254
Thackeray, William Makepeace (1811–1863), Indian-born English novelist 272
Theroux, Paul (1941–), American novelist & travel writer 2, 101, 102, 117, 118, 285, 286
Thomas, D M (Donald Michael) (1935–), English novelist & poet 8, 106
Thomas, Dylan (1914–1953), Welsh poet & playwright 60, 150, 156, 176, 178
Thomson, George Malcolm 15
Thompson, Hunter S (1939–), American novelist 107
Thoreau, Henry David (1817–1862), American writer 148, 155, 161, 163, 191, 205, 250, 253, 258, 271
Thubron, Colin (1939–), English travel writer 101
Thurber, James (1894–1961), American humorous writer & artist 22, 86, 164, 167, 172, 215, 225, 243
Tlali, Miriam (1933–), South African novelist & journalist 118
Tolstoy, Leo (Count Lev Nikolayevich) (1828–1910), Russian novelist, short story writer & philosopher 40, 47, 200, 258, 262, 322
Toplady, August Montague 105
Toynbee, Philip (1916–), English novelist & editor 281
Trapido, Barbara (1941–), South African-born English novelist 201
Trevor, William (William Trevor Cox) (1928–), Irish novelist & short story writer 41, 103
Trillin, Calvin (1935–), American writer 297
Trilling, Lionel (1905–1975), American academic, critic & writer 106
Trollope, Anthony (1815–1882), English novelist 45, 166, 170, 230, 236, 244, 248, 259, 267, 268, 276
Trollope, Joanna (1943–), English novelist 7, 91, 265
Troyat, Henri (1911–), French novelist 193, 258
Tucholsky, Kurt, American writer 138, 192
Tuchman, Barbara (1912–), American journalist & historian 49, 63
Turgenev, Ivan Sergeyevich (1818–1883), Russian novelist & playwright 248, 255
Turner, Graham, English journalist 208
Twain, Mark (Samuel Langhorne Clemens) (1835–1910), American novelist & humorist 11, 156, 162, 172, 173, 174, 212, 280, 289, 307, 322
Tyler, Anne (1941–), American novelist 20

Tynan, Kenneth (1927–1980), English theatre critic 305, 317

U

Uhnak, Dorothy (1933–), American police officer & crime novelist 205, 218, 231, 239
Untermeyer, Louis (1885–1977), American poet 54
Unwin, Sir Stanley (1884–1968), English publisher 105, 291
Updike, John (1932–), American novelist & short story writer 18, 50, 119, 166, 181, 200, 224, 300, 306, 315, 319
Uris, Leon (1924–), American novelist 3, 266

V

Valency, Maurice (1903–) 188
Valéry, Paul (1871–1945), French poet & essayist 5
Van Heerden, Etienne (1954–), South African novelist 204, 254
Van der Post, Sir Laurens (1906–1996), South African novelist & non-fiction writer 78, 153
Veblen, Thorstein (1857–1929), American social scientist 174
Versfeld, Martin (1909–1995), South African philosopher & writer 210
Vidal, Gore (1925–), American novelist & non-fiction writer 13, 15, 49, 114, 145, 148, 185, 219, 223, 278, 292
Voltaire (François-Marie Arouet) (1694–1778), French poet, playwright & satirist 13, 73, 208, 235, 257, 289
Vonnegut, Kurt (1922–), American novelist 1, 16, 26, 36, 77, 80, 101, 143, 145, 188, 190, 202, 225, 231, 236, 250, 261, 288 291, 295, 326

W

Wace, Master Robert (1115–1183), Anglo-Norman poet 211
Wain, John (1925–1994), English poet, novelist & critic 5
Walker, Alice (1944–), American novelist 109, 110
Wallace. Edgar (1875–1932), English crime novelist 215
Wallace, Irving (1916–), American novelist 50, 232, 288
Wallace, Mary C 124, 159, 187, 189
Wallechinsky, David (1947–) 78
Walpole, Horace, 4th Earl of Oxford (1717–1797), English writer 136
Walters, Minette, English crime novelist 19, 98
Wambaugh, Joseph (1921–), American policeman turned crime novelist 22, 26, 34, 143, 230, 245
Wantling, William 112
Ward, Artemus (Charles Farrar Browne) (1834–1867), American humorist 171
Warner, Marina (1946–), English novelist, writer of art & historical works, & critic 124
Warren, Robert Penn (1905–1989), American academic & writer 37, 236
Watson, Graham, English literary agent 73, 294
Waugh, Evelyn (1903–1966), English novelist 14, 59, 151, 153, 155, 157, 223, 230, 277, 281, 313
Weldon, Fay (1933–), English novelist & screenwriter 119, 161, 187, 192, 195, 242, 267, 290
Weill, Kurt (1900–1950), German composer 67
Wellington, Arthur Wellesley, Duke of (1769 –1852), English general & statesman 298
Wells, Carolyn (1862–1942) 305
Wells, H G (Herbert George) (1866–1946), English novelist & short story writer 86, 233, 259
Welty, Eudora (1909–), American novelist & short story writer 18, 49, 225, 256
Wescott, Glenway (1910–), American novelist, poet & short story writer 133
Wesley, John (1703–1791), English preacher who founded Methodism 157

Wesley, Mary (1912–), English novelist 89, 93, 128, 236, 326
West, Morris (1916–), Australian novelist 79, 130, 131, 257
West, Jessamyn (1907–1984), American novelist 95, 130, 131 257
West, Dame Rebecca (Cicely Isabel Fairfield Andrews) (1892 – 1983), English novelist & playwright 50, 130, 210, 282
Westheimer, David 257
Wheelock, John Hall (1886–1978), American poet 88
White, E B (Elwyn Brooks) (1899–1985), American journalist & humorist 22, 40, 41, 68, 167, 186, 193, 216, 217, 220, 221, 241, 264, 268
White, Edmund, American literary critic 62
Whitney, Phyllis A (1903–), American editor, novelist & writer, mainly of children's books 140, 273
Wiesel, Elie (1928–), American human rights campaigner & Nobel peace prize winner 49, 144
Wilbur, Richard (1921–), American poet & critic 143
Wilde, Oscar (1854–1900), Irish poet, playwright & wit 24, 35, 195, 292
Wilder, Thornton (1897–1975), American novelist & playwright 59, 104, 219, 314
Wilhelm, Peter (1943–), South African editor, poet, novelist & short story writer 59, 104, 219, 314
Williams, Joy (1944–) 154
Williams, Tennessee (1911–1983), American playwright 21, 24, 47, 87, 92, 96, 112, 113, 124, 180, 217, 220, 225, 233, 314
Williams, Dr William Carlos (1883–1963), medical doctor turned poet, essayist & short story writer 94, 271
Wilson, A N (Sir Angus) (1913–1991), English novelist & short story writer 77, 202, 209, 291
Wilson, Colin (1931–), English novelist & critic 42
Wilson, Edmund (1895–1972), American critic & writer 72, 214
Wilson, Ethel (1890–1980), South-African born Canadian novelist 36
Wilson, Sloan (1920–), American novelist 83, 90
Winder, Robert (1959–), English journalist & editor 103
Winterson, Jeanette (1959–), English novelist 323
Wodehouse, P G (Sir Pelham Grenville) (1881–1975), English humorous novelist 127, 180, 316
Wolfe, Thomas Clayton (1900–1938), American novelist 295
Wolfe, Tom (1931–), American journalist, novelist & critic 98, 214, 228, 230
Wolff, Tobias (1945–), American academic & novelist 37
Wood, Charles (1932–), English playwright & scriptwriter 214
Woolf, Leonard (1880–1969), English publisher & political writer 203
Woolf, Virginia (1882–1941), English novelist & critic 13, 20, 91, 249, 315

Yeats, W B (William Butler) (1865–1939), Irish poet, playwright & critic (Nobel Prize for Literature, 1923) 8, 69, 111, 159, 249
Young, Edward (1683–1765), English poet 306
Young, Elizabeth 133
Young, Marguerite (1909–), American novelist & poet 232

Zinsser, William (1922–), American writer 65, 105, 182, 250, 263
Zola, Emile (1840–1902), French novelist & critic 3, 52, 191
Zuckerman, Albert, American literary agent 40, 71

NB While we have tried to make it as accurate as possible given limited research facilities, this index is incomplete. The compiler and publisher welcome additional or corrected information.